ST. LUKE'S HOSPICE, P

OTHER LIVES, O

G000321145

This book is to be returned on or before
the last date stamped below.

22/5/00

ST. LUKE'S HOSPICE, PLYMOUTH

About the Author

Dr. Roger J. Woolger is a graduate of Oxford University and a certified Jungian analyst. He has been a past life therapist for eleven years, researching and developing his own Jungian-based technique.

OTHER LIVES, OTHER SELVES

A Jungian Psychotherapist
Discovers Past Lives

ROGER J. WOOLGER, PH.D.

Aquarian
An Imprint of HarperCollins*Publishers*

Aquarian
An Imprint of HarperCollins*Publishers*
77–85 Fulham Palace Road,
Hammersmith, London W6 8JB

This edition published 1994
First published in the USA by
Dolphin/Doubleday, Inc., New York, 1987
1 3 5 7 9 10 8 6 4 2

© Roger Woolger, Ph.D. 1987

Roger Woolger asserts the moral right to
be identified as the author of this work

A catalogue record for this book
is available from the British Library

ISBN 1 85538 311 X

Printed in Great Britain by
Mackays of Chatham, Kent

All rights reserved. No part of this publication may be
reproduced, stored in a retrieval system, or transmitted,
in any form or by any means, electronic, mechanical,
photocopying, recording or otherwise, without the prior
permission of the publishers.

To all my clients,
for having "the dignity of daring"
in our work together
. . . and, of course, A.D.M.G.

ACKNOWLEDGMENTS

Much of my work as a therapist is private and not even talked about outside of my office, but I am grateful to have had the opportunity to demonstrate some of my findings to the general public and to colleagues at workshops. I would therefore like to record my thanks to the following persons and organizations who have so kindly and loyally supported this somewhat controversial work: Tom Valente, Elizabeth Rechtschaffen, and Omega Institute; Ralph White and the New York Open Center; Nancy Lunney and Esalen Institute; Michael Owen, Larry Rooney, and Helen Keeler and Therafields Association in Toronto; John and Marilyn Rossner at the Spiritual Science Fellowship and Denise Rousselle in Montreal; Rebecca Browning and TARA in Boulder; June Singer and the California Institute of Transpersonal Psychology; Marie Tari and the East West Center in Syracuse; Rick Rosen and Sahni Hamilton at Bodyworks and Libba Beerman in Chapel Hill; and Charlotte Alexander in Portland. Special thanks, too, to Helen Williams, Rosemarie Delahaye, and Connie Stafford for encouraging me through the more difficult times. From the early days, thanks and recognition to our fearless Vermont research team: David, Larry, Carol, John, and Kim, and warmest thanks to Sara and Sam, fellow explorers.

Last but not least, thanks to Byronia, our trusty word processor for holding on to it all, to Mother for all cups of tea and to my beloved wife, colleague, and critic, Jennifer, for lovingly typing, discussing, and sharing every part of this book with me.

CONTENTS

FOREWORD

Comfort and security levels often cloud our abilities to move deeper into knowledge of the images that impel and regulate our lives. Yet we yearn for ways to clear the clouds of unknowingness. In ourselves and our society, we are bound up with patterns that perhaps no longer serve us. If anything, these patterns which focus on materialistic values and self-centered orientations seem to create ecological havoc within ourselves and on our planet. On the other hand, these patterns have given rise to crises that are forcing individuals, groups, and nations to question old assumptions, models, and structures—and to develop a different perspective in order to deal with the perennial problems we face. As Ilya Prigogine, who won the 1977 Nobel Prize for a theory describing transformations, emphasizes, we are perhaps at a turning point where the stresses and conflicts of our time can thrust us into a new higher order. He is stating what Thomas Kuhn, a science historian and philosopher, calls a movement toward a paradigm shift—a paradigm being a scheme held by a community of individuals for understanding and explaining certain aspects of reality. We are presently emerging from a materialistic, control-oriented, self-centered scheme of reality into one which perceives life as an inseparable web of relationships. This new paradigm supports an awareness that there are intrinsically dynamic processes (forms of consciousness) that articulate the patterns and structures of our lives. We are still hesitant to give up the belief that science deals with absolute truth rather than with a limited and approximate description of reality. It must be considered that personal truth is never an objective endeavor within the realm of science, but rather a personal path and inner revelation which all great spiritual teachers have revealed.

If we can understand that transformation is what we are seeking, we will see that the basic tenet of this book is not about past life therapy, but about personal transformation. By weaving his knowledge and understanding of the poets and philosophers who provide intimations of an open, creative universe with his own clinical material, Roger Woolger presents a transformational perspective exploring the creative possibility that we are related to a pattern of consciousness that goes beyond ordinary awareness.

Roger has had the courage to undertake this book as a participant-observer of the past life therapy process. In that role, he discloses his own doubts and the pathways of self-examination he traveled trying to make sense of the material of past life images. In doing so, he finds himself, like others who have journeyed beyond socially accepted conventions, having to discard traditional models of the universe and human nature. Whether we believe in past life imagery or not, it is of little consequence. In his use of literary and philosophical metaphors, Roger Woolger creates an understanding of the images which bind us in a universal way to one another. He brings to the reader a cluster of ideas which serve as a catalyst for personal change.

This book is timely. Several years back, it could easily have been disregarded and placed in the category of the occult. But now it has personal relevance outside of that

category. In *Other Lives, Other Selves* Roger addresses
the issues of our relationship to the process of life, the
question of our own personal identity, and the issue of the
purpose of life as we witness it. This book, in many ways,
gives a pathway to those who want to find their own
natural depth and a form of self disclosure that provides
an added dimension to the therapeutic process. The hope
of past life images is that they provide a vision that all of
us, whether we choose to recognize it or not, are living
within a spiritual ecological terrain which embodies our
sense of humanity.

RONALD WONG JUE, PH.D.
President, Association for
Transpersonal Psychology

PREFACE

The ability to remember past lives has been the subject of systematic research by psychologists for nearly thirty years now. Dr. Ian Stevenson of the University of Virginia has on record hundreds of painstakingly investigated cases of previous lives spontaneously recalled by children. Psychotherapists and hypnotherapists like Morris Netherton in California and Joe Scranton in England have demonstrated on film and television the extraordinary work of past life regression in adults. While in trance their subjects writhe as they remember agonizing deaths, weep copiously at the loss of loved ones, or burst into foreign languages they've never even heard of.

And yet for all this widespread publicity, to say nothing of the huge success of the Edgar Cayce readings, Jane Roberts's Seth books, and Shirley MacLaine's recent bestsellers, past life research and therapy are quietly ignored if not scathingly dismissed by most psychologists and intellectuals in the major universities in America and Europe.

Why is this?

One possible reason is that "past lives" suggests to most people reincarnation, and reincarnation immediately conjures up images of occultism, exorcism, and spirit possession; it is "of the Devil," as fundamentalists say. Or maybe it is because famous Hollywood movie stars are always being quoted in the popular tabloids as having remembered lives as Egyptian priestesses, or else their marriages in previous lives to other famous people.

Or perhaps it is because reincarnation sounds suspiciously oriental to a public that has become jaded and skeptical about gurus from India with their huge Swiss bank accounts, Rolls-Royces, and mindless followers.

So, when Mike Wallace interviewed Shirley MacLaine on the television program "60 Minutes," about her very personal beliefs in spirit guides and reincarnation, he may have thought he was speaking for the average viewer when he said, "Oh, come off it, Shirley. Surely, you don't believe that?"

But was Mike Wallace as close to public opinion as he thought? Some surprising statistics seem to indicate significant shifts in popular beliefs.

A 1982 Gallup poll, for instance, revealed that nearly one American in four believed in reincarnation while in Britain polls by the conservative *Sunday Telegraph* showed that belief in reincarnation by the general public had risen from 18 to 28 percent in a ten-year period. Could it be that our expert psychologists and media pundits have fallen a little bit behind the times? It may be that serious thinking about reincarnation is taking over from skepticism and Christian orthodoxy in much the way that the new physics has taken over from classical Newtonian physics.

The pioneering quantum physicist Max Planck once made a remark that could well apply to the rise of belief in reincarnation:

A new scientific truth does not triumph by convincing its opponents and making them see the truth; but rather be-

cause its opponents eventually die and a new generation
grows up that is familiar with it.

Do we indeed stand on the verge of a radical reevaluation
of what the human personality is? Is there a new psychology emerging that can once more encompass the immortal component traditionally called "the soul"? Can the
ancient doctrines of karma and reincarnation be understood in terms that make sense psychologically to modern
Western men and women without the blind acceptance of
yet more dogma or degeneration into fashionable pop
psychology?

I believe that they can, and it is the purpose of this book
to show how, as a practicing psychotherapist and critical
investigator, I have arrived at these conclusions.

For convenience of orientation I have divided the book
into four parts. Part I briefly charts my own personal and
professional evolution from Jungian analyst to Jungian
past life therapist. I attempt to sketch the historical background to our growing interest in past life phenomena in
order to distinguish my work as a therapist from three
other equally legitimate but quite different perspectives
on past lives: the approaches of the psychic, the parapsychologist, and the reincarnationalist.

Part II describes how I have developed a synthesis of
various ideas and techniques currently favored by certain
transpersonal psychotherapists. My own foundation remains Jung's concepts of the complex and the archetype,
but I propose a third term, *the past life complex* or *samskara*, adapted from Hindu psychology. A sixfold map of
the unconscious is proposed and illustrated with cases.

Part III looks at two specific factors that I find to be
essential in past life work: bodily consciousness and the

configuration of psychic opposites that appears among past life personality fragments.

Part IV describes the momentous and pivotal experiences of birth and death as they occur in past life work. The final chapter tries to put the work in the broader perspective of spiritual development and Jung's concept of individuation.

I wish that I could have presented much of the material in simpler ways and used fewer technical terms, but the picture *is* a complex one and I have attempted to do it full justice. A glossary of terms is included for the reader's convenience, plus extensive notes and readings for those with a more professional or scholarly interest.

Like early maps of the New World, this is only a sketch of new and unfamiliar territory. In charting these unknown coasts there are more than a few inspired guesses, with the result that some parts may be hopelessly out of proportion, or just plain wrong. I hope future explorers will correct my misperceptions and unwitting distortions.

PART I

INTRODUCTORY

Only within yourself exists that other reality for which
you long. I can give you nothing that has not already its
being within yourself. I can throw open to you no picture
gallery but your own soul.

Herman Hesse   *Steppenwolf*

Every man beareth the whole stamp of the human
condition.

Michel de Montaigne   *Essays*

CHAPTER 1

A SKEPTIC ENCOUNTERS PAST LIVES

He fished by obstinate isles . . .
Ezra Pound

From Behaviorism to Jung

When I graduated from Oxford University in the mid-sixties with a joint degree in behavioral psychology and analytic philosophy, my mind had been put into a carefully tailored straitjacket, though I hardly knew it at the time. If anyone had suggested something like remembering past lives to me then, I would have dismissed the very idea as self-contradictory. Remembering entails a remember-berer, I would have said, and only one person has access to my memories, namely me. Logically "I" can no more remember the memories of another life than the memories of the man sitting opposite me on the bus.

With a few more linguistic cuts and logical thrusts, I would have had my reincarnationalist friend fumbling for a satisfactory definition that would stand up to my philosophical swordsmanship. Behind me stood the great voices of rationalism and empiricism. "Metaphysics is dead," Professor A. J. Ayer had said, and that was the end of it. Rest in peace, Plato, Aristotle, and Hegel![1]

As for psychology, Oxford was groping in the Dark Ages, if I had but known it. The word "consciousness" had been successfully banished from our vocabulary and there was strong resistance to the invasion of subversive American neologisms like "cognitive" in those days. Experimentalism and sterile statistics reigned supreme. The only candidates who might have shown the remotest interest in reincarnation were probably the rats. Better the cosmic maze than a wire mesh one!

Like many a disillusioned psychology major, I was unable to face more of this intellectual wasteland in graduate school. After all, what had statistics to do with the heart and the soul? with the supreme spiritual achievements of mankind: the mystics, Shakespeare, Dostoyevsky? Instead, I spent a few years as a teacher in West Africa and then went back to graduate school at London University to study comparative religion. Here at last I could breathe more freely and immerse myself in the scholarly study of Hinduism and Christian mysticism. I had meditated since I was a teenager, finding it a mental hygiene as self-evident as brushing my teeth. So here was a chance to broaden my background.

Perhaps I should say I have never had a guru nor been attracted to finding one. My pursuit of other religions has always been a mixture of the scholarly and the down-to-earth. In texts, I always looked for the originals without commentaries, whether the Bhagavad Gita or the Gospels. In meditation, I only use what is practical and useful to me regardless of tradition. Some might see this as rather arrogant, but I like to think I have always been guided by the words of the Buddha when he said, "Be ye a light unto yourselves."

The subject of reincarnation, however, never really arose during my graduate studies. Classical Hinduism seemed to assume the doctrine without making a fuss about it. After all, it is the higher self, the *"atman,"* not the "ego," that keeps coming back, in the Hindu perspective.

Even in the classical methods of yoga and meditation, I never came across any mention of the necessity to meditate on our past lives. The idea of karma, that every man reaps what he sows, seemed mainly to belong to a philosophical vision of our place in the universe and to have little practical application. I was struck, as many are, by a distinct "fatalism" in much of the popular Hindu thought.

No doubt it was this same need for practical applications, which had originally led me to meditate some years earlier, that now led me to Zürich, Switzerland, where I was to immerse myself in a type of psychology that I was temperamentally most suited to. This was the school of depth psychology founded by Carl Gustav Jung, the Swiss psychiatrist who had originally collaborated with Freud. Jung later broke away from Freud to form his own school, based on a broader conception of the unconscious mind. Where Freud's unconscious had been entirely peopled by complexes, mainly derived from early childhood experiences, Jung added another layer common to all mankind, inhabited by the archetypes or universal symbol patterns common to myth, religion, and art.

That part of the unconscious mind containing Freud's repressed childhood memories Jung referred to as the *personal unconscious,* the place where all psychotherapy must begin, but the underlying layer of the archetypes he termed the *collective unconscious,* [2] a pool of transforming

symbols available to us all. Here, for me, was the explanation for why great works of drama and literature like
Oedipus Rex and *King Lear* and *The Brothers Karamazov*
move us so deeply. Our personal tragedies of abandonment and loss, bitterness and rage are magnified and potentially transformed in the greater struggles of these su-
perhuman characters because a part of us can identify
with the transpersonal power of the archetypes. All great
art is psychotherapy if experienced the right way; and all
good psychotherapy must engage our artistic and creative
selves at some level.

Finally I had found in Jung a psychology that respected
and nourished both my intellectual and my creative and
intuitive being—the two parts later to be identified as the
left and right brain functions. Without both sides we cannot be truly whole, complete persons. I began to understand why academic psychology had seemed so arid to
me. A young German romantic poet, Novalis, had anticipated this problem in 1800 and had, amazingly, foreseen
the very way that Jung and others were to take a century
later:

> When pure statistics and measured features
> Are no more keys to living creatures,
> When dancing and bursting into song
> Proves our most learned scholars wrong,
> When all the world is fresh and new
> And once more Nature to herself is true,
> When light and darkness merge their love,
> Into a higher unity above
> When fairy tales and legends old
> Tell the true history of the world
> Then, but a single, secret phrase
> Shall put to flight our mixed up ways.[3]

The more I immersed myself in Jung's writings and in my own analysis and dreamwork, the greater the effect he had on my thinking and my personal and professional development. He seemed to offer a bridge—and a very broad one—that allowed the different traffic of psychology, religion, literature, and science all to pass over and do productive business with each other. He is one of the great synthesizers and visionaries of this century.

Jung himself had remained skeptical about reincarnation for most of his life. When in 1938 he wrote a commentary to *The Tibetan Book of the Dead,* a text saturated with the doctrine of karma, he maintained bluntly that "there is no inheritance of prenatal or pre-uterine memories," adding instead his own theory that "there are undoubtedly inherited archetypes which are, however, devoid of content."[4]

Jung was writing long before Dr. Ian Stevenson's rigorously researched cases of children who spontaneously remembered detailed facts from the lives of deceased individuals they claimed to have been. It was also long before Dr. Thomas Verney collected an impressive amount of scientific evidence for in utero memory in his bestseller, *The Secret Life of the Unborn Child.*[5]

But back in the 1970s, knowing nothing of this, I preferred to follow Jung's considered position that reincarnation was in principle unprovable but was nevertheless one of the most widespread of all religious beliefs and must in itself be accorded the status of an archetype, a universal psychic structure.

This was still how I thought in 1971, when I was sent a book called *The Cathars and Reincarnation* to review for the prestigious *Journal of the Society for Psychical Research* in London.[6] I had been a member of this long-established society—the first ever to scientifically investigate mediumship, telepathy, apparitions, etc.—since college days and Renée Haynes, the *Journal*'s editor, knew that I tempered my interest in such matters with a healthy skepticism.

As it happened, *The Cathars and Reincarnation*, by Arthur Guirdham, proved to be an event which Jungians call "synchronistic" because it anticipated a path I was later to take. (A *synchronicity* for Jung is, among other things, a coincidence that has a personal meaning beyond the immediate facts of the situation.)[7]

By way of explanation of the title of this unusual book, I should say that the Cathars, also called the Albigensians, were a heretical medieval sect that flourished in Italy and southern France in the thirteenth century. The Cathar heresy became so widespread that eventually the Church had to mount a full-scale crusade to exterminate it. It was during this crusade, incidentally, in which upward of a half million people were burned or otherwise massacred, that the so-called Holy Inquisition was set up.

Dr. Guirdham, a practicing psychiatrist, recounts in his book how a certain woman patient came to him with a series of dreams of thirteenth-century France. The dreams had very precise historical details in them which were later verified by French experts on Cathar history. Guirdham himself began to get parallel dreams and concluded eventually that he and his patient had been lovers in the horrible milieu of the Cathar persecution and had died fiery deaths together.

To a psychoanalyst in training it all sounded like what we call in the trade "transference" and "countertransference." Transference is the patient's unconscious emotional involvement with the therapist, and countertransference is the therapist's reciprocal feelings, if they exist. In a good analysis, the therapist's job is to spot when this is happening in both himself and the client. If the therapist misses it, they both get sucked into an elaborate *folie à deux*, a shared delusion.

This is pretty much what I said in the review of Guirdham's book, and Renée Haynes agreed with my conclusions. Guirdham went on to write several more books about other reincarnated Cathar friends, and the whole thing began to sound like a reincarnational soap opera.

A Very Unglamorous Past Life

This was in the early 1970s. More and more absorbed in the psychology of Jung, I forgot all about Guirdham, Catharism, and reincarnation. By 1976 I had settled in America, Vermont to be precise. I had been attracted to that beautiful state during a temporary teaching post at the University of Vermont in Burlington and decided to work in the same area as a psychotherapist.

The next time the subject of past lives came up was when a colleague of mine suggested experimenting with a technique for regressing oneself to a past life. I was skeptical, but agreed to the experiment. Jungian training had taught me much about working with visualization and dream imagery in a relaxed, meditative state. So why not?

Imagine my surprise, now eight years after that review, lying on a sofa in a remote farmhouse in Vermont, when images, at first dimly, then very vividly began to form, and I not only found myself in southern France, but in the thick of the Albigensian crusade! Here I was, now a practicing Jungian analyst, having visions that my own training had told me were not possible. Had the visions resembled the stories in Guirdham's book, my skepticism would immediately have been alerted. But my story, as it unfolded, was not at all focused on the persecuted minor lords and ladies of Languedoc. Quite the reverse. I found myself almost grunting out the story of a very crude peasant-turned-mercenary soldier of that same period. This rough-and-ready character I seemed to have assumed was originally from the south of Naples and ended up in the papal army raised by the King of France to exterminate the heresy in the South. As this highly unsavory individual, I found myself in the thick of some of the most hideous massacres, in which the inhabitants of whole French cities were hacked to pieces and burnt in huge pyres in the name of the Church.

Images from that first remembrance haunted me for years, and it took three more two-hour regressions to complete a story I was, and still am, loathe to look at. Yet, amazingly, it started to explain to me disturbing fragments of torture and killing that had come in dreams, meditation, and unbidden fantasy over the years, images that no amount of psychotherapy had ever really touched. Also, the way the story ended seemed to explain a phobia, a fear of fire, I have had all my life. After one of the sieges, the mercenary I seem to have been, deserted and joined the heretics, eventually only to be caught and burned at the stake himself.

As I reflected on the story more and more, other pieces of my personal history in this life started to fall into place. Since adolescence I had developed a very cynical attitude to almost all orthodox religion, especially Christianity. I found it hard to see any Church as anything but authoritarian and dogmatic, denying people the freedom of personal inquiry and experiment. But even more adamant had been my early rejection of all forms of militarism and a strong inclination toward pacifism. I even refused to join the Boy Scouts for reasons I could scarcely articulate as a teenager. Could it be that from early on I had unconsciously been reminded of parts of that soldier's brutal experience?

The most painful recognition of how that soldier still lived in me was remembering one fight I had gotten into at school at around twelve years of age. In a classroom one day, I had become so wild with rage at a boy I considered a hypocrite that four other boys had to drag me off of him. I had been ready to kill. I vowed never to lose my temper again; a part of me recognized how easily I could kill.

Why did such a painful "past life" memory come to me and not something more edifying, glamorous, or reassuring?

Part of the answer lies in the experience of self-examination I had learned from my training as a Jungian analyst while in Zürich and from my years of meditation. Jung insisted that all would-be analysts undergo analysis themselves, so that they would not project their less acceptable qualities onto future patients. "Physician, heal thyself" remains the first maxim of all psychoanalysis, Freudian or Jungian. Jung once put it even more radically: "We do not become enlightened by imagining figures of light, but by making the darkness conscious."[8]

In my own personal analysis in England and Zürich, I had begun to own many pieces of my less sociable, violent, angry, brutal self, the opposite, or *shadow*, of my nice, amenable, sociable self or *persona*. So I had already had glimpses of my brutal mercenary in dreams over the years, but never until this "memory" were the glimpses so vivid or disturbing. I was reminded, too, that the work of analysis and self-analysis, in whatever form, is a life's work and that just getting a certificate or a Ph.D. from a prestigious school or institute is by no means a guarantee of psychological maturity. To this day I continue to struggle with that soldier and his unfinished guilt. As a shadow, he is to me, as Jung again put it so wisely, "a moral problem that challenges the whole personality."

I was later to learn that most people, when they first have past life regressions, rarely get such violent or horrible memories. As a rule, the unconsious mind—which I now believe to carry past life memories, as well as forgotten childhood events and archetypes—will, in its wisdom, only send us past life memories that we are ready to deal with and are able to integrate into our conscious personality structure. Those who have little experience of therapy or meditation more often start gently. The first past life memories that come tend to be more benign. Beginners not subject to pressure or neurosis are usually shown other selves from the past, that can be more easily assimilated and dealt with. This is as it should be.

In the workshops my wife Jennifer and I give, we often remind our students of the oriental image of *the guardian of the threshold,* a frightening monster depicted at the gates of a temple or bordering a sacred *mandala,* or meditation picture. These guardians are images of our own fear and are there to prevent us entering realms of the psyche we are not ready for. Whether we are aware of them or not, each of us has our own inner guardians of the threshold to prevent us from going too deep, too fast. There is a subtle inner economy of psychic and spiritual unfoldment in which every individual proceeds at his or her own pace, governed by these inner guardians and guides. These inner figures become very clear when we learn to understand our dreams.

I tell my story of my first past life encounter as both a warning to the unwary and a stimulus for those who are ready to explore. Any psychological work that goes into the deeper layers of the unconscious mind is likely to bring up powerful emotions, disturbing memories, and fantasy material. Such often overwhelming psychic contents may seem to the uninitiated and even to experts to belong to the realms of classical madness. Past life exploration can be like taking the lid off Pandora's Box; it can unleash potent forces over which we may have little control. For this reason, it is my firm belief that *guiding regressions and research into past lives should only be undertaken by those fully trained in psychotherapy.* This is not a parlor game, simple as the procedures many seem when first witnessed.

At the same time, there is powerful learning to be had from this extraordinary process. It is no exaggeration to say that there are among my clients those whose whole life orientation has been changed by only one or two past life sessions. The opportunity to confront one's true self, naked and unadorned, to see the essence of one's "stuckness" in even a single story, is unparalleled in any other psychological discipline that I know.

For example, a very successful businessman consulted me once and described himself as a Type A personality, one of those who is driven in everything he does. This man felt constantly inadequate, that he was not strong or assertive enough, and described how, despite more success than most men ever achieve, he punished himself by overwork. In addition, he had a history of physical accidents in which he had broken his ankles, hip, shoulder, and wrist at one time or another. One accident to his shoulder seemed to bring out inexplicable feelings of injustice in which he found himself thinking, "Why me?"

When directed into a past life connected in some way with this, his body became tense, he clenched his fists and jaw, and uttered the following words:

> *It's no use. I can't do anything. I'm not strong enough. I won't let go. I won't let go. I can't hold on anymore. I don't want to die. I'm falling . . .*

What he was reliving were the last agonizing moments of a soldier on the edge of a cliff, unable to muster the strength to climb to the top. Another sadistic soldier was taunting him with the words, "You're weak. You're no good. If you were really strong, you'd make it." When he failed, the soldier hit him on the head with a rifle butt and he fell to his death, shattered on the rocks below.

In the last agonizing moments before letting go, he has the following thoughts:

> *It's a test . . . I've failed. I wasn't strong enough. I was weak and helpless. I'm ashamed. I could have done better. I didn't deserve to die. I'll never do that again. I'll never give up again. Anything but failure. I'm gonna hold on.*

The death, as he relived it, was over in an instant, and after the titanic struggle his body suddenly became limp. A flood of insight came as he saw that his whole life had been a constant repetition of the soldier's dying thoughts: "I'll never give up again. Anything but failure. I'm gonna hold on." It was obvious to him that these thoughts had been governing his life metaphorically, and that he could now choose to change them, and was no longer doomed to relive an old story that was no longer his.

Unfinished Dramas of the Soul

From nearly a decade of taking clients and colleagues through past life experiences and continuing my own personal explorations, I have come to regard this technique as one of the most concentrated and powerful tools available to psychotherapy short of psychedelic drugs.

Not every client goes directly to dramas like that relived by this businessman—he had an extensive background in other therapies—but almost everyone I have worked with can easily identify two major ways in which past lives seem to be influencing current behavior. The first is a recognition that these characters from previous eras are recognizable as *other selves,* that we dimly know have always been there in the background of our consciousness. Often in the rap part of our session, I will say: "Do you know that character?" And be he or she rebellious slave, depressed scullery maid, arrogant overlord, obsequious courtier, or likable charlatan, my client will inevitably reply with a sigh or an embarrassed smile, "Oh yes, I know *him* (or *her)!"*

The second feature that stands out almost universally is an inescapable feeling that this character's past life *story* is somehow being reenacted in this life and that it still remains unfinished:

—A woman client still cannot have children because of guilt about abandoning an infant during a famine.

—A man remembers being sexually humiliated as a young servant by older women to whom he is indentured and withdraws into the company of men, a pattern today repeated in homosexual relations.

—A woman who has successfully had three children in

her current life suffers from severe premenstrual cramps which lead her into a past life memory of her painful death in childbirth in a tribal life.

Each other life that comes to us, however brief or fragmentary, is a piece of another self. The personality is not single, it is multiple—not in the psychiatric sense of multiple personality, but in that there are many levels to the self like many skins to an onion. We peel off these selves as we look into our past lives or as we look into our own dreams.

Jung's approach was through the dream. There are many selves running around in our dreams, many secondary personalities. Jung believed, as Fritz Perls (originator of Gestalt Therapy) did, that, most of the time, every personality in the dream is me. I may be dreaming about my mother or my father, my grandfather, my boss, but they are all me. I have a mother in me—I can "mother" my little girl. I can "boss" people around. I can feel like a lord executioner when I want to kill someone, or I may get a man with a gun running around in my dreams wanting to kill me. Each is another self, another part of me, and all these selves are present in us.

I had studied and practiced dream work for many years. Dream work is not easy to learn, nor is it easily taught, because just as we all have different handwriting so we all have different dream styles. I spent many years leading dream groups, and I found it very hard work. I had to interpret and learn every single person's dream style in the group to help each person get a handle on their own dreams. When I stumbled upon past lives, I found they contained similar material, material we can learn to interpret ourselves without an expert on symbolism. When they surface, our past lives are immediately obvious to us *because they are stories*. It is not hard to understand a story. It is harder to understand a dream. That takes training. So, what I describe in the following chapters is a different approach to Jung's idea of the multiplicity of the unconscious. My approach is through stories rather than dreams. And it is through the stories that come through our "other lives" that we learn to accept the many selves that compose our common humanity.

To give the reader some idea of the remarkable range of human problems that have responded to past life regression in my psychotherapy practice, here is a list of some of the more common psychological issues I have treated. Many of these will be elaborated in later chapters.

Insecurity and fear of abandonment. Often related to past life memories of literal abandonment as a child, separation during a crisis or a war, being orphaned, sold into slavery, being left out to die in times of famine, etc.

Depression and low energy. Past life memories of loss of a loved one or parent, unfinished grieving, suicide memories, despair as a result of war, massacre, deportation, etc.

Phobias and irrational fears. Every kind of trauma in a past life: death by fire, water, suffocation, animals, knives, insects, natural disasters, etc.

Sadomasochistic behavior problems. Usually related to a past life memory of torture, often with loss of consciousness, usually with sexual overtones; the pain and rage seem to perpetuate hatred and a desire to revenge oneself in the same way.

Guilt and martyr complexes. Commonly stem from

past life memories of having directly killed loved ones or from feeling responsible for the deaths of others (e.g., in a fire): human sacrifice of one's child, having ordered the deaths of others unnecessarily, etc. The entrenched thought is most often, "It's all my fault. I deserve this."

Material insecurity and eating disorders. Often the rerunning of past life memories of starvation, economic collapse, or inescapable poverty; manifests as anorexia, bulimia, or obesity.

Accidents, violence, physical brutality. Repetition of old battlefield memories from warrior lives; unfulfilled quests for power, love of adventure cut off; common in adolescence, the time historically when many soldiers met their deaths.

Family struggles. Usually there are old past life scores to settle with parents, children, or siblings: betrayal, abuse of power, inheritance injustices, rivalry, etc.; includes most Freudian Oedipal dynamics.

Sexual difficulties and abuse. Frequently problems of frigidity, impotence, and genital infections have past life stories of rape, abuse, or torture behind them. Many incest and child abuse stories turn out to be reruns of old patterns where emotional release was blocked.

Marital difficulties. These often derive from past lives with the same mate in a different power, class, or sexual constellation: e.g., as mistress, slave, prostitute, concubine, where the sex roles were reversed.

Chronic physical ailments. Past life reliving of traumatic injuries or deaths to the head, the limbs, the back, etc. Therapy often relieves chronic pain in these areas; headaches may relate to intolerable mental choices in other lives; throat ailments to verbal denunciations or unspoken thoughts; ulcers to memories of terror, neck-aches to hanging or strangling.

From this list, which is far from exhaustive, it is clear that one person may have several themes and related past life stories that will need to be worked through in the course of therapy. Exactly how this is done I shall describe in more detail in later chapters. For the moment this list will suffice to give some idea of what past life regression entails and how it is not something for idle amusement.

From Death to Rebirthing

After my first experience of remembering the past life of the medieval French mercenary soldier I decided to continue experimenting with the technique. The same colleague and I exchanged sessions on and off for nearly a year, then, as other interested colleagues and friends became curious, we formed a small experimental study group. Six of us paired up to work with each other and agreed to come together every other week and share our findings. At the same time, since three of us in the group were omnivorous readers, we set out to read everything we could find on past lives or reincarnation, ranging in our search from *The Tibetan Book of the Dead* to Seth to Dick Sutphen. We also tried out the various methods and techniques for regression that psychologists and hypnotherapists have described in the small number of books that had then been written on the subject.

In my own case, once I had cleaned out all the visions of my medieval storm trooper I got a more benign and peaceful memory of being a feudal lord in fourteenth-century Brittany. Next, I recalled a number of military lives and lives of travel which alternated with monastic or priestly lives. There even seemed to be a pattern in the remembered lives: a swinging between opposite themes of engagement and retreat. This certainly appeared to fit my own emotional dynamic as well as explaining many of my interests and pet aversions.

A new dimension was added to our informal experimentation as a group when we all decided to undergo the very powerful therapeutic technique called rebirthing, the discovery of Leonard Orr in California. Rebirthing is a highly intensive process of quasi-yogic breathing which has the effect of releasing emotions, attitudes, memories, and physical holding patterns said to originate with the trauma of birth.[9] Although I had myself previously done a certain amount of therapy designed to release physical energy blocks associated with emotional attitudes—an approach derived from the brilliant pioneer work of Wilhelm Reich back in the 1930s—I was to find that, for me, rebirthing went even further.

My own shattering experience of letting the breath take over completely had me spluttering, choking, and weeping my way out of the birth canal as tingling streams of energy burst through my head, arms, and legs. I seemed to be taken to a crucial new level of residual emotional patterns that psychoanalysis and Reichian therapy had failed to touch. But most surprising of all, I found myself muttering the desperate words: "I don't want to be in this world." My rebirthing guide said: "Why not?" and immediately I had a vision of a mutilated body lying on a pile of emaciated corpses in a burial pit of some kind. And I began to weep bitterly and uncontrollably again, as though racked with some cosmic suffering on behalf of not just my own but of all human suffering. For what I instantly knew was that I was seeing a body that "I" had in some sense just left, the body of a German Communist dissident who had died in one of the early concentration camps in the early 1930s (before the Jewish persecution, as it turned out). Later reworkings of this painful theme led me to the astounding realization that I had been born depressed and that all later childhood experiences, so carefully unraveled in psychoanalysis, were not the origins of my depressive temperament but rather the reawakening of a deep pessimism and despair "I" seemed to have died with in 1933. Clearly, whole new dimensions of therapy were hinted at here and with them a complete revisioning of the origins of mental illness and the very nature of personality. At the time, as our group discussed our similar experiences, we did not realize the full import of what we had stumbled upon.

Unknown to our little group in Vermont, at least two other researchers, Dr. Stanislav Grof at Esalen Institute[10] and Dr. Morris Netherton in Los Angeles,[11] were also observing and experimenting with the interface between the birth trauma and past life regression, consistently noting how the one is mirrored in the other. As Grof recently put it, this kind of willingness to go fully into such a level of emotional trauma also typifies a whole new kind of psychotherapy which he calls *experiential therapy*.[12] I was later to learn that Grof too had to go through a period of discarding certain received psychoanalytic theories of development eventually to embrace what is now broadly called a *transpersonal* view of the human psyche.

Grof's own route to these realizations was through his extensive LSD research rather than through rebirthing or hypnotic regression, though today he too uses cathartic breathing, of a sort very similar to rebirthing breathing, in his Esalen workshops. He has also observed many examples of reincarnational scenarios in the reported visions of his subjects.

Dr. Morris Netherton, who must be counted one of the leading pioneers of research into past life remembering for therapeutic purposes, had also been finding for many years that particular aspects of the birth trauma would directly trigger past life traumas in the unconscious. So, for example, someone who reexperiences their birth with damage to the head from a forceps delivery will frequently remember a death from a blow to the head in another life. These memory traces will be found to underlie persistent headaches in the present life.

As I have evolved my own style of working over the years, I have studied and borrowed from many of the acknowledged masters in the field of psychotherapy. The professional reader of this book will detect, as well as Jung, the influence of Gestalt therapy, psychodrama, and Reichian therapy in my approach. In Chapter 4 I elaborate in more detail on my own psychotherapeutic method, but for the moment I simply want to describe a fairly typical session from my practice to give the reader who has never attended a past life workshop a somewhat fuller picture than the glimpses I have given up till now. The case that follows is by no means one of the more complex or grimly traumatic, but it illustrates very well the range and intensity of the process. In the commentary that follows, I discuss some of the philosophical and psychological questions that people most frequently ask about the whole phenomenon of past life recall and reincarnation when they have seen it demonstrated in our workshops.

CHAPTER 2

PAST LIFE THERAPY: HOW IT WORKS

> What seest thou else
> In the dark backward and abysm of time?
>
> Shakespeare, *The Tempest*

> The unconscious is the unwritten history
> of mankind for time unrecorded.
>
> C. G. Jung,
> *Psychology and Religion:*
> *West and East*

Peter's Story: A Nineteenth-century Migrant Worker

It is a Monday evening. A small group is sitting in a circle on the thick carpet of our living room in the old stone farmhouse in upstate New York where my wife, Jennifer, and I live. It is a recently formed past life therapy group. A young, slightly built man in his early twenties, whom I shall call Peter,[1] lies on the carpet with his eyes closed. His body is slightly contorted; he turns his head to one side and grimaces. His fists and jaw are clenched.

The group has just done a short exercise to find an

image of a character from another lifetime that they each
feel identified with. In this guided imagery exercise performed with closed eyes, each of them have found themselves briefly imagining themselves as another person in
another time with another body. After briefly sharing
their images, which ranged from an Italian woman in a
church to a Roman slave, the group chose to hear more of
this young man's image.

> "I'm a boy in my early teens," he says, jaw still clenched,
> "and I'm being whipped by this farmer."
> "What else is happening?" I ask.
> "There are these two farmhands. They're holding me by the
> arms while he whips me. I hate the sonofabitch."
> "Do you cry out?"
> "No, I don't," he says, still grinding his jaw. His face is now
> contorted with what certainly looks to all observers like pain
> and rage.
> "What would you say if you could let it out?" I urge.
> "I wanna kill that sonofabitch. I ain't got no right to say no
> to him, but he can hit me when he chooses. I hate you. I HATE
> YOU! I just wanna get the hell outa here. But I can't go. He'd
> kill me."
> By now Peter is breathing heavily and spitting out his
> venom at this farmer who, it seems, abuses him. For a while I
> encourage him to repeat the most venomous phrases, to say
> what his clenched fists want to, to let it all out.
> "I've had enough of you, you bastard. I'm gonna kill you.
> I'm gonna punch you real good. I used to be scared of you but
> I'm bigger now. I could kill you."
> As he shouts and writhes, his breathing deepens and his
> knuckles whiten; the whole story begins to emerge with only
> the slightest prompting from me, because he is so deeply in it
> by this point.
> "I'm just a farmhand on this farm; in my early teens, but

big. I'm sort of indentured to this man. It's Missouri. I don't remember my parents. I think they must have died when I was young. I've always resented him pushing me around the way he does, but I never say anything. But today it was too much. He told me to go feed the chickens and I told him no. So he hit me in the face and I took a swing at him. He won't stand for that so he sent two older farmhands to hold me. They're holding me by the arms against a fence, while he's getting his horse whip. He's whipping me (he winces, contorts), but I don't cry out."

This time, as he screams out his loathing, his body is noticeably less tense, his jaws and fists less clenched. He has verbally expressed his hatred. The affect is lessened. Now Peter becomes quieter, more reflective.

"I don't know what I done. I must have done something. It ain't fair. I ain't got the right to say no.

Now that he speaks less heatedly I am aware that he is speaking with a very distinct accent, one different from day-to-day Peter. And as he continues his story a kind of bitter sneering tone enters into his voice as well as a strange kind of mannerism of looking to one side.

The remainder of his story is both poignant and disturbing. Never having learned to read, and bitter at this humiliating punishment, he eventually leaves the farm at seventeen, when the farmer dies. Legally no longer bound, he takes to the roads to become a migrant laborer and a social misfit. For a while he works in a mine, but he is so secretive and his mannerisms so odd that he makes people nervous: *"They think I'm funny,"* he says. He wanders for years, most of his life in fact, until he eventually dies, at eighty-four, just after the turn of the century in a charity bed in a state hospital somewhere in the Midwest.

There are big gaps in his story, so I ask him, "Are there any other important events you need to look at?" With a little guidance, his eyes still closed, he reports a field of dandelions with a house in it.

> *"Yes, I go to this house. There's an old woman there. The men in the town hate this woman. They're giving me money to beat her up and threaten to kill her. I'm at the house. She invites me in and offers me this tea cake. She's really nice to me—the first person in my life who has ever been kind to me. I don't know if I can do it, but I'm all worked up. Those men knew I was crazy enough to do it, so maybe I can. I go into the kitchen. It's a big house. The maid's there. She says I look funny. That riles me. I blurt out that I'm gonna kill the old woman. She just laughs at me. I get really mad now. I punch out at her. The tea tray goes flying and I punch her real bad. I've killed her; what am I gonna do? I don't wanna go but I gotta. I drag her body off and dump it in the pond outside the house at the back. Then I hit the road. They never catch me. I never tell anyone what happened."*
>
> *Tears come to Peter's eyes: "The old woman, she was the only one who was ever kind to me. The first place I was treated right. I had no one, no one."*

All the loneliness of this derelict's years on the road, his terrible unspoken humiliation on the farm, his remorse at the murder and his hunger for a few crumbs of human kindness well up inside and he weeps for his empty life.

All of those watching are deeply affected. I lay a hand on Peter's shoulder, still talking to him as the Midwesterner. "It's all over now, you can let it go," I say.

Peter is now back in the hospital bed.

> *"I'm leaving now. I'm out of that body, just looking down on it lying on the bed. Oh, it was so lonely. I was so full of anger. That's why I could never face anybody. I was angry at*

the whole world. The maid got what had built up inside me all those years . . . I'm reaching up. There's an angel. He's come for me."

Peter smiles and I leave some moments of silence for him to inwardly commune with whatever the angel brings him in his after-death vision. Then I ask him: "How does this story relate to your current life, Peter?"

"I have always had a problem with anger," he says, "and I am fascinated by violence and war. Part of me is afraid I might lash out if I get really angry. And authority figures—I always rub them the wrong way up."

"Could you be carrying something of that man in you today?" I ask.

"Oh yes, that makes a lot of sense. I tend to be a loner in this life too."

We talk for a little about the need to feel some compassion for the pain and wretchedness of this man's life but above all to realize that this unhappy personality in Peter no longer needs to run his life from the background, as it were. Peter agrees that it is as though he has been unconsciously challenging authority figures in order to play out the humiliation and resentment that really belongs to the laborer's life and not to this one.

Finally Peter opens his eyes and looks around the room. A circle of rather stunned and concerned faces greets him. He smiles. *"I'm fine,"* he says, as if to reassure them. *"I feel very different."* The whole remembering has taken about forty-five minutes, but to most of us it has seemed quite a bit longer.

A Typical Past Life Session in Therapy

Although Peter's session took place in a group session, it follows the general lines of how I now practice in individual therapy. Usually I start with an interview to explore any current or recurrent problems. In the first session I take a detailed personal history from birth through childhood up to the present, noting illnesses and emotional upheavals of any kind. Then I give my client a simple relaxation exercise with eyes closed and begin to focus on whatever issue seems central. Sometimes I encourage the client to focus on an image, a recent memory or a person and start to say whatever comes to mind as if they were confronting that situation. I may feed them, Gestalt-fashion, a phrase to sum up or intensify the affect, such as "I've had enough of this. Leave me alone." Sometimes we may focus on a pain in the body, such as a backache or stomach cramp, and allow images to emerge from that area.

As soon as images, words, and feelings start to intensify, I suggest they follow them into any story that emerges, this life or another life. I tell my client: "It doesn't matter whether you believe in reincarnation or not; simply follow the story *as if* it were real for the duration of the session."

Very soon the client will find him or herself in a different body and personality, like Peter, recounting the story quite dramatically *as that other self.* Then, following the principles of psychodrama, I encourage my client to relive in their fullness the major events and turning points of that other life, assuming that the most catharsis and release will come at these crucial points of conflict. Whatever arises, however confusing, incoherent, or bloody, I will take him or her through it to completion. If the climax of a particular story is in fact a violent death, I will ensure that it is fully relived at a physically conscious level on the same principle that has been successfully used with shell-shock victims, namely, that only a remembered trauma can be let go of.

In most sessions I will attempt to complete the memory of a life story by taking the rememberer through the death of that particular personality. This brings a sense of completion and, more importantly, of detachment. The death transition is an opportunity to let go *consciously* of the obsessive and repetitive thoughts, feeling, or fears of that other self. In the after-death period there is usually a valuable opportunity to compare the themes of the past life with unresolved issues in this one. As with Peter, every client is encouraged to see the story as now finished, a pattern that need not be repeated. Naturally there will be painful, even shameful aspects of the self that may have to be faced. In Jung's perspective this is what is called *shadow* work: looking at unpleasant and often negative characteristics and not repressing them further.

Because I always insist that the past life story be experienced fully in the body—not from the viewpoint of a detached observer—there will often be quite intense bodily convulsions and contortions that are part of the somatic process of spontaneous release. Sweating, hot and cold flushes, cramping, temporary paralysis, sharp pains, erotic sensations, numbness, trembling, shaking, or tingling may all occur. I tell clients that this is the release of blocked energy associated with an old trauma. The trauma at a physical level may be from birth, a past life, or an operation in this life, and often all three. Whatever it is, the body is encouraged to express and let go of the shock and the trauma. Although to an observer seeing a session for the first time this may seem frightening or even a little crazy, it has been the repeated and consistent finding that such release at a somatic as well as emotional level is absolutely crucial to the full healing process.

Mostly I work with an individual client for two hours. This gives adequate time for the three stages of the process: 1) interview, 2) intensive work, 3) reflection and reentry, or what some therapists call "processing." From the foregoing and later descriptions of sessions it will become clear what an extraordinarily concentrated and intensive form of therapy this is. I know of nothing other that psychedelic work that operates at so many levels in so short a period of time. Generally no more than five to ten intensive two-hour sessions are necessary to work through major issues therapeutically. This is, of course, a radical departure from longer psychoanalytic methods of treatment, which are very often slow because they fail to engage experientially and remain at an intellectual and interpretive level only.

Past Lives: Memory or Fantasy?

Anyone witnessing a session like Peter's or even reading about one like it may well want to raise the question "Did Peter make this up or was he really remembering?"

This is a very reasonable question and one often asked, but like many a simple question about a highly complex phenomenon it is not one to be answered with a straightforward yes or no. Consider how you might remember and recount your most cherished childhood adventure, some special vacation or perhaps a family tragedy. Are you simply remembering, or does some degree of embroidering or exaggeration creep into your account? Do you dramatize your story at all? Are certain events run together or possibly transposed slightly as you tell your story? What about your emotional response? If we reflect on these matters alone it immediately becomes clear that remembering is by no means a simple matter, particularly when the practice of narration is examined. In actual fact, all kinds of literary and philosophical criticism has been written about this very tricky issue.

Most of us, if we are honest with ourselves, will admit that some degree of confabulation nearly always enters into any story we tell about events we have experienced or witnessed. We sometimes come to realize this when someone else present has a different version of the same events.

But even if we grant this, we nevertheless retain a strong sense that it was, after all, a memory that we have been recounting and not a fantasy. We don't, for instance, say to a friend who slips up on a detail: "Well, if your aunt wasn't actually in Chicago for the wedding, you must have imagined the whole thing."

So the first thing to emphasize about the assumed opposition between memory vs. fantasy is that memories which we all agree are memories actually contain quite a lot of fantasy in them. I point this out because many people tend to dismiss reports of past life remembering by saying that they cannot be authentic because they contain certain historical inconsistencies. And yet these skeptics probably would not dismiss the "reality" of their own childhoods simply because certain details of their memory of it proved to be false. In both past and current life remembering our imagination will often fill the gaps and round out the story in all kinds of subtle little ways. Where the picture is not clear the unconscious mind may well touch it up for us.

The second thing to emphasize about Peter's story is that it was much more than just a retelling, a narration; *it was a reexperiencing.* To the extent that Peter's voice, his face, his mood, and his mannerisms all changed, Peter had *become* the Midwesterner from the last century; he had taken on, if temporarily, a quite different identity or other personality.

Was he acting or performing? Certainly not consciously. Peter had never had an acting lesson in his life. As it happened, there was present in that particular group a professional musician who had had considerable acting training. "Boy, I know some acting teachers who would give their eyeteeth to get a performance like that" was his reaction to the session.

Thanks to movies like Alfred Hitchcock's *Marnie* or Peter Schafer's *Equus* most people today are familiar with the idea of therapeutic regression to a forgotten childhood trauma. Therapists have repeatedly demonstrated that, by regressing a patient to a particular age when a violent or emotionally disturbing event took place and having him or her relive it, most if not all of the painful symptoms associated with the event can be removed. After World War II many psychiatrists relieved shell-shock victims of severe residual symptoms of terror and shock with great success.

Yet age regression to events in this life is one thing, the skeptic might say, regression to *another* life, however similar in appearance and effectiveness, must surely be another. For what does it mean to reexperience *another person's* life?

It means, I think, much more than simply imagining the

life of another person in the sense of making it up. Out of the hundreds of thousands who have been "regressed" to another lifetime, by far the vast majority seem to agree that it is not simply a matter of invention or imagination. Many, like Peter, find themselves deeply in the story, with what is very clearly a different ego consciousness. Novel words and emotions, they report, spontaneously erupt into awareness, and with little or no prompting from the guide. Some have even described it as like a mild possession, like being taken over temporarily by another personality. The difference from being possessed, however, is that these "other lives" seem very much to belong to the regressed person; there is a strong sense of familiarity, not the feeling of alienness that comes with even the mildest possession state.

What past life remembering entails is a kind of deep identification with an inner or secondary personality, an identification which does indeed involve imagination, as all remembering does, but in the fullest sense. Shelley described this when he said that "one must imagine intensely and comprehensively" and that a man "must put himself in the place of another." (See also Chapter 12.)

When we read novels or watch films and plays we practice varying degrees of this imaginative identification with the major characters; we are moved to terror or pity by imagining the story *as if* we were in their shoes, *as if* we were ourselves suffering their joys and sorrows. This is possible, psychologically, because we already have within us our own versions of these characters and their stories. Jung believed that our disposition to experience the heroes, villains, lovers, and despots in ourselves derives from archetypal, which is to say, ancient, universal character formations that are the root structures of our psyches. We are therefore born with a disposition to imagine other human beings in these characteristic forms. Literature, drama, and film provide us with various kinds of elaborate Rorschach ink blots onto which, Jung would say, we project our own versions of these inner figures. Naturally the authors of such stories are trying to describe their *own* inner figures in a realistic fashion, but the important point is that in the process of reading or watching *we* activate our own inner cast of characters. What past life remembering seems to do is bring these characters to the surface of consciousness with remarkable clarity, detail, and consistency by using the device of offering the psyche a blank screen called a "past life" to project them onto.

To acknowledge and, even further, to experience the other in ourselves is the first step, in my view, toward genuine psychological reflection and toward knowing for one's self that in our deeper or fuller consciousness *we are multiple beings,* that we have many personalities within us. Some of these other selves are surprisingly close to consciousness and can be awakened quite easily by the use of theater games and guided imagery exercises. What has not been recognized in psychotherapy until quite recently is that these secondary personalities turn out to be every bit as complex and rounded as our ego personality, even to the point of having detailed histories stretching from birth to death.

Past Lives: Romance or Reality? The Cases of Helen and Alice

No doubt there are some who will object to the description of these selves as past life personalities by pointing out that the characters in a good novel can also have biographies that are as complex and unpredictable as any human being but still remain the products of imagination rather than memory. I would have been inclined to agree with this objection at one time but for the case of a woman who once consulted me who was in fact by profession the writer of popular romances.

The writer, whom I shall call Helen, found herself in her regression back in the nineteenth century as the only daughter of a respectable middle-class family in the North Country of England. It was a small seaside town and the young woman lived a very circumscribed and proper life with her family. She had not married, for lack of any acceptable suitor, nor had her parents insisted on her marrying, although she was, at the starting point of the regression, in her mid-twenties.

The event that changes her life is the visit of an attractive young merchant from London with whom, given the barrenness of her provincial life, she falls hopelessly but silently in love. The lover is distinctly worldly and clearly symbolizes the possibility for Helen to escape from her dull existence. Yet she begins to doubt his sincerity, and although they become engaged to be married he makes no effort to follow through on his commitment. There is a stormy scene in which her father intervenes on her behalf, accusing the fiancé of being a user. In her romantic longings she had not allowed herself to see his true intentions, but now she becomes angered and lets her father ask him to leave.

For a while she rages at her lover's betrayal, at the restrictions of her life, and at being a woman in such a world. Her father will not tolerate her outbursts of what he calls hysteria, and she buries her emotions. Her mother had died years earlier and now she finds herself alone with a father who becomes slowly infirm and more and more domineering.

After her father's death she inherits the house and experiences terrible loneliness. Her anger at both men turns to bitterness. Her hatred stays with her until her death. Reflecting on this life when it is over, Helen sees it as a huge waste and that she had made the mistake of letting others control her life.

Upon emerging from the regression Helen had a look of astonishment on her face. "My God," she said, "that was the plot of my very first novel. *But it didn't end that way!* In my novel the young man does return, marries her, and takes her to the city. But he turns out to be somewhat of a scoundrel in my version. Their marriage breaks up and is simply the springboard for her to go off and have all sorts of other amorous adventures."

From the sound of it, her actual novel fulfilled all the expectations for a typical romance novel; by contrast, the plot of her past life story was mutely tragic and inconsequential. Perhaps a Balzac or a Henry James might have made a poignant novel out of such a slight story, but Helen did not aspire to such literary heights. What struck me after listening to her comparison of the two stories was that her recent novel could well have served as a *fantasy compensation* for the anguish and loss experienced in a genuine past life memory whose full events had not emerged because they were too painful. I was also led to wonder whether her other novels might too be compensations for this buried memory of unrequited love.[2]

Seen therapeutically, what the session brought out was that it was hard for Helen to face and untie that inner knot of grief, rage, and heartbreak surrounding the story of this lonely jilted young woman who lived in her unconscious mind. Her novel writing had no doubt helped her to relieve much of this sadness and give expression to yearnings she was too timid to live out in this life. To that extent her chosen profession provided her with a form of self-healing, but the core of her complex, with its wrenching and bitter images of loss and abandonment and its unthinkable thought, "I am not loved or lovable," remained untouched.

Similarly, in Peter's story, reliving the farmhand misfit's wretched life revealed deeply buried feelings of humiliation and severely wounded self-esteem coupled with murderous rage and accompanying guilt. I find it hard to believe that Peter would choose to invent such a complex and unheroic story just to impress either me or the group. If anything, his story had the nature of a painfully wrought confession that obliged him to look squarely into his tendency to isolate himself from others, his distrust of authority, and his unresolved fear of and fascination with violence.

Peter's and Helen's cases are by no means untypical of the thousands of remembered lives that my own clients report. They are also very similar to cases other past life therapists have in their files. Contrary to the popular stereotype of past lives fostered by the tabloid press, the vast majority of past lives are *not* those of Egyptian priestesses or wives of Henry VIII. Most of the lives that are reported are barely identifiable within the known framework of history. We encounter African tribesmen, nomadic hunters, nameless slaves, Middle Eastern traders, anonymous medieval peasants, and so on, from all times and places; often they can barely name their chieftain or lord, let alone place themselves upon some totally irrelevant time map of European or ancient history.

As another example of how very *un*romantic certain past lives can be I will briefly mention the case of Alice. In her regression Alice experienced herself as a young boy in nineteenth-century industrial England. The boy was a ragged street urchin of six or seven who slept in alleyways or under bridges, begged for or stole his food, was chased, beaten, and was ever on the move in an utterly miserable life of pure survival. As one wretched scene succeeded another, I waited for the event that would fortuitously change everything and bring him new hope or direction. In the back of my mind, for sure, images from *Oliver Twist* and *Les Misérables* had already started to present themselves as I listened.

"So what happens next?" I asked, waiting for his wheel of fortune to turn a little more kindly (this time it was I who was the romantic, looking for compensation).

"It's blank . . . dark . . . nothing," said Alice.

Many years of guiding regressions have taught me about the phenomenon of "overshoot" when moving forward in time in a past life. Darkness or lack of images is nearly always a sign that death has occurred, so I said to her: "Go back and see what happens before it goes dark."

"I'm crossing a street. I'm tired and weak. It's winter and I haven't had enough to eat. Not paying attention . . . Aah! I'm hit. It's a wagon. My head, my chest is crushed . . . It's all black. Suddenly I'm above my body. It's all over. What a sad, pointless life."

Other clients report lives cut short by famine, plague, or disease at an early age. There are also countless lives of young men dying on the battlefield barely in the first engagement, leaving their bodies feeling bitter and cheated by all the false promises of glory and honor. Perhaps the most striking of all in this regard are memories of dying at birth and even before birth; dying as a fetus from an abortion or a miscarriage are hardly glamorous subjects for cocktail party conversation, or images gleaned from watching too much television.

In sum, it is not romance that most characterizes the majority of past lives I meet in therapy, but bitter and unrelenting realism. I am often reminded of the bleak words of philosopher Thomas Hobbes when he wrote that "the life of man is solitary, poor, nasty, brutish and short."[3]

Three Explanations of the Past Life Phenomenon

After many years of witnessing, guiding, and recording hundreds into thousands of past life stories like those of Peter, Helen, and Alice, I cannot pretend that I have not speculated a great deal about the tantalizing questions of whether all this is memory or fantasy, whether these are really *our* other lives and whether there truly is a continued existence of the soul, as so many religious traditions assert. But as a therapist and not a philosopher I am perhaps fortunate in that I am not shackled by the problem of belief or disbelief; I am not obliged to delay my sessions until the learned jury of parapsychologists and metaphysicians is in on these matters. Not that they do not have important observations to make—we will look at their contributions in the next chapter—but for the therapist there is another kind of truth, psychic truth: *that which is real for the patient.*

To ask each of my clients, when he or she is in a state of

focused awareness, to treat whatever images arise *as if* they were real merely asks him or her to make an experiment, to entertain a hypothetical stance for the duration of the session. Neither I nor my clients are in any way committed to any doctrine or philosophical position except to take what arises with utmost seriousness and not devalue it as "just imagination." As I always tell my clients: *"It doesn't matter whether you believe in reincarnation or not.* The unconscious mind will almost always produce a past life story when invited in the right way." Indeed, I am sometimes inclined to think that even if the conscious mind is highly skeptical about the reality of past lives as historical memories, the unconscious is a true believer and is simply waiting to be asked.

Yet even though the purpose of this book is not to prove the reincarnation hypothesis, as I stated earlier, it might nonetheless be valuable to end this chapter with a brief sketch of what have emerged, during my investigations, as the three main theoretical positions most people take when attempting to explain past lives. Then the reader is free to decide which position he or she feels most comfortably aligned with. My own prejudices will emerge during the course of the book.

The first position is what I call *the positivist or tabula rasa position.* This position takes it as a fundamental axiom that the mind is a blank slate *(tabula rasa* in Latin) at birth, that we have only one life or identity, and that therefore all psychological disturbances must be the result of experiences in this, our only life. The only way the positivist is commonly prepared to explain past life reports, however historically accurate, is to see them as the result of unconscious imagining and confabulation derived from long-forgotten stories, TV shows, or family

gossip overheard or read early in childhood. This capacity
of the mind to confabulate such elaborate other identities
quite unconsciously is called *cryptoamnesia* (see next
chapter). Following the work of in utero remembering
surveyed by Dr. Thomas Verney in *The Secret Life of the
Unborn Child,* some positivists are now prepared to say
that cryptoamnesia may even take place before birth. The
orthodox Freudian position today—Freud himself was
much more open—is that all these stories are infantile
fantasy projections arising from emotional conflicts associated with the parents: the celebrated Oedipus complex.
In general, positivists of all shades of opinion tend to have
fairly strict standards about what is real and what is fantasy or imagination.

The second position on past lives commonly proposed is
what I call *the Great Memory position.* By this I mean the
belief that we all have access, in dreams, meditation, or
hypnosis, to a stratum of the unconscious mind which is
universal and consists of not just our own forgotten experiences or fantasies. This position holds that we all have
the capacity, rightly prepared, to dip into the vast collective memory bank of mankind. This universal memory
has been called variously the Akashic record, the collective unconscious (Jung), or simply Great Mind. The
psychic Joan Grant coined the phrase "far memory" to
describe the active faculty of tapping into other lives.
Parapsychologists cautiously term this ability "retrocogni-
tion." Here is how the poet W. B. Yeats, from whom I
borrow my preferred epithet, describes how he came to
this view:

Before the mind's eye, whether in sleep or waking, came
images one was to discover presently in some book one had

never read, and after looking in vain for explanation to the current theory of forgotten personal memory, I came to believe in a Great Memory passing on from generation to generation.[4]

The important thing to notice about this position compared to the one that follows, the reincarnationalist position, is that, to change the metaphor a little, the Great Memory does not require reincarnation for us to be able to tune into the historical airwaves. This is clearly an attractive position for those who believe, with Hamlet, that "there are more things in heaven and earth than are dreamt of in your [positivist] philosophy." Yet it fails to explain why specific memories seem to come repeatedly to certain individuals and not to others or why these memories have such a ring of uncanny familiarity to many of those who recall them. The experimental consensus to date is that past life memories are by no means arbitrary or random; we cannot just access the cosmic computer at will and pull out any life we choose. Like it or not, certain of them really do seem to belong to us individually. "Aye, there's the rub," as Hamlet would put it.

The third or *reincarnationalist position* is a familiar one these days whether we subscribe to it or not. Roughly stated, this position asserts, along with Wordsworth and other Western Platonists, that "our birth is but a sleep and a forgetting." The soul that rises at birth has lived many lives in numerous bodies accumulating merit or demerit as the karmic consequences of actions previously performed. Selfishness sown in one life is reaped as misery in another according to the universal law of psychic cause and effect called karma.

Eloquent testimony to this belief is to be found in nearly

all religious traditions at one time or another and possibly it is as old as man. In the West the theory of reincarnation has attracted a long line of distinguished minds, among them Goethe, Benjamin Franklin, David Hume, Schopenhauer, Tolstoy, and T. H. Huxley, to name but a few.[5]

The Influence of Theosophy

In my own thinking I have found myself swinging back and forth between the second and third positions; as a Jungian I am naturally attracted to the Great Memory idea as was Jung, while at the same time feeling tempted to go the whole hog and embrace reincarnation in all its sublime simplicity. As for the positivist position, I find that it takes too narrow and too materialist a view of the psyche. It seems to me arrogant simply to ignore the hundreds and thousands of past life reports now on record even as phenomenological data on the grounds that they can't be anything but fantasies or to nitpick about historical discrepancies. Positivists remind me of flat-earthers who refuse to go too close to the edge and see for themselves because they might fall off.

At the same time, I find myself with many serious reservations about the theory of reincarnation as it is mostly presented by Western writers and thinkers. What holds me back most of all from reincarnation as a popular doctrine is the fact that few reincarnationalists are aware of just how thoroughly their ideas are saturated with the truisms of nineteenth-century Theosophy. This enormously influential pseudo-religion, as René Guénon, the great French historian of sacred tradition calls it,[6] was largely the synthetic creation of Madame H. P. Blavatsky (1831–1891), a remarkable Russian trance medium and

writer. Appearing as it did as a late Romantic reaction
against both scientific materialism and a spiritually mori-
bund Christianity, the Theosophical movement seemed
to offer nourishment to a generation that was hungry for
"ancient wisdom" and mysticism. What they got, however, was Madame Blavatsky's endlessly intriguing but
ultimately unsatisfying mishmash of authentic teachings
and occultist clichés. As Guénon puts it:

> [Theosophy] is, in short, no more than a confused mixture
> of Neoplatonism, gnosticism, Jewish Kabbalah, hermeticism,
> and occultism, the totality being arranged around two or
> three ideas which, like it or not, are entirely modern and
> Western in origin. Originally this heteroclite system had been
> presented as "esoteric Buddhism," though it is all too easy to
> see that it has only the vaguest of connections with genuine
> Buddhism.[7]

The "modern and Western ideas" to which Guénon
alludes are none other than the twin nineteenth-century
shibboleths of evolution and progress, archetypes still
very dear to our Western myth of ourselves. As Guénon
also said:

> Theosophy attaches considerable importance to the idea of
> "evolution," an idea which is very Western and very modern;
> and like most branches of spiritism, with which it is closely
> linked on account of its origins, Theosophy associates this idea
> with reincarnation. This particular conception of reincarna-
> tion seems to have arisen among certain [French] Socialist
> visionaries in the first half of the nineteenth century.[8]

A major consequence of the pervasive influence of Theosophy is that apologists for reincarnation still continue to
paint a certain rather sentimental picture of the evolving
soul and its progress through karmic high school—under

the tutelage, of course, of a distinguished coterie of "Ascended Masters" in various guises. Such presentations invariably play into a certain grandiosity or what Jung called "ego inflation." For lack of very much serious grounding in traditional spiritual psychology such as Yoga or Buddhist meditation, writers of popular metaphysics frequently fail to make the proper distinction between the ego personality and the greater self or soul and so unwittingly encourage the sort of cocktail party karma-babble like "I know that this is my last time around." Strictly speaking, the ego self does not reincarnate at all, only the soul, and even then it is far from clear to what extent progression is linear and historical.

My own beliefs, which will play in and out of what follows, have been nourished by the masters of the psychoanalytic tradition, in particular Freud, Jung, and Reich, and by my contact with an authentic tradition in the form of Theravada Buddhism, with its practice of vipassana meditation. Intellectually and spiritually I am most at home in what is now called transpersonal psychology, a movement which tries to bring psychological and spiritual perspectives together.

For me, the ego personality is but an evanescent fragment of the Greater Self, to which it owes love and obedience and whose laws of dissolution and re-formation remain a *mysterium tremendum et fascinans*- -an awesome and overwhelming mystery, to loosely render the Latin.[9] Blavatsky's images of linear soul evolution or Rudolf Steiner's higher spiritual leagues do not appeal to me. I prefer to remain dumb before the vast and miraculous interweaving and reabsorption of soul and the myriad heights and depths of psyche seeking to know itself. Goethe, in *Faust*, put it much better:

> Formation, transformation,
> Eternal Mind's eternal re-creation.

CHAPTER 3

TERRA INCOGNITA
EXPLORING UNKNOWN
PSYCHIC REALMS

I am aware that you are driven by the innermost
inclination to the study of the occult and I am sure that
you will return richly laden. Just don't stay in the tropical
colonies too long: you must reign at home.
Freud, letter to C. G. Jung, 1911

The Stigma of the Occult

Early in the history of psychoanalysis there is a famous
moment, reported by Jung in his memoirs, when Freud,
his newly found mentor, very solemnly asked him never
to abandon the theory of infant sexuality. "That is the
most essential thing of all. You see, you must make a
dogma of it, an unshakable bulwark." If the word
"dogma" wasn't enough to arouse the young Jung's skepticism—he had already rejected the dead theological
maunderings of his father, a Swiss Reformed pastor—the
metaphor of seige fully aroused his astonishment. "A bulwark," Jung replied, "against what?"

"Against the black tide of mud—of occultism," replied
the founder of psychoanalysis.[1]

This incident was to be a turning point in the relationship between the two men, for Jung was eventually to break with Freud, and the dogma of sexual theory, and to found his own school. It was not that Jung wanted to devote himself to occultism but that he realized that Freud's narrow rationalism was excluding not just the occult but vast unknown areas of philosophy, religion, and parapsychology from the much more comprehensive perspective that Jung was developing. Jung himself had a number of what might be called psychic experiences which he knew were not to be explained away. He also considered himself more widely read in religious and spiritual matters than Freud. To the end of his life he was prepared to write learned if somewhat cautious commentaries on what were in his day obscure religious texts, like the *I Ching* and the *Tibetan Book of the Dead*. He tried, too, to keep an open mind about psychic phenomena.

The tension between Freud and Jung over the occult wasn't simply a disagreement over the proper study of psychology or even a matter of incompatible temperaments. Their struggle epitomizes the conflict between science and religion, orthodoxy and heresy, rationalism and superstition that has endlessly divided Western civilization. Some historians see its roots in the rise of rationalism among the Greeks and the subsequent demise of the gods and their cults. For others, the origin of the split lies in the clash between the pagan religions and the eventual dominance of Christianity as the official state religion of Rome under the Emperor Constantine. Archetypal psychologist James Hillman observes a fundamental archetypal opposition between modes of monotheism and polytheism that dogs the whole of our culture right down to contemporary disputes in psychology.[2] Even today orthodoxies such as Freudian ego psychology, Behaviorism, and psychiatry try to exercise monotheistic control over proliferating alternative schools of psychology like Reichian, Gestalt, parapsychology, and Feminist psychology, schools that collectively express the new polytheism. These new heresies are subtly persecuted by licensing laws, insurance companies, and doctrinaire research. Occasionally the American Psychological Association will declare a whole field anathema, as it did a few years ago with parapsychology.

Much as we all proclaim a liberal tolerance of other points of view, it is all too easy to fall into an obsessively righteous demand for *the* truth, for the *real* meaning of this or that phenomenon, as though there can be an ultimate Archimedean point from which the human psyche can be understood. A belief in the final interpretative power of rationality and science to explain everything is itself a pernicious form of monotheism and only leads to all kinds of irrational, inexplicable, and even occult reactions from the repressed polytheistic unconscious. It is no accident that the seeds of the revival of psychism and a psychology of the unconscious were sown by Mesmerism during the eighteenth-century Enlightenment. They blossomed as spiritualism, Theosophy, and the Gothic revival at the height of nineteenth-century scientific materialism and positivism. Jung commented on this antithesis as follows:

Rationalism and superstition are complementary. It is a psychological rule that the brighter the light, the blacker the shadow; in other words, the more rationalistic we become the more alive becomes the spectral world of the unconscious.[3]

What so disturbed Freud as "the black tide of the occult" could well be seen, to use one of his own terms, as the return of the repressed side of Western spirituality: the Greek mystery schools, the Christian Gnostics, the medieval heretics and witches (really healers and shamans), the alchemists, mystics, and psychics of all shades whose visions failed to conform to prevailing Christian orthodoxies whether Catholic or Protestant.

Many contemporary followers of Jung seem to be just as terrified of "the black tide of the occult" as Freud was, to judge by the number of Jungian associations that have politely but firmly dropped me from their lecture and workshop programs once my past life interests became known.[4] Some degree of stigma attaches to the investigation of past lives and psychic phenomenon in general. Most people—even highly educated ones—tend to shy away from it, or patronize it in subtle ways. Many of my colleagues seem to think I have sold out to the palm readers and the occultist lunatic fringe until I explain my approach. Risking the chance that this book may confirm their direst predictions, I nevertheless stand firm in trying to keep an open mind about important phenomena that have been banished to the hinterlands of our known psychic universe.

Past lives, spirit possession, near death experiences, psychic powers, and so on are part of a vast psychic *terra incognita* like lost temples in South America that have been overtaken by centuries of jungle growth. As creative innovations in psychotherapy make more and more inroads into that huge continent of the psyche we call the unconscious, more of these exotic structures will be unearthed. In common with many a lone explorer, I have become accustomed to my stories of fabulous discoveries

being scoffed at a little. Nevertheless, to be fair to my
more skeptical colleagues, I will admit that it is quite easy,
to stay with the metaphor, to get lost in the jungle of
occultism and to hallucinate things that are not really
there. For this reason I try to provide in this chapter some
preliminary compass bearings to help investigators and
readers orient themselves in this huge and tangled territory.

From my far from exhaustive research I have found
there to be four main ways of looking at past lives:

1. The *psychic approach:* this includes past life readings and trance mediumship.

2. The *parapsychological approach:* this favors a scientific and experimental investigation of past life
claims.

3. The *religious approach:* this expounds or elabo-
rates reincarnation as an article of faith.

4. The *psychotherapeutic approach:* this uses past
life regression in the service of therapeutic change.

Although these approaches obviously overlap in practice—a psychic may take part in parapsychological research, a reincarnationalist may be a therapist too—they
do help us avoid counterproductive disputes about truth,
falsehood, methods, and aims. When we look at each of
these categories in turn it becomes clear that each carries
fundamental differences of perspective both with regard
to their philosophical assumptions and especially in the
goals that they project, practical or otherwise.

Thus the psychic aims to channel past life *information*
from a paranormal source; the parapsychologist is concerned with proving or disproving the *truth* of past life
memory claims; the religionist is occupied with ex-
pounding reincarnation as a *doctrine* received through a

religious tradition; and finally, the psychotherapist uses past life regression as a practical technique for the purposes of *psychological healing*. With these general qualifications in mind, let us proceed to look at the first three approaches. The fourth, psychotherapy, will be treated in the next and succeeding chapters, since it is the predominant approach I am using in this book.

The Psychic Approach

My work has naturally brought me into contact with many who call themselves psychics. Often clients come to do past life work after a psychic reading, for instance. For several years I worked closely with a woman psychic healer who was sensitive to past lives, subtle energy imbalances, and the presence of what she called entities. I would complement her work by finishing unfinished past life scenarios that she had detected, using my own psychodramatic skills to guide them to completion and resolution. When I felt particularly stuck I would consult her for readings and suggestions. From our joint work I developed great respect for her perceptions at the subtle level. Whether it was how she read dreams, physical complaints, or past life traumas, she always offered extremely precise and useful input into the immediate issues of the clients in question. In psychological language, I would say she had the gift of direct access to the unconscious; what for me was a dimly lit cellar with vague shapes that I groped among was for her a brightly lit space with psychic objects whose shape and nature were clearly illuminated.

Now, I don't for a moment claim psychic abilities for myself. From years as a therapist working with dreams and "listening with the inner ear" as Theodor Reik, a

Freudian, once put it, I have a well-developed intuitive sense, but not what would be called telepathic or clairvoyant. A psychic like my friend has a faculty I don't possess, what used to be called second sight but is nowadays called extrasensory perception or, for short, ESP. The latter term is preferable because a psychic may not only "see" extrasensorily but also "hear" voices and messages and "sense" physical events not immediately perceivable.

To the extent that a psychic exercises these powers when giving a reading, I find this a most valuable adjunct to my work as a psychotherapist. What psychics see clairvoyantly also confirms the research that Jung and others have made into the collective unconscious, whose many layers now seem almost incontrovertibly to include traces of past life memories. But many psychics claim a great deal more than this, placing their perceptions within the greater framework of what is loosely called "metaphysics." Here we are dealing with what nowadays is called "channeled teachings," which assert, more often than not, the existence of higher spiritual planes, spirit guides, ascended masters, reincarnation, and karma.

It is at this point that I find myself distinctly uncomfortable about the psychic approach. I feel obliged to accept not only psychic perceptions and impressions regarding past lives and other data but also to subscribe to a highly elaborated set of doctrines. It is as though in reaction to their exclusion from the mainstream of religion in the West, the psychics have produced their own theology, as well as an alternative form of ethics, cosmology, and metaphysics, and even a discarnate hierarchy of teachers and masters.

My main reservations about many channeled teachings are that: 1) They are frequently inconsistent with other psychic teachings, 2) They are often as dogmatic as any other theology, to be accepted without any critical discussion, and 3) They are often quite derivative of other occult or psychic teachings.

Despite these criticisms, there is much that is of immense value in the teachings of writers like Rudolf Steiner, Alice Bailey, Edgar Cayce, and Jane Roberts, to name some of the more influential writers of this century. Jane Roberts's guide Seth is, from my own reading, quite exceptional in many ways: his teachings are clear, internally consistent, and free of well-worn Theosophical platitudes; above all, they are highly sophisticated psychologically.

From a cursory study of many of these readings I cannot agree that there is a single common doctrine called metaphysics that they have in common. Each of these doctrines—Steiner, Cayce, Bailey, Roberts—has its own distinctive emphasis when it comes to higher planes, masters, soul evolution, and so on. The Christian emphasis in Steiner, Cayce, and Bailey is quite absent in Roberts/ Seth, for example. Also, Seth seems to reject the idea of soul evolution called progress, so inimical to the other more Theosophical derivatives.

While there is some commonality among the various versions of reincarnation that appear in these writers, they don't have nearly as much in common as they claim, as I learned when I researched it. Contrary to the impression given in Annie Besant's *Esoteric Christianity* and Head and Cranston's otherwise valuable compendium *Reincarnation: The Phoenix Fire Mystery,* there is not an unbroken esoteric or underground tradition in the West through which teachings such as reincarnation were passed down. All we have are sporadic revivals, usually ending in persecution.[5] It is true that in the twelfth century the Cathars imported the belief from the Middle East, but after their extermination in 1210–1244, Christian orthodoxy prevailed and it completely disappeared. As for the Knights Templar, nothing is known of their beliefs with any certainty. With the Neoplatonic revival during the Italian Renaissance, reincarnation reappears briefly in veiled form, later to be absorbed into the Rosicrucianism of that time, but it does not appear at all prominently in the Masonic traditions of the eighteenth century. The real appearance of the psychic doctrine—to distinguish it from the Eastern traditions of reincarnation (see below)—is intimately bound up with the emergence of the schools of spiritualism, Theosophy, and the so-called French occult revival in the mid-nineteenth century. It is this background that I will briefly sketch.

Reincarnation in Spiritualism, Occultism, and Theosophy

Spiritualism as a movement is usually dated from 1847, when the Fox family in Hydesville, a small town near Rochester, New York, moved into a house where mysterious rapping noises had been heard. The two daughters and the mother discovered a way to communicate with the rappings by knocking back. Eventually they developed a code to talk to the so-called spirit, who revealed that a man had been murdered in the house. Word got out and visitors flocked to the house. Mrs. Fox and her daughters found they could speak to other spirits of the dead in other houses they visited. So the modern séance was born. It was an immediate success and soon imitators were legion. Before long, tables began to turn, objects to levitate, and scripts to be produced by automatic (i.e., trance) writing. By 1853 the craze had spread to England, Germany, and France. The latter part of the century became the era of the great mediums, like Florence Cook, Stainton Moses, and Daniel Dunglas Home, who produced all kinds of paranormal feats. Many mesmerists, already familiar with the use of trance, also supported the movement.[6]

In France the spiritualist movement acquired the name of *spiritism*. There it was largely the inspiration of a former schoolteacher, Hippolyte Rivail, who under the name of Allan Kardec, published the famous *Book of the Spirits* (1857), compiled from trance readings given to him by two women mediums in Paris. This was to be the prototype for all future books of "channeled" readings. Spiritism later migrated to Brazil, where it is still very much alive today.

What stood out from my research into this movement was that reincarnation as a doctrine was at the very beginning a basic tenet of only the French spiritist movement, but *not*, however, of spiritualist groups in the English-speaking world. Spiritualists there were only interested in immediate survival of spirits of the departed and not with their subsequent return to earth. If anything, English and American spiritualists seemed anxious to find psychic evidence of life after death which would confirm previously held and quite conservative beliefs about the afterlife. The English medium D. D. Home, for example, vehemently attacked the French doctrine of reincarnation and to this day many spiritualist churches still reject reincarnation. French spiritism, as René Guénon points out, early on became enmeshed in socialism and the widespread revival of occultism with which it is exactly contemporary. The mediums who channeled for Kardec had almost certainly been influenced by the current vogue for occultism in which reincarnation was prominently featured.

Occultism owes its popularity and influence to the ex-seminarian Alphonse-Louis Constant who, under the name of Eliphas Lévi, published a number of books on magic and "the great mysteries" from 1856 onward. Lévi had studied Kabbalah, Jakob Boehme, Emanuel Swedenborg, and many eighteenth-century *théosophes* and freemasons who taught the "Egyptian" mysteries (Mozart's *The Magic Flute* is an example of this earlier interest). In his youth Lévi had been influenced by Balzac's novels of spiritual quests, notably *Louis Lambert* (1832) and *The Search for the Absolute* (1833). As the eminent historian of religion Mircea Eliade writes, Lévi's books "met with a success difficult to understand today, for they are a mass of pretentious jumble."[7] Yet there is hardly a popular work on the occult and on magic that does not echo their contents.

Nevertheless, it was Lévi's popular occultism that fed directly into Kardec's spiritist teachings in France and became the primary source of every subsequent modern revival of reincarnation as a doctrine. One reason for its ready acceptance in France was that the various social upheavals since the Revolution had spawned a variety of socialist movements and inspired great Romantic exposés of social injustice such as Victor Hugo's *Les Misérables* (1862). Reincarnation as filtered through Balzac, Lévi, and Kardec, himself a disciple of the great Swiss social reformer Pestalozzi, naturally took on a strong socialist flavor. Reincarnation seemed to provide for the disaffected and the downtrodden a doctrine that accounted for social inequality and provided ultimate justice for rich and poor alike through its revolutionary system of karmic checks and balances.

How then did reincarnation find its way from France to an English-speaking spiritualist world which, as we saw, was more conservative in its metaphysics? The answer lies with the ever-resourceful Madame Helena Blavatsky, herself a trance medium and an early student of French occultism.

In 1873, while investigating two renowned mediums in Chittenden, Vermont, Madame Blavatsky met a certain Colonel Henry Steele Olcott, a passionate follower of spiritualism. Two years later, the two of them founded the Theosophical Society in New York. Madame Blavatsky's first major work, *Isis Unveiled* (1877), which focused mostly on Egyptian mysteries and western Hermeticism (i.e., astrology and alchemy), rejected reincarnation. More in line with spiritualist teaching, she saw only the ascent of the departed soul at death to higher planes of spirit. "Reincarnation," she writes, "is a violation of the harmonic laws of nature" (vol. II, p. 351). With the publication of *A Secret Doctrine* in 1888, however, after spending many years in India, Madame Blavatsky had reversed her position and now included a quasi-Hindu/Buddhist version of reincarnation strikingly similar to Kardec's. René Guénon in his authoritative critical histories of spiritism and Theosophy is of the opinion that Madame Blavatsky appropriated the doctrine of reincarnation from Kardec's spiritism in view of its popular success in France.[8] Given the enormous amount of material Madame Blavatsky has been shown to have plagiarized from occult sources, this is not altogether surprising.[9]

Plagiarism was by no means the only scandal surrounding the colorful life of Madame Blavatsky. A disgruntled housekeeper in Bombay had exposed how she "materialized" her so-called Mahatma Letters through a false backing in a certain shrine, and for a time the Theosophical Society seemed thoroughly discredited. Yet it is a measure of Madame Blavatsky's extraordinarily charismatic personality that by the turn of the century, barely ten years after her death, her writings had once more become invested with an aura of sanctity and Theosophy continued to attract millions.

The evolutionary content in the version of reincarnation Blavatsky adopted from Kardec was as attractive then as it is today. For, as I remarked in the previous chapter, the idea that we are evolving progressively life-by-life toward greater perfection on this earth resonates powerfully with the nineteenth-century myth of progress and with current visions of the New Age. Yet this picture of reincarnation remains a Romantic and singularly Western myth replete with optimism and new frontiers; the Eastern vision of rebirth in traditional Hinduism and Buddhism is by contrast profoundly pessimistic and ahistorical, as I shall show when we discuss the religious approach.

A rather ironic footnote to Madame Blavatsky's championing of the doctrine of reincarnation appears in the well-known book on mediumship by C. A. Wickland, *Thirty Years Among the Dead*. In one of his sessions with a medium, Wickland writes, the spirit of the departed Madame Blavatsky was contacted. Eager to settle the question of reincarnation once and for all Wickland asks the distinguished spirit's opinion from "the other side." The spirit's reported reply is as follows:

> Reincarnation is not true; I have tried and tried to come back
> as somebody else, but I could not. We cannot reincarnate. We
> progress, we do not come back.[10]

Was Wickland's medium in fact mirroring back to him his
own unconscious skepticism as a spiritualist about reincarnation? Or was it genuinely Madame Blavatsky's spirit
hoist upon her own petard of "progress"? Or perhaps, as
she was prone to do, the ever-colorful H.P.B. had changed
her mind once again!

Contradictions notwithstanding, there is hardly a corner of psychic metaphysics that Madame Blavatsky's Theosophy has not infiltrated. With the possible exception of
Jane Roberts/Seth almost every recent metaphysical book
on reincarnation shows its direct or indirect influence.
Edgar Cayce's famous trance readings about the karmic
origins of mental and physical disease were certainly at
odds with his conscious Christian fundamentalist beliefs,
yet it is known that Cayce was a voracious reader of occult
and Theosophical books in his youth, having once worked
as an assistant in a bookshop presumably carrying such
titles. So Cayce himself manifests yet another split between the orthodox and the heterodox, the conscious and
the unconscious selves, with regard to the occult.

There is no question that spiritualism, occultism, and
Theosophy have provided thousands of men and women
of psychic or visionary temperament with both a metaphysical framework for their experiences and a social milieu to which they could comfortably belong. In recent
years the scholarly study of shamanism by religionists and
anthropologists like Mircea Eliade, Michael Harner, and
Stephen Larsen have helped us see that the visionary who
in trance visits other realms, encounters spiritual and de-

monic beings, and is empowered by them has always been recognized in traditional societies as an expert in the supernatural.[11] From the very earliest days in the Christian West, however, visionaries and healers have been subjected to one wave of intolerance and cruel persecution after another. From the suppression of the Gnostics of the first centuries to the medieval heretics to the witchcraze, Christianity has proved largely inimical to independent spiritual exploration. Even a recognized mystic like Meister Eckhart suffered excommunication, while St. John of the Cross barely escaped execution by the Inquisition. Of all the major religions, Christianity alone has failed to countenance an inner esoteric order. By contrast, Judaism has always retained an esoteric dimension, in the form of the Kabbalah, and has never lost contact with the doctrine of reincarnation.[12]

For all my reservations about the elusiveness and derivativeness of many popular psychic teachings, I don't want to let this obscure the extraordinary achievements of psychics as a class of individuals and the implications their highly evolved shamanic faculties have for a comprehensible picture of the psyche. Colin Wilson, in his book *The Occult,* has neatly summed up these paranormal abilities as Faculty X, the unknown psychic faculty that presumably we all have to some degree. Just as we can sharpen our vision, extend our auditory acuity, and develop superfine tactile sensitivity—the pulse-reading skill of the acupuncturist is a good example of the latter—so too, Wilson and the psychics like Joan Grant imply, we can all develop Faculty X.

It may help us, therefore, to conceive of a continuum of consciousness as follows: from our outer sensory perceptions to the inner observation of thoughts, feelings, and images onward to the spontaneous flow of images and to intuitive understanding, and, finally, at the end of the continuum to psychic perception. Whenever people in our workshops do exercises of any sort to develop their intuition, they find that all kinds of telepathic tuning to their partners or to others in the group take place. Equally, therapists who work closely with imagery, body symbolism, dreams or subtle energy systems frequently have insights whose provenance has to be called psychic.

If there is one thing psychics are natural experts in it is trance states. Meditation and hypnosis both use trance for traversing this continuum from outer to inner states and likewise these practices tend to develop Faculty X when they are followed regularly. So the psychic approach is not solely restricted to those with psychic faculties but is one with which we are all equipped to experiment with and develop. As more people let go of the encrusted prejudices of the centuries regarding the occult, witchcraft, and mediums, more will find themselves using and developing these faculties. Past life remembering has already proved easy for many people to learn. In our workshops, my wife and I have a 90 to 95 percent success rate in teaching our particular method of doing this.

Other groups and trainings, like the Silva Mind Control and DMA, as well as many forms of hypnosis, directly or indirectly are also teaching people that intuitive and psychic skills are within their reach experimentally. And yet, if these are experiments, they are nevertheless *subjective* experiments, and herein lies the fundamental difference between the psychic approach to past lives and other realities and our second approach, that of parapsychology, to which we now turn our attention.

The Parapsychological Approach

It was perhaps inevitable as more and more mediums reported semi-miraculous materializations or levitations, and made clairvoyant predictions of future events, that a skeptical reaction would set in among the rationalists and scientists of the nineteenth century. Certainly there were phenomena, as eminent scholars like Frederick W. H. Myers and later the philosopher William James were prepared to agree, but how to interpret them, this was a different matter.

Toward the end of the century more and more investigators of what was eventually to be called "psychology" were looking at spirit phenomena in terms of hypnosis and suggestion and using the recently developed concept of the "unconscious mind" to explain what went on. As early as 1854, for example, a French investigator, Michel-Eugène Chevreul, demonstrated that the movements of the divining rods, pendulums, and even tables were produced by the unconscious muscular movements of the practitioners. He concluded that the alleged messages of the "spirits" are the expression of the unconscious force of the mediums.[13]

In a similar but even more damning vein, René Guénon, in his radical critique, *The Spiritist Error* (1926), maintained that the mediums used by Allan Kardec for his *Book of the Spirits* were little more than "psychic mirrors" who reflected back to Kardec from his unconscious mind beliefs he had already absorbed from early French writers on the occult and reincarnation.

F. W. H. Myers, whom I have mentioned, was part of a group of interested skeptics in Cambridge, England, who began a number of private investigations of clairvoyance, precognition, and communication from the dead in the 1870s. In 1882 a physicist, William Barrett, a clergyman, the Reverend Stainton Moses, a philosopher, Henry Sidgwick, and Myers himself, a young classical scholar, formed the Society for Psychical Research. This society—the SPR for short—has attracted numerous psychologists, scholars, and scientists, such as William James and Gardner Murphy, both psychologists, Sir Alistair Hardy, the biologist, Gilbert Murray, the classicist, and Arthur Koestler, the writer, to name only a few of the better known. The SPR still flourishes today, along with its American counterpart, the American Society for Psychical Research, and continues to stand for an open-minded, scientific, and non-doctrinaire approach to paranormal phenomena. Reincarnation, however, was never the subject of much SPR or ASPR investigation, since, as I noted in the last section, reincarnation tended to be a fairly restricted belief in the English-speaking world in comparison with Continental Europe. Early SPR investigators in England were much more occupied with the question of whether there was personal survival after death, spending their energies trying to find spirit guides or controls who could come up with verifiable data about the lives they or other departed spirits had once led on earth.

A certain Swiss investigator, the physician-philosopher-psychologist Theodore Flournoy (1854–1920), is important to mention here because he established a skeptical paradigm, namely cryptoamnesia, which remains to this day one of the positivist's most devastating weapons in dismissing the claim that past life memories are in fact derived from historical events unknown to the subject. The theory of cryptoamnesia claims, simply stated, that the unconscious mind has recorded all sorts of overheard conversations, pictures, stories from books, and, nowadays, films and television programs, that are now forgotten. These forgotten stories or images, it is claimed, become the basis for historical romances that mature in the unconscious and later emerge disguised as fully elaborated past life "memories."

Flournoy's investigation of the trance medium he called Hélène Smith, published in his book entitled *From India to the Planet Mars* (1900), shows how her mediumistic "reversions" (today we would say regressions) to the time of Marie Antoinette and then to a life as a Hindu princess could be entirely accounted for by books she had read or come across as a child. She also claimed to have had a life on Mars, which she supported by a strange "Martian" script. However, when this was analyzed it proved to have the syntax of French. As for the spirit control, Leopold, who mediated these "other lives" to Hélène, Flournoy believed him to be an unconscious subpersonality of Hélène herself.

In my own work I naturally entertain the possibility of cryptoamnesia on those rare occasions where a client recalls a life as a well-known historical personage. Certain characters have even appeared more than once to different clients. Two women I worked with independently remembered having been Anne Boleyn, the ill-fated wife of Henry VIII, while two other women recalled the life of Joan of Arc. Still two others both independently saw themselves as the French Countess de la Motte Valois, the adventuress responsible for the celebrated "diamond necklace scandal" at the court of the queen, Marie Antoinette.

In all six of the sessions the quality and apparent verisimilitude of the lives as remembered was barely distinguishable from other more typical past life regressions of quite obscure persons. In contrasting the two Joans or the two Anne Boleyns each woman emphasized quite different aspects of the life, but in accordance with their present characters, much like two actresses playing the same role. One of the Annes came up with such precise historical details that I was tempted to go leaping for my history books. But since I was practicing therapy and not research the drama and passion of these remembrances eclipsed any real historical interest for me.

In speculating about what my clients had produced, it seemed to me that these were all examples of cryptoamnesia in which the dominant motivation had been a deeply felt identification with one or other aspect of these famous women's lives; they each had had tragic, heroic, and adventurous stories. And even if they hadn't literally been these famous women in other lives, I am left to wonder if there were not similar but less illustrious past life stories that had gotten grafted onto the famous, known historical outlines. An obscure and ignominious witch-burning memory lingering in the unconscious of either of these women could easily have been aroused by childhood reading of Joan of Arc's fate, for instance. In this way the almost archetypal stories of the famous become vehicles for moving, amplifying and bringing to a head emotional conflicts dormant in the unconscious minds of those attracted to them.

Cryptoamnesia was invoked in the fifties in one of the most famous cases of all, that of Bridey Murphy, the Irish past life personality of the housewife Virginia Tighe. Mrs. Tighe was regressed by the businessman and amateur hypnotist Morey Bernstein in the 1950s. Despite copious details from Mrs. Tighe's hypnotic regression sessions which were verified in the course of painstaking investigation, the triumph of the skeptics seemed to come when it was discovered that the subject had early on lived with an aunt of Scottish-Irish descent who had often told her niece about the old country. Even though the aunt's knowledge of Irish history in no way matched up to "Bridey Murphy's," it was sufficient to demolish all past life claims in the minds of skeptics. Possibly the fairest summary of this fascinating case is to be found in D. Scott Rogo's excellent parapsychological survey of the issue, *The Search for Yesterday,* where he writes, "Few partisans realize that perhaps the case represented a mixture of both elements—a tightly woven fantasy based on cryptoamnesia, role playing, *and* paranormally acquired information."[14]

Another investigator of mediumistic phenomena was Carl Jung. The title of his M.D. dissertation, "On the Psychology and Pathology of So-called Occult Phenomena" (1902), reveals the basic skepticism of his approach. He follows Flournoy in attributing all the material he collected from a young trance medium in his family to cryptoamnesia and split-off subpersonalities.[15]

The key idea of sub- or secondary personalities was to become for Jung the basis of his mature psychology of the total Self, which he saw as a complex structure of many secondary personalities. This idea, already implicit in much early nineteenth-century psychological thinking, remains one of the most fruitful models of the psyche. In this view, we own our "spirit world" as the other or inner world of our own unconscious, to which we have unique access as part of the greater Self.

Another of Jung's major contributions to modern psy-

chology and parapsychology is his idea of the collective
unconscious, the shared repository of the experience of
the human race recorded in universal symbolic form he
called archetypes. Although there is nothing explicit
about past lives in this theory—in fact Jung denied the
possibility of such personal memory early in his career—
there is obviously room to extend this theory to include
past lives. Above all, the concept allows us to entertain the
notion of a universal psychic substrate to human experience which unites us all nonspatially, which is to say, beyond the brain and the body. This idea, a commonplace of
Hinduism and Buddhism, has generally found little favor
among Western philosophers and has been relegated to
one of their shelves reserved for metaphysical curiosities
bearing the label "idealism." It is nevertheless a profoundly liberating concept when fully understood. Without it, we are left to piece together all kinds of fragmentary paranormal information and strange phenomena
with the none-too-sturdy glue of rationalism and the limited framework of experimental science.

Possibly no one has tried harder to "prove" reincarnation by the rational and empirical standards of parapsychological science than Dr. Ian Stevenson of the University of Virginia. Since 1960 Dr. Stevenson has been
indefatigably collecting past life memory reports from
various parts of the world, notably India, Sri Lanka, Tur-
key, and Lebanon.[16] He much prefers reports from children who spontaneously talk of having lived elsewhere in
another body and so on. Stevenson dismisses hypnotic
regression as hard evidence on the grounds that the subject too easily mirrors the bias, conscious or unconscious,
of the hypnotist. Generally, he or his research assistant
collect as much data as they can find, first from the child,

then from the family and from witnesses. Then he visits the alleged site of the previous life to verify the information.

One of the double binds that Stevenson's research has created for itself is that he has tended to conduct his investigations mostly in cultures that openly believe in reincarnation, obviously because it is mostly here that the past life stories of young children will attract serious attention. The problem comes when he wants to corroborate these stories. It seems a strong possibility that the child learns unconsciously to confirm the descriptions of the deceased person he was in a previous incarnation. When Stevenson is checking out purported past life memories, a child is typically taken to the village of his or her supposed previous incarnation. But during the matching up of the child's memories with the reminiscences of the villagers who knew the deceased, the child often seems to unconsciously mirror the expectations of the informants, for whom reincarnation is a received teaching. Such social pressures are ignored in Stevenson's research design. Many books on reincarnation quote Stevenson's work as solid proof, and at first sight it is impressive, but considerable doubt has been thrown on it by certain of his former research assistants, who have failed to replicate his findings and have also noted the above experimental defect. A useful survey of Stevenson's work is to be found in Rogo's *The Search for Yesterday.*

One of the criticisms sometimes leveled at Stevenson is that he is somewhat of a fanatic regarding reincarnation; with him it has become a fixed idea, an obsession. Certainly anyone who spends nearly thirty years pursuing a single idea could be accused of that, though the same could be said of Einstein or Freud. Such single-minded-ness does not detract from the truth of the idea, but it does tell us something about the psychology of the pursuer. My own discomfort with Stevenson's and similar investigations is that they are excessively mental and abstract. To look for evidence in a purely scientific fashion necessarily excludes the observer; he or she can't be a subject for that would admit to bias. This is to deny the *subjective factor*, which is to say, the complex or fixed idea that drives the parapsychologist to investigate in the first place. Why does the investigator himself not try to remember a few past lives of his own? Why not reserve the objective question of truth until later, and then decide on the basis of his own experience? Somehow there is a quality of intellectual defensiveness against inner emotional or psychic experience that clings to much psychical research.

The Religious Approach

If the psychic appeals to the authority of spirit guides and to paranormal perceptions when talking of past lives and the parapsychologist invokes the scientific canons of rational consistency and empirical proof, what is the religious approach? Here the appeal is to a third kind of authority: tradition—a word derived from the Latin, meaning "handed down." For millions of people in the world reincarnation is part of an ancient belief system, and a fundamental assumption in their worldview.

In cultures where traditional religions such as Islam, Taoism, Hinduism, and Buddhism flourish, individuals with psychic talents find their way to teachers of Yoga, to meditation masters, or to comparable spiritual authorities who have many generations of insight, teaching, and experience behind them. Psychic powers and past life memories which arise spontaneously during meditation tend to be treated lightly as features along the path but not the true destination of the seeker. In tribal societies, the shaman, shamaness, or witch doctor usually recognizes such individuals in adolescence and removes them from the tribe for secret initiation. In all such societies the ordinary popular beliefs of the mass of the people and the secret practices of the yogi, the monk, or the shaman are not in conflict.

In the West, however, this has not been the case. From the very first centuries, what was to become Christian orthodoxy vehemently suppressed those Christians of psychic, shamanic, or visionary temperament called the Gnostics. The authorities of the early institutional Church soon established a strict orthodoxy of doctrine against which all contrary views were stigmatized as heretical. When in 313 the Emperor Constantine made Christianity the official state religion, attempting to syncretize it with various sun-god cults, Christianity was left to deal with the many cults—of Isis, Cybele, Mithras, etc.—that swarmed within the Roman Empire. The monotheistic zeal to convert and eradicate the diversity of polytheism gave the Church an authoritarian character that has plagued the West ever since with schisms, councils, inquisitions, and witch-hunts. As D. H. Lawrence once remarked, "the fear of the pagan outlook has ruined the whole of Christian consciousness."[17]

As a doctrine, reincarnation or the transmigration of souls was apparently known to many of the early Christian Gnostic sects who had inherited it from ancient Egypt. It was also held by Neoplatonists and the Greek Orphic sects and was closely associated with the Pythagorean Brotherhood. Pythagoras had, according to his biographer, Iamblichus, been initiated in the mystery schools in Alexandria and had also traveled in the East, where reincarnation is a universal belief. From the sixth century B.C., when Plato's Academy flourished and the Buddha was still alive, all the way through to A.D. 529, when Justinian closed the University of Athens and the last Neoplatonist scholars fled to Persia, there were nearly a thousand years of spiritual and cultural cross-fertilization between Orient and Occident: Indian sculpture reflected classical Hellenic style; Christian art borrowed Buddhist auras or halos for their icons of saints.

Contemporary Christian theologians don't seem to be able to agree, despite mountains of scholarship, on whether early Christianity accepted the doctrine of reincarnation or not. Leslie Wetherhead maintains that "reincarnation was accepted by the early church for the first five hundred years of its existence." Head and Cranston provide texts to support him. John Hick, on the other hand, claims this view to be totally erroneous and misleading, saying "reincarnation was taught within the Gnostic movement from within the Church but that it early distinguished itself and was treated as a dangerous foe."[18] Equally controversial is whether or not the Church father Origen, deeply immersed in Neoplatonism (as was St. Augustine), believed in reincarnation proper or simply the preexistence of the soul—which is not the same thing. One of the favorite texts cited to support the idea that Jesus taught reincarnation is from the Gospels. In John 9:2–3, we read:

"Rabbi, who sinned, this man or his parents, that he should have been born blind?" "Neither he nor his parents sinned,"

Jesus answered, "he was born blind so that the works of God might be revealed in him."

Following this, Jesus heals him. Does this example support the idea that Jesus taught reincarnation? A strong case can equally be made, says Hick, that Jesus is explicitly rejecting any idea of karma or that misfortune is a punishment caused by some previous sin. In fact, his words seem to indicate that this is a "just so" story, not the result of either his parents or the previous sin.

But whatever the true nature of Jesus's teaching or the beliefs of the early Church, there is no doubt that reincarnation had totally disappeared from orthodox Christian teaching by the Middle Ages. Despite the neo-Gnostic rumblings of the Cathars in the twelfth and thirteenth centuries, reincarnation remains beyond the Christian pale to this day. Judaism, which has never been as authoritarian as Christianity and which has maintained a healthy esoteric tradition—that of the Kabbalah—accepts reincarnation but has never made it an open teaching. So, given a largely barren climate for both reincarnation and esoteric learning in the West, it is not at all surprising that those of psychic temperament have been drawn to the pseudo-religions of spiritism and Theosophy in the nineteenth century and to Alice Bailey, Edgar Cayce, and others in our own day. In short, the West seems to lack any authentic esoteric tradition in which the more complex spiritual teachings—of which reincarnation is but a part—can be authoritatively passed on. Perhaps it is this kind of hunger, unrecognized for what it is, that drives an Ian Stevenson in his focused research and accounts for the massive popularity of the Seth books and, recently, Shirley MacLaine's autobiographies.

From the global perspective of the history of religions, we in the West may well be spiritually impoverished. The recent revival of interest in reincarnation could be a symptom of our recovery of a dim awareness of a much richer picture than our predominantly Christian world-view has offered us over the centuries. It is hard for us to see ourselves from within, so instead I quote the words of the eminent Hindu scholar Alain Daniélou, who returned to the West after many years in India:

> I spent more than twenty years in the traditional Hindu world as far removed from the modern world as though I had been miraculously transported back to the Egypt of the Pharaohs. On returning to Europe I was amazed at the childishness of the theological concepts, and the barrenness of what is called religion. I found a rudderless humanity, clutching the dying tree of Christianity without even understanding why it was dying. Those people feeling this vacuum were searching for their equilibrium in a visibly threatened world but could find no help.[19]

Since reincarnation as a doctrine does not belong to any established Western tradition, the form in which it has reached us through Theosophy and popular metaphysics is inevitably distorted. Not only has it been filtered through our Western myths of progress and evolution, as I discovered, but today it all too easily becomes yet another piece of consumer-ready spiritual psychology which does nothing but feed the insatiable narcissism of our rootless culture. Alice Bailey rightly warned against the glamour that spiritual practices have for Westerners, and no subject is more prone to this than reincarnation. The clinical psychologist Dr. Ronald Wong Jue, who has been prominent in establishing past life therapy as a reputable form of psychotherapy, has perceptively put it as follows:

> I believe that the West has bastardized reincarnation. In the East incarnations are for God to know himself; reincarnation is a vehicle for spiritual evolution. But in the West there's more emphasis on the ego. This is like concentrating on the way you dress rather than the person beneath the clothes. People are more interested in the content of the images than in the process of spiritual evolution.[20]

When we turn to the two Eastern traditions with the most extensively articulated doctrines of reincarnation, namely Hinduism and Buddhism, we find a radically different view of ego, of time, of history, and of salvation from what we are accustomed to in Western religion and philosophy. And we also find a picture substantially different from that of popular metaphysics. Instead of a linear progression of lives through history where the moment of enlightenment is expected to occur conveniently sometime in the twentieth century, we encounter in the Hindu vision, for instance, a vast panorama of endless cycles of history where whole civilizations and even universes come and go like raindrops on a pond. For the Hindu, reincarnation represents the prison of eternal return, from which the wise man seeks *moksha:* escape, deliverance. Spiritual evolution in this perspective is vertical, not linear or horizontal through time. The moment of enlightenment may come at any point in the endless cycle.

Scholars have always issued warnings that Hindu terms like *atman* are barely translatable into Western notions of "soul" or "self," just as *brahman* cannot simply be rendered as "God." In Buddhism too there are no easy equivalences; in fact, the very notion of *atman*—loosely,

the divine essence at the heart of every being—was carefully avoided by the Buddha lest his disciples become
egoically attached to the fruits of good or evil from previous incarnations. To illustrate the subtlety and tone of the
Buddhist approach, here is a typical teaching story on the
problem of who or what actually reincarnates; King
Milinda is questioning the monk Nagasena:

The king asked: "Venerable Nagasena, is the person who is
reborn the same person [who died], or a different person?"

"He is neither the same person nor is he different."

"Give me an illustration."

". . . Suppose, your Majesty, a man were to light a lamp.
Would that lamp burn all night?"

"Yes, Venerable Sir, it would."

"Well, your Majesty, is the flame that burns in the first
watch of the night the same flame that burns in the second
watch of the night?"

"No, Venerable Sir, it is not."

"Is the flame, your Majesty, that burns in the second watch
the same that burns in the third watch?"

"Venerable Sir, it is not."

"Then, your Majesty, was the lamp in the first watch a
different lamp in the middle watch and an even different one
in the third?"

"No, Venerable Sir, the light comes from the same lamp all
night long."

"In just this way, your Majesty, a human being is the unin-
terrupted succession of physical and mental states. As one
state passes away another is born, and it occurs in such a way
that there is no differentiation between the preceding and
succeeding states. Therefore, it is neither the same person
nor a different person that goes to the final summation of
consciousness."[21]

In Buddhism it is strictly incorrect to speak of "my karma" or "your karma," since notions of "mine" and "yours" belong to the illusory sense of individual self which we call ego. In the end there is only karma, the psychic inheritance of the accumulation of mankind's thoughts and actions, as passed on through the great cycle of rebirth. My karma is your karma and yours is mine, or, as John Donne put it, "No man is an Island." We are all a part of the great psychic continent that is humanity. Perhaps this is what St. Paul meant when he enjoined us to "carry each other's burdens."

The religious approach we find to past lives in the East is immensely complex and is consequently one not to be undertaken lightly by Westerners not steeped in one or more of these ancient traditions. I cannot claim competence to review the past life issue from such a perspective, but as a longtime student of Vedanta and an intermittent practitioner of Buddhist meditation, I know that these perspectives hold a profound significance for me. In recent years there has been an enormously creative rapprochement between psychology and traditional spiritual disciplines which bears the name Transpersonal Psychology.[22] Dr. Jue, quoted above, and Dr. Stanislav Grof are among the small but industrious groups of scholars, meditators, and therapists trying to find new paradigms that can integrate the finest achievements of Western psychology with the profundity and range of spiritual psychologies found in Eastern traditions. Jung, with his enormously thoughtful commentaries on Chinese alchemy, *I Ching*, Yogic texts, and certain Zen writings, was of course a pioneer in the many-faceted approach. It is perspectives such as these, as well as the inspiration I have derived from certain writers and poets, that will provide the background for succeeding chapters.

PART II

THE EMERGING SYNTHESIS

What is sought . . . is not some flamboyant new form of consciousness that will seize men's minds and revolutionize the world, but an almost imperceptible inner change—a willed suspension of conventional judgments, a poised awareness, a *stillness*, in which long-smothered voices that speak the language of the soul can be heard again. It is a quiet secret.

But do not be misled by this. For it is also a terrible secret. The inner life of the mind has its nightmares, as well as its golden dreams and wayward fancies. To become purely receptive, to create an inner silence, is to unlock a dangerous door, opening upon a world from which faint hearts would do wisely to keep away. It is to set out on a solitary journey whose end is still unsure.

Alan McGlashan,
The Savage and Beautiful Country

CHAPTER 4

THE FOURTH WAY
A PSYCHOTHERAPIST'S
APPROACH
TO PAST LIVES

Since then, at an uncertain hour,
That agony returns:
And till my ghastly tale is told,
This heart within me burns.

Coleridge, *The Rime of the Ancient Mariner*

One integrates life as story because one has
stories in the back of the mind.

James Hillman, *Healing Fictions*

Psychotherapy and the Unconscious Mind

We have now taken a critical look at three major ways of
exploring and understanding past lives: the *psychic,* the
parapsychological, and the *religious.* How exactly does
the psychotherapist's stance differ from these perspectives, and where does it overlap?

First, and most obviously, the psychotherapist is mainly
concerned with helping the patient get better, not in

proving a theory or in promoting a doctrine. As I said earlier, I tell all my clients that *it doesn't matter whether you believe in reincarnation or not* for past life therapy to be effective. On the other hand, I do ask them to believe in something else, in a factor which is central to almost all schools of psychotherapy deriving from Freud and nineteenth-century hypnosis: *the healing power of the unconscious mind*.

When a psychic gives a reading and tells me about my former lives as he or she clairvoyantly envisions them, this may provide me with valuable insights into other levels of my personality but it mostly remains at the level of psychological information. As with a well-constructed psychological test or an astrological reading, I am left to decide what to do with this information. In therapeutic work, any such assessments can often provide a rich starting point for further work. Ultimately, the usefulness of such readings will be judged by how the client's unconscious mind responds during our subsequent work together in therapy.

Although I make no claims myself to being psychic, I have found it quite easy to spot dreams that contain past life material. For example, a female client of mine, whom I will call Peggy, found herself in part of one of her dreams in a dingy institutional dormitory with an iron bedstead. In the dream the idea of slaves came to her and she saw a sewing machine and part of a Bible. The whole issue of past lives had never been raised in Peggy's therapeutic work; we were actually engaged in more traditional Jungian analysis involving intensive dreamwork. Failing to find any personal connection to either slavery, dingy dormitories, sewing machines, or Bibles I remarked: "It sounds to me like a past life fragment is woven into your dream." I would hardly want to call this a psychic reading, but it was certainly, in my estimation, a highly feasible interpretation.

Peggy's reaction to my remark was simply a blank "maybe." But in the next session she brought the following short dream:

> *A friend says there's a man from the Irving Trust. He says it's time to wake up. The bank is upset that there are hundreds of people involved.*

Peggy immediately recognized the symbolic meaning of the Irving Trust as a reference to Washington Irving's *Rip Van Winkle.* It sounded to both of us as if a person from another era was about to emerge from her memory bank where the "accounts" of hundreds of people were stored. Sure enough, in the intervening week she had the following dream:

> *It is the sixteenth century. I am a wandering priest. Some-one has died of leprosy and I am at his house during the cleansing ritual and later I wash someone else's hands and feet with the same water. A voice says: "This was probably the most significant event in putting an end to the realm." I understand this to mean I was responsible, though inno-cently, for spreading leprosy.*

This was clearly a past life dream and led to further investigations, which I will not pursue. The point is that no formal past life exploration had been made when the dreams had occurred, yet a single remark on my part had had the effect of triggering this past life memory which lay dormant in the unconscious. Good psychic readings often have the same effect.

Even from this short example it may be clear that the

therapeutic approach to past lives places primary value on the subjective experience of the client and leaves the question of historical truth or doctrinal orthodoxy entirely to one side. I never encourage my clients to investigate the historical background of a past life memory, since this can drain energy from the immediate power of the image or story that is emerging. When a past life memory is evoked or occurs spontaneously in therapy, I do not see it as an end in itself but simply as a means that may help further the emotional catharsis, self-understanding, and healing that are, in my estimation, the true goals of psychotherapy.

This is precisely where, as a psychotherapist, I differ from my academic colleague, the parapsychologist, who wishes to see if these experiences will stand up as evidence.

Since proof is uppermost in the parapsychologist's mind, his or her whole style of conducting research is very detached to avoid "leading" the subject. While the therapist creates a supportive atmosphere and trusts the unconscious to produce whatever is needed for the growth of self-awareness, the researcher remains highly suspicious of imagination, hypnosis, and suggestion.

If they do use hypnotic regression, questioning is mostly focused on external cultural and historical details that can be independently verified. Some researchers become so caught up in their historical detective stories that the rememberer's feelings are sometimes callously ignored. There is a rather shocking part of the well-known Bloxham tapes in which the hypnotherapist, Arnall Bloxham, regressed a certain Graham Huxtable to a life as an eighteenth-century sailor. In a deep trance, reliving a battle at sea, Huxtable, as the sailor, has his leg blown off and screams uncontrollably. Bloxham apparently slaps his face to bring him out of trance and assures him that his leg is still intact. According to Jeffrey Iverson's book *More Lives Than One?* which documents Bloxham's work, both men were clearly shaken by the experience.[1]

In a therapeutic session, the subject is never brought back so suddenly or left with the unfinished impressions of that pain. Instead, very precise cathartic working through is used to help him let go of and fully clear the trauma at all levels: physical, emotional, and mental. The focus is on the person and not the events. As it is, the Bloxham tapes provide copious historical data but very little which is personally, that is to say psychologically, valuable from a therapeutic standpoint.

This leads me to another important difference between the psychotherapist's approach and the parapsychologist's. Skimming through the cases in this book might give the impression that all past life stories are miserable and traumatic. Are there no happy and successful lives? the casual reader might ask. Of course there are, but they do not constitute the immediate focus of therapy. People go into psychotherapy because they are emotionally disturbed, depressed, overwrought, and so on. As a result, the lives that surface in the beginning will directly reflect and often explain the core of such symptoms. It would be as valuable to someone in distress to focus on happy past lives as it would be for a physician to treat a mangled left leg by examining the healthy one.

In this respect parapsychological research actually provides a healthy counterbalance to the focus on pathology of therapists like myself. There is now a large and growing accumulation of transcribed past life regressions which have been made without focusing on emotional issues.

These records provide a pretty accurate average cross
section of achievements, failures, joys, and sorrows of almost every period of history. Dr. Helen Wambach describes in her books how she regressed several thousand
volunteers without any reference to problem areas or
therapy by asking her subjects simply to survey century
after century while in trance. Her findings provide us
with a much more balanced picture of past lives in general and a useful and healthy corrective to purely therapeutic cases. She even estimates from her research sample that 70 percent of the people in history may have died
in their beds and that the most common cause of all death
has been pneumonia![2]

Nevertheless, my own approach as a therapist is to at
least begin with the more traumatic past life stories that
lie near the threshold of consciousness and not to attempt
to make my client "feel better" by seeking out happy
stories to compensate for their pain. Pain, whether physical or psychic, is always an indication that the organism is
out of balance in some way; the pain must be addressed
directly if possible. While there are some psychotherapists
who believe that the summoning of beautiful and transcendent imagery—spirit guide figures, gurus, angels, the
Higher Self, etc.—is sufficient to alleviate psychological
distress, I must confess I am not among them. It is too like
sending in the spiritual cavalry to rescue the beleaguered
ego. Sometimes the death of the old ego is precisely what
is required, so that a new one can be born.

The Greeks understood tragedy in Aeschylus's words as
"transformation through suffering" and it is their spiritual
sense of the healing power of story and drama that I am
most aligned with. Jung emphasized the positive value of
suffering again and again in his writings, summing up his

philosophy of the therapeutic enterprise with words worth pondering: "We do not become enlightened by imagining figures of light but by making the darkness conscious." This is not to say that memories of happy and fulfilled past lives do not play a significant part in past life therapy, as we shall see in cases in the latter part of this book, but that they should not be invoked prematurely or at the expense of what has wisely been called "the healing crisis."

Hypnotic Regression, Active Imagination, and Trance States

I described in the previous chapter how clinicians such as Freud, who practiced psychotherapy at the turn of the century, were quite skeptical of things that smacked of the occult. Whenever contents appeared in unconscious fantasy that might possibly be past life fragments they were treated with great caution. Usually it was held safer to call them "split-off" or "secondary" personalities and avoid metaphysical speculation.

Only one clinician who took past life memories literally appears in the annals of early psychotherapy. In the early years of the century French therapist Colonel Albert de Rochas found that hypnotized subjects could be regressed not only to earliest childhood memories but also to fetal memories and, before that, to previous lives. He claimed his subjects alternated between male and female lives as he took them further backward in time. He also found he could take subjects forward into future lives. His claims aroused skepticism then, as they do today, and unfortunately his findings and method quickly dropped out of sight.[3]

The first recent revival of interest in past life regression came with Morey Bernstein's experiments with Virginia Tighe in 1956—the famous Bridey Murphy case we mentioned in the last chapter. But Bernstein was not a therapist and was essentially practicing as an amateur parapsychologist searching for proof of a past life memory through hypnosis.

It was the psychiatrist Denys Kelsey and his wife, Joan Grant, who was a psychic, who first made public the therapeutic use of past life and prenatal regression in recent years.[4] The work was initially greeted with skepticism, but gradually, in both Britain and the United States, more and more hypnotists and psychotherapists—doctors Joe Keeton, Morris Netherton, Edith Fiore, to name the better known—have published their accounts of therapeutic past life regression and their strong belief that this is the most thorough and effective therapy known to them.[5]

The debate about whether past life stories are actual memories—the literalist view—or whether they are truly fantasies will doubtless continue for many years to come. On the whole, the psychoanalytic schools deriving from Freud and Jung have inclined toward the fantasy view, while hypnotherapists have tended more toward the idea that these stories literally happened.

My position is somewhere in the middle. I believe that the unconscious produces all kinds of fantasies, which are attempts to resolve psychic conflicts at a symbolic level. Mostly, as with dreams, fantasy products are highly condensed and require delicate unraveling to be fully understood. A single dream, for example, may contain elements from two or three periods of a person's life—childhood, adolescence, current life—all wound around one specific complex which has an archetypal theme underlying it. But just as dreams and fantasies contain elements from *this* life—i.e., memory traces of actual events—I believe that fragmentary memories from past lives are also woven into them. So when dreams like Peggy's, with very specific historical details, appear I am prepared to treat them literally and not just as symbolic condensations.

Possibly the most significant difference between a psychoanalyst and a hypnotherapist is how he or she approaches the unconscious. The analyst for the most part listens passively and offers insightful interpretations; the hypnotherapist by contrast actively directs and helps rework the stories, images, and fixed ideas that arise from the unconscious in trance states. In this respect, the hypnotherapist is much closer to a psychodrama director, in that he or she becomes actively engaged in the inner melodrama.

Jung developed a method which is neither as laissez-faire as the Freudian method nor quite as directive as hypnotherapy. His technique, which he called *active imagination,* is best described as an interaction with the unconscious. We learn to sit, as in meditation, and simply observe a fragment of a dream or hypnagogic image without any attempt to guide, control, or interfere with it. The aim is to allow the image to come to life of its own autonomous psychic energy, our ego letting go of all expectations, presuppositions, or interpretations. After a certain period of practice and initial coaching by the therapist, this inner image will start to move in some way and our observing ego learns to participate in the story very much as the dream ego in normal dreaming. This waking dream ego is encouraged to encounter the dream situation as directly as possible, not to retreat, and to fully allow any emotions such as fear, anger, sadness, longing, etc., to arise during the inner psychodrama.[6]

Jung's technique has the invaluable effect of stimulating, focusing, and training the "inner senses," so that dreaming and waking meditation on images becomes enormously enriched. Since there was no special provision for either memory images or past life images in his original formulation, everything that arises is treated the same way. We are simply instructed to follow and participate in the imaginal story and, in some instances, dialogue with inner figures that emerge. The key instruction remains "to stay with the image."

This powerful technique differs from past life regression in a number of ways. It does not distinguish between stories where I have a physical body or when I have a spirit form, nor between memories and fantasies, nor does it allow for past life traumas where I go out of body or escape into a compensatory fantasy to avoid some violence or injury in the story. The differences can be illustrated by the following excerpt from a client's active imagination:

> *I am walking through some dark woods. I see and hear some soldiers emerging from the trees. They are clearly planning to attack and rob me. They come closer. In terror I climb a tree. The tree turns into a stairway. I find myself in a childhood attic where I used to play with toy soldiers.*

It would be hard to take this as anything but a fantasy as it stands. The tree transforming into a stairway is clearly a fantasy event, and since this client has no memories of being attacked by soldiers in his lifetime the conclusion is further reinforced.

By contrast, a past life therapist might simply ask questions to guide the story as if it were an actual memory and not a fantasy or a dream. When we are asked to imagine a story as if it were real, we limit our imaginings to the historical constraints of time, space, and personal identity. In other words, we cannot suddenly grow wings, as in a dream, or change magically from a peasant to Sir Lancelot, as we might in a guided fantasy. Also, in historical memories death is often painfully realistic; in a dream, death is rarely experienced so vividly.

Here, then, is how this piece of active imagination might turn out as a past life memory guided by a therapist (TH). The client (CL) is lying down with his eyes closed:

TH: *What are you doing?*
CL: *I'm walking through the woods.*
TH: *How are you dressed?*
CL: *Seems to be ragged clothes, a leather belt and pouch, a floppy hat, sort of medieval.*
TH: *What kind of physique?*
CL: *I'm thick-set, coarse, muscular. A peasant, about thirty.*
TH: *What happens in the woods?*
CL: *There are three soldiers coming out of the trees. Their swords are drawn.*
TH: *What are they doing to you?*
CL: *They're cutting my throat. Oh, I'm choking on my blood (coughs). I'm dying (convulses). I'm gone (body relaxes).*
TH: *What are you aware of now?*
CL: *I'm floating above my body. There's blood all over it. I'm quite detached now. It's all over. I'm leaving.*
TH: *Where do you go?*
CL: *I'm in a peaceful place above the earth. There are these beings with me. Very warm and comforting.*
TH: *Are they human?*

CL: No, not at all. They seem to be helpers. We communicate without talking. I don't seem to have a body now.

This brief scene is typical of thousands of past life regressions. It contains many of the elements common to the dream but it is also a drama where the complexes are personified, a crisis is generated, and catharsis occurs. It acts as what Jung and James Hillman have called a "healing fiction," but a realistic one nevertheless. Facing the real death experience—and the peace that accompanies it —has great therapeutic value.

The technique of active imagination and the examples of past life sessions I have given so far also resemble the guided imagery exercises no doubt familiar to many people today from personal growth workshops. In the end, there is much in common between all these approaches. The real difference is the emphasis on how the story is developed. Past life therapy's particular bias is toward the production of realistic scenarios.

Whether or not the term hypnosis is used to describe all these ways of working with images from the unconscious, one thing is certain: each of them does entail some degree of trance. Simply closing one's eyes or paying attention to a part of one's body or a mental image or phrase is enough to put many people into a light trance. There seems no question that, although Freud himself gave up formal hypnosis, every Freudian client on the couch is drifting in and out of trance states. The recent work of Milton H. Erickson, a master hypnotherapist, has demonstrated how all kinds of subtle changes of voice tone, verbal stimuli, body and image awareness are constantly taking us in and out of trance.[7]

Today the only important disagreement about trance

states in therapy is not whether they occur but how deep a trance is necessary for effective work to take place. For myself, I rarely use a specific technique to induce hypnosis for past life work. I find clients can easily attain a light trance state by simply paying careful attention to inner images or words once their eyes are closed. Some hypnotherapists claim that it is essential to put their clients into a full hypnotic trance for past life work to be possible. I suspect, however, that how one arrives at the unconscious material is purely a matter of personal style. J. L. Moreno, it is interesting to note, maintained that trance is a key element in a good psychodrama, but he never used any technique remotely resembling hypnosis.

In recent years, more therapists have come to recognize the extraordinary variety of levels of consciousness that can fruitfully be used in healing work—trance states, biofeedback, guided fantasy, waking dreams, yoga, Zen. As a result, our vision of the things that psychotherapy shares with traditional shamanism and healing has also expanded. For example, anthropologists have long shown how shamanic healing and the temple dance rituals of Bali are conducted in trance.

To find a broader framework for understanding these heterogeneous approaches and to begin to profit from the spiritual wisdom of ancient traditions, many psychologists, like myself, have been drawn to a loosely formed school that calls itself transpersonal psychology. The inklings of what this approach might possibly encompass—a cross-fertilization of Western psychology and Eastern spiritual disciplines—are to be found in the celebrated *Tibetan Book of the Dead*. First published in 1927 in a translation by W. Y. Evans-Wentz, it acquired a number of extra commentaries, such as Jung's important "Psycholog-

ical Commentary" in 1935. Just as striking as any of these
Western reactions to this material is the "Introductory
Foreword" by the great German scholar and convert to
Tibetan Buddhism, Lama Anagarika Govinda, who makes
the following remarks:

> There are those who in virtue of concentration and other
> Yogic exercises are able to bring the subconscious into the
> realm of discriminated consciousness, and thereby to draw
> upon the unrestricted treasury of subconscious memory,
> wherein are stored not only the records of our past lives but
> the records of the past of our race, the past of humanity, and
> of all prehuman forms of life, if not the very consciousness
> that makes life possible in this universe.[8]

Such a degree of inner control of trance states and access to the unconscious is still quite rare in the West. But as
hypnotherapists continue to refine their methods, as analysts identify further categories of unconscious material,
and as more people, professional and nonprofessional, discover the huge potential of meditation, I believe this access will become more common.

How I Work: The Case of Elizabeth's Cats

What I have evolved in my own practice over the years is
a personal blending of a number of therapeutic techniques and perspectives: Freudian, Jungian, Reichian, Gestalt, and more. I have absorbed from these schools a
number of disciplines and attitudes which call upon subpersonalities, body language, psychodramatic role playing, trance work, catharsis, symbol awareness, and meditation. If there is a dominant metaphor to my approach to
the unconscious, and especially past lives, that holds all

these approaches together, it is probably the story. It seems to me, from the many cases I've treated, that the unconscious mind strongly resembles the figure of the Ancient Mariner—it wants to tell its story.

As I sit and listen to each client's elaboration of worries about career, money, relationships, sex, family, or whatever, I have trained my awareness to listen for the other stories—the stories behind or beneath the story presented. By letting my intuitive imagination cast a wider net, I have learned that behind every personal complaint —compulsive eating, fear of flying, impotence, money worries, depression, and so on—there lurk older, fuller stories with events often far more devastating and cataclysmic than the surface fears my clients find themselves enumerating.

Nothing illustrates the power of this approach more than the case of a professional woman in her early forties, whom I shall call Elizabeth.

A major issue in Elizabeth's life was her anxiety about the three cats who lived with her in her city apartment. What she felt was that she could never leave them for very long—so much so that she was virtually unable to take vacations. Once she had asked an acquaintance to feed them so she could get away, and one of the cats somehow got stuck in a closet for nearly a week and almost died. This, of course, confirmed her worst fears.

The more I probed, there seemed to be all sorts of relationships with animals in her life that were surrounded by disasters of one sort or another: a dog that was killed when she was a child, a cat she had rescued that was later killed, and more.

What was it that made her certain of further disasters to her pets? As our interview proceeded I became aware of two strongly related thoughts running through the various animal sagas she related: "I can't leave them, because something will happen to them" and "It's all my fault, I didn't do enough for them."

As soon as we had passed through the preliminary focusing that put her in touch with the past life level of her unconscious, she began, with tears in her eyes, to tell the following story:

> I'm an old woman living in a large bleak stone house. It's northern, maybe Scotland. There's a storm outside. I've been fighting with my husband. He says I don't care about the children. Perhaps he's right. I swore I'd never have children because I don't want to take care of them. But we've got two now, three and four years. He's outside screaming. I'm not letting him in. Let him take them if he knows better. I'm not letting them in.
>
> The storm's getting worse but he has stopped screaming now. It's quiet for a while, an hour or so. Now it's knocking, it sounds like my little boy. Oh, no he won't, he's not doing that one. He's just sent the boy because he thinks I'll relent. Well, I'll show him. They're not coming in.
>
> Now it's morning. The storm's over. They didn't come back. I'll bet they went to the inn. But I don't want to go to the door. Something's wrong.
>
> I go to the door finally; it won't open. Oh, my dear lord. It's the children blocking it! My little girl is dead. My boy is unconscious, my husband's nowhere to be seen. (She weeps bitterly.)
>
> It's all my fault! It's all my fault! They must have been so scared out there, so weak and helpless! (deep sobbing and remorse).

The rest of the story emerged slowly and painfully. The little boy died within hours. The poor woman in Elizabeth's unconscious was later to learn that her husband had loaded the children onto a handcart and while heading for the inn at the height of the storm had collapsed and died of a heart attack. The children had come back to the house to tell their mother, only to be shut out by her. In the extremity of her shame and remorse, the woman never tells her neighbors, letting them think that her husband was responsible. Her guilt torments her for the rest of her life and she dies with the thought, "I don't trust myself to take care of anyone."

This, then, was the appalling story that lay behind the fear of leaving her cats. The catharsis and insight gained brought her enormous relief. Most encouraging of all was that shortly after the session Elizabeth took a two-week vacation, leaving a friend to feed her cats. She sent me a card afterward. "I had a wonderful time," she wrote. "I never thought once about the cats."

Authentic and Inauthentic Suffering

Had we stayed at the reality level of the story of Elizabeth's cats we might have gone nowhere. Any outside observer could easily suggest half a dozen ways for Elizabeth to get her cats taken care of, but that would not have relieved the residual guilt that would have ruined her vacation with worry. Most of us would tend to be impatient with her complaints as neurotic overattachment of some sort.

For the therapist, what is important is not the literal truth of a story but its psychological truth. Jung once remarked that neurotic suffering is inauthentic suffering, implying, so it seems to me, that the pain experienced is out of proportion to the supposed event that apparently occasions it. We all know of cases of inauthentic, neurotic suffering: the clinging and hysterical wife who finds all kinds of reasons why she cannot take a job in the world; the lower-echelon administrator who complains endlessly about his bullying superior and yet who tyrannizes others in his own charge; the fiercely independent man or woman who labors in the woods in a half-built cabin with frozen pipes all winter. These are all dramas of inauthentic suffering, feeble cries for help or sympathy that, as the uninvolved listener, we often turn a deaf ear to. Somehow we know the situation is transparently phony, a setup, and that these intense and intractable situations are what Eric Berne calls "games people play."

In taking the perspective of past lives in therapy I listen intently to these neurotic life patterns with the unvoiced question *"What is the authentic suffering behind this?"* What is the deeper, archaic, lurking fear or trauma *beneath* this displaced surface story?

Using the various methods I shall describe below, past life therapy probes to a deeper layer of the complex, where things are more raw, more extreme, and where, in the controlled, safe environment of therapy, the authentic pain at the heart of the complex can emerge and be released.

Behind the fears of a clinging housewife, for example, we may find a historical story of a black slave life complete with auction, humiliation, sexual brutality, and maybe even suicide, all adding up in her unconscious fantasy to a terror of the marketplace which she is now acting out by refusing to go out into the world.

Beneath an administrator's petty tyrannies may lie a feudal story of land dispossessed and an unsatisfied longing for revenge, so that the unfinished story of power, control, and defeat is played out again and again in this man's work life.

At the back of a young man's or woman's retreat into the woods we may find an old story of a native American tribe where a young child ran into the woods to escape massacre only to return to find the mutilated corpses of his parents and villagers. So present life becomes structured around the fear of being fully in the world, and although it is seemingly safe and protected in the woods, he or she puts out desperate but ambivalent messages about being helpless and alone.

So the purpose of telling the past life story is to return the individual's neurotic suffering to its authentic psychic roots so that it may be detached from the contemporary situations to which it does not properly belong. As in the case of Elizabeth's cats, once seen in a new, truthful perspective the anxiety usually is resolved and disappears, leaving the client free to live his or her current life unfettered.

The Body Tells Its Story Too

Freud has shown how hysterical symptoms like a paralyzed arm may be an arrested symbolic expression about some painfully repressed story to do with touching or embracing. More recently, popular psychology has accustomed us to the notion of body language and psychosomatic complaints.[9]

When I listen to my client's story I also watch and empathize with his or her body language as well as carefully take a history of his or her physical illnesses, noting especially what each coincided with in my client's life. I have learned that for every chronic physical symptom—particularly those that resist conventional treatment, e.g., back pain, premature ejaculation, asthma—buried in the symptom is an older story of disaster, deprivation, or violent death. Back pains produce images of stabbing, beating, crushing, being broken, burdens; premature ejaculation evokes memories of shame, humiliation, sexual torment; asthma brings with it fears of drowning, asphyxiation, death from smothering, and so on.

The body and its various aches, pains, and dysfunctions is a living psychic history book when read correctly. My therapeutic approach is very simple. All I do is ask my client "What is your pain *like?*" In the search for a fitting word to describe it, my client will focus on the embodied complex and find metaphors that swiftly begin to reveal the elements of a story. A pain may be strikingly specific: "It's as though it goes through my left eye and out of the side of my neck," one client said. In seconds the image of an arrow sprang to his mind and he was suddenly on a battlefield struck down by enemy fire. "My arm feels as though it's being pulled, wrenched," another client said. "What's pulling it?" I asked. "Oh, help! It's an animal, a lion. I'm in an arena. They are tearing me apart." In no time at all the grisly end of a Christian martyr was reenacted with the amazing release and relief of chronic aches and pains that had before been quite unrelated to each other as physical symptoms.

Even though the physical ailment may have very specific origins in a person's current life, I have found more and more that there are several layers to every major syndrome of physical illness, accident, or weakness. If Freud's observation was that behind every slip of the tongue there lies a buried complex, why not behind every slip on the ice, every car accident, every illness that strikes us out of the blue? If there is a buried complex behind each accident in this life, could there possibly be an old past life injury behind the complex?

The existence of a past life level of physical problems has been confirmed over and over again in the cases I have seen. So much so that I have learned when taking a psychological case history to ensure that we include all major illnesses, accidents, and chronic ailments and especially the chronological ages at which they occur.

Working with a woman client in her early forties named Jane, for instance, I helped her relive an unfulfilled life as a woman in pioneer days which ended tragically when a horse and trap overturned and she broke her back and died. In the regression I had not thought to ask her age until our session was almost completed. "How old were you?" I asked. "Twenty-seven," she said with certainty. "Does twenty-seven remind you of anything in this life?" I queried. Suddenly a look of astonishment came over her. "My goodness," she exclaimed, "it was at twenty-seven that I was in the hospital with a very serious kidney infection they couldn't properly diagnose. I nearly died." She reached down the left side of her back. "The pain was terrible, just here, *exactly* in the place where I broke my back as that pioneer woman." As we talked further it was clear that twenty-seven was a crisis point both in this life and the past life. Gnawing self-doubt about the direction of her life and her failure to marry had surfaced at this juncture in the past life and it had taken a fatal turn. When similar issues emerged in her current life it was as though her body had started to repeat and reenact the old story.

Occasionally, as in the case of a young writer who consulted me once, the physical problem is the first thing we look at. This young man had had a number of ski accidents as an adolescent, leading to several major operations on his right knee which still left him in his late twenties with recurrent bouts of pain. By probing the pain we found no less than three past lives associated with his legs. First, an amputation in the trenches during World War One. Before that, he remembered dying on an eighteenth-century battlefield with the same leg blown away below the knee, and then an even more terrible glimpse of torture to the right leg much further back. It seemed that he was reliving old battle wounds once more in this life, even though his chosen career was of a quite different sort.

Another of the more striking of the cases I have treated where a part of the body carried a deeply buried past life complex was that of a man who was tormented by impotence. The man, whom I shall call Gregory, had tried other therapies to little effect. When he was interviewed, it seemed that the predominant feeling connected with his genitals was one of shame. Physically, his genitals were extremely sensitive.

> No sooner had Gregory been invited to fully feel the shame connected with his genitals than he found himself in a château at the time of the French Revolution. He is dressed as a jester, but with his genitals exposed. Before him are an angry mob who have just burst through the doors of the château. They rush at him, beat him savagely, and castrate him. He puts up no resistance and dies with the thought: "I deserved all that." When taken back to an earlier time in that life, the origins of his death and his sexual shame become fully evident. As a servant early singled out to be the jester by his masters in the château, he finds himself being forced into the drunken debauches of these degenerate and bored nobles who retained him. One of their practices that deeply revolts

him was having to stand by and make jokes about their sexual and sadistic abuse of young peasant girls who have been kidnapped and brought to the castle for the perverted pleasures of the men. Often after they have been appallingly used they are murdered and secretly disposed of. Powerless to protest and deeply identified with the victimized women who were of his own class, the jester eventually achieves some kind of expiation for his powerless complicity by offering up his own genitals to the revolutionary horde of peasants who storm the château. He feels that he has betrayed his class, that he has betrayed these women, and that he has betrayed his own natural sexuality. These were the thoughts and feelings that were unconsciously triggered every time he wished to make love to his wife. Telling this terrible story greatly helped Gregory regain much of his natural self-respect and improve his conjugal relations with his wife.

Some of my most powerful and effective therapeutic work is done when the past life story is held at the bodily level in this way. There is no question that for many people the body is a very unconscious area and therefore stores some of their most residual or deeply buried complexes. The very metaphor of complexes having physical residues is a significant one from the viewpoint of karma. The Tibetans talk of the present era of human history as "the age of impure residues," for example. Certainly this kind of work adds new and provocative dimensions to the whole area of so-called psychosomatic medicine. In a later chapter I will explore the implications of this in more detail. For the moment we will continue to keep the body in mind, so to speak, since it is an integral part of every person's full spectrum of awareness, as experts in Reichian therapy, Alexander work, movement, voice, and sensory awareness have so brilliantly demonstrated for a generation or more. The movement therapist Anna Halprin has rightly remarked that "every part of the body has a story to tell." What I would add to this is that many of these stories turn out to belong to past lives.

CHAPTER 5

THE MULTIDIMENSIONAL PSYCHE

But thought's the slave of life, and life time's fool;
And time, that takes survey of all the world,
Must have a stop.

Shakespeare, *Henry IV, Part 1*

The time of soul is not to be presumed continuous . . . It
is discontinuous, not simply as having breaks or gaps . . .
But as having many avatars, many kinds and modes. The
polycentricity of psyche demands no less than this,
namely, a polyform time.

Edward S. Casey, "Time in the Soul"[1]

A New Refutation of Time

Many people who observe a past life session for the first
time are amazed to see that within minutes a person finds
him- or herself experiencing their birth, back in the
womb or perhaps in a story that belongs to ancient Sume-
rian history millennia ago. How is this possible, they say,
when it takes years of psychoanalysis to uncover one or
two early childhood traumas? I would answer that they

have unconsciously assimilated from psychoanalysis and our language structure as a whole a certain way of conceiving time, such that ancient Sumeria or early childhood are assumed to be "distant" and "hard to reach" the way Outer Mongolia, say, or Australia are difficult to get to from America.

Jorge Luis Borges draws our attention to this in his brilliant essay "A New Refutation of Time":

> Our language is so thoroughly saturated and animated with the notion of time that quite possibly not a single sentence in all these pages fails to require or invoke it.[2]

So it is with practically all psychological thinking that concerns itself with the past. Even "cause and effect," a root metaphor of Newtonian science (on which most psychology still models itself), is loaded with the irreversible image of forward moving time.

In fact, we psychologists are so caught up with this kind of thinking that we frequently assume that our failure to arrive at causes or origins is bound up with the passage of time. The cause of the complaint, we say, is *so far back* in early childhood as to be inaccessible to consciousness. It is no small wonder then, with highly trained psychoanalysts getting stuck on this stumbling block, that most people, professionals and nonprofessionals alike, are unwilling to even consider looking for origins in previous lives. If we can't get back as far as the beginning of *this* life, so the argument goes, why bother with lives millennia ago? But for all this I think that if we stay with Borges's very suggestive observation we may begin to see that we are trapped in an illusory labyrinth which is entirely the construction of our language. For as the philosopher Immanuel Kant observed, "we represent the time sequence by a line to infinity . . ."[3] Here precisely is the clue: we *conceive or imagine time spatially*. Consider the following: "a *long* time," "*distant* events," "*going back* to a previous life." Each phrase relies on an image of space or movement through space. It actually turns out that the very word "origin" conceals a spatial metaphor in its derivation, for the Latin *origo,* whence it comes, means spring or source.

Once we are able to rid ourselves of the cumbersome notion of linear time we can begin to move swiftly and freely to all possible realms of the psyche. We can each become, as Hamlet wished, "a king of infinite space."

In one of his short stories Borges describes how several occult explorers stumble upon what is known as an Aleph, which is a very tiny place on the earth where the energy is such that a person placed there is able to envision all human history *in an instant.* I can think of no better metaphor for what many recent pioneering researchers of the human psyche have also stumbled upon. After his experience of Zen meditation, Fritz Perls went on to emphasize in his Gestalt therapy the supreme importance of the "now." Stanislav Grof has observed the multidimensional psyche many hundreds of times in his LSD research; Milton Erickson's ground-breaking work in inducing hypnotic trance has called our attention to the importance of minute shifts in the moment-by-moment flow of consciousness. What these and many other therapists are emphasizing more and more is the *primacy of immediate experience*—not the symptom, the diagnostic category, the family history, the Oedipal constellation, the reality configuration, the behavioral dysfunction, or any number of other abstractions. What practically all of these descriptions do is subtly mold a client into the intellectual system of the therapist, a tactic which, however well intentioned and sympathetically administered, tends to slow down the process of therapy. Time and time again, before I had fully grasped the importance of this principle, I found myself slipping into well-meaning discussions *about* the client's experience rather than directly and empathetically staying with the here and now of his or her immediate awareness. For the fact is that as soon as we begin to talk about events as if they were actual, we are very close to reexperiencing them. It is only the time structures built into our language and the false "linear access" view of memory that comes with them that distance us from the events.

Currently emerging in psychotherapy is what Stanislav Grof calls a "new paradigm," a view of the human psyche that rejects the old Newtonian-Cartesian mechanistic dualism of mind and body, cause and effect, solid space and linear time in favor of the holographic or holonomic model of psychic process—a model, incidentally, that the writings of Jorges Luis Borges have anticipated poetically for many years.

For a fuller and more competent survey of holography and holonomics than I am capable of, I refer the reader to Stanislav Grof's recent important statement *Beyond the Brain* (1985), but I will briefly mention a provocative illustration of the holonomic principle that he cites from the Hwa Yen School of Buddhist thought (as a metaphor of space and dimension it neatly complements Borges's image of time in the Aleph). In Grof's summary:

> The Empress Wu, who was unable to penetrate the complexity of Hwa Yen literature, asked Fa Tsang, one of the founders of the school, to give her a practical and simple demonstration of the cosmic interrelatedness. Fa Tsang first

suspended a glowing candle from the ceiling of a room, the entire interior of which was covered with mirrors, to demonstrate the relationship of the One to the many. Then he placed in the center of the room a small crystal and, showing how everything around it was reflected in it, illustrated how in the Ultimate Reality the infinitely small contains the infinitely large and the infinitely large the infinitely small, without obstruction.[4]

Difficult and unfamiliar as these principles are to those who are still slumbering on in what William Blake called "Newton's sleep" (i.e., looking for causes in childhood, places in the brain, trying to hold body and mind together with bits of conceptual string, etc.) they nevertheless make possible some radical and fresh ways of practicing psychotherapy. For if, according to the holonomic principle, everything in the psyche mirrors everything else, therapy is no longer limited to any one point of entry into the complex. It no longer matters whether I start with childhood, or the body, or the reality situation, or the birth trauma, or past lives; each or any of these aspects can take us into the feeling core of the complex when properly pursued. Simply by paying careful and unprejudiced attention to the contents of my client's immediate experience and listening for the symbolic resonances in his or her verbal or bodily language, it is astonishingly easy to open up to all of these other levels in no time at all (pun intended).

Whether we start with a thought, a fragmentary memory, an ill-defined feeling, a dream image, a pain, or a breathing pattern, we swiftly find ourselves moving in and out of several levels of psychic reality into worlds within worlds, within worlds. In a single two-hour session a client's inner journey may take him or her from recent distressing events to a past life, to a birth memory, to a childhood incident, and even to some level of transpersonal or archetypal awareness.

The Case of Susan: A Dutch Artist's Residual Guilt

A particularly vivid example of how such multidimensional unfolding may occur in even one two-hour session —more often it is spread over several—is provided by the case of a young woman I shall call Susan.

Susan was thirty-four, a professional painter, who sought out therapy with a confused bag of complaints about her marriage, feeling bad about her mother, whose home she had moved away from, and the notion that it was all connected to a past life fragment as a painter in Holland she had glimpsed. As she told her story I was struck by how terribly rigid and tense her shoulders were. It was as though they were held two or three inches higher than necessary.

During the introductory part of my focusing procedure she had great difficulty in letting go, so I offered to massage her neck and shoulders. When she agreed, I worked a little on her very tight trapezius muscle and her neck, encouraging her to pay attention to any images that arose. Very soon she slipped into a male life as an impoverished Dutch painter during the seventeenth century. The painter had a wife and a very young baby whom he could barely support. In his obsession with finishing a certain painting, he severely neglected both wife and baby even when the baby became sick. To his horror, the baby grew worse and died and, to cap it all, his embittered wife deserted him. The key scene in our work was as follows:

TH: *Where are you now?*

SN: *I'm wandering along the canals. I can't find my wife. She's left me for good.*

TH: *Where do you go now?*

SN: *I think, back to the house. Oh, no! I don't want to go back there. (Her shoulders begin to tense up very noticeably.)*

TH: *Breathe deeply and go back to the house and see what happens.*

(At this point Susan shot up from lying on the couch to sitting position, grabbed her neck, and screamed.)

TH: *What just happened?*

SN: *O God! I hanged myself. (Sobs deeply.)*

For a short while we worked on releasing the death experience and the shattering emotions connected with the loss of wife and child. But this was not all. When asked where she found herself next she spontaneously began reexperiencing her birth in this life—*with the cord wrapped around her neck!* Full understanding came moments later when, as a baby, she looked up at her mother, having survived this second trauma:

SN: *I know why I'm here.*

TH: *Why are you here?*

SN: *To be close to my mother (sobs). I know who she is now.*

TH: *Tell me who she is.*

SN: *She's the baby who died. I see that I've been trying to make it up to her all these years.*

What is remarkable about this already exceptionally condensed session is the way in which all the guilt about the neglect and death of the baby had been lodged, or psychically imprinted, at the very moment of the Dutch painter's remorseful suicide. Mirrored in the birth trauma and carried in the young woman's body language to the present day, all her unconscious feelings about the baby in the past life which had become identified with her mother had remained locked in her neck and shoulders. She had continued to punish herself unconsciously and had not been able to let go of feeling responsible for her mother for this reason. In subsequent sessions she was able to do precisely this and felt enormous pressure taken off her marriage, to say nothing of her shoulders that had by then noticeably dropped a couple of inches.

It is not hard to see the many levels or aspects operating within Susan's complex. What had struck me first of all was her body language, what I will call the somatic level of her complex. My strong intuition was that her shoulders had to be telling a story of some kind, but what it was I had no idea initially. What I learned when I took her through a simple focusing exercise was that this part of her would not let go. So already I was alerted to some symbolic resonance to do with either "holding on," "carrying," or possibly "don't hurt me."

At this point I had only my hunches, which were quite premature, so, following the principle of immediate experience, I got her to focus her attention on her shoulders with the aid of some therapeutic massage. (This was simply my own method of choice for focusing on her body. I might have used a number of other methods with the same effect. Employing a Reichian approach, for example, I might have encouraged her to exaggerate her posture, so as to reawaken feelings unconsciously locked in the rigid musculature of her shoulders. Or I might have used a Gestalt technique of asking her shoulders to simply say what they were feeling, producing words like: "I've got to carry all this. It's too painful. I mustn't do it again. I mustn't let go. It's all my fault," etc.)

The rapidity with which Susan found herself at the past life level of her complex surprised me at the time. I had half-expected her shoulder tension to be connected with the recent conflicts in her marriage as she had begun to describe them. Pursuing this tack might then have taken us to what I call the existential level of the complex: what's going on for a person right now in his or her life. But, no, the massage had taken Susan to a different level of her unconscious, where the complex had a number of powerful symbolic resonances that strongly wanted to emerge. It is true she had reported getting a glimpse of the very same past life from meditation, but at the time her conscious mind had no idea how it connected with her marriage, her mother, or her shoulders.

The reason why her shoulders were so intimately bound up with her mother only started to make sense when she started to relive the trauma of the suicide by hanging, at the past life level of her complex (the shoulders, incidentally, typically hunch up reflexively to protect the head and neck regardless of a conscious intention to kill oneself by hanging. I have found a similar pattern with numbers of past life deaths that involved decapitation and strangulation as well as hanging. Also, memories of severe beatings or blows to the head will produce pronounced hunching of the shoulders as a self-protective posture. (See Chapter 7 for a further example.)

With both the somatic and the past life aspects of the complex strongly activated, the pitiful story of the impoverished painter and his guilt at neglecting his wife and baby provided an enormously powerful opportunity for the cathartic release of residual feelings of guilt, despair, and self-hatred. The symbolic resonance of "taking it in the neck" at the moment of death now took Susan into her birth experience, or part of what Stanislav Grof has termed the perinatal aspect of a complex. Here she re-lived the anguish of nearly choking as she was delivered. The somatic memory had acted as a bridge between the death and the birth experiences. (Often the movement is the reverse: from a birth trauma with choking on the mucus it is common to flip directly into a past life memory of death by drowning, for example.)

What happened to Susan immediately after her birth is another striking example of the multilevel awareness that will often occur when the complex is allowed full range of expression. As well as feeling herself a helpless baby that has barely made it into the world after a perilous passage, she was also conscious on a level of almost transcendent understanding; she received a deep and meaningful insight into her destiny, her karma, we might say. I call this the archetypal level because it has to do with meaning in a broader spiritual and symbolic sense. Susan somehow "knew" she had a debt to her mother (karma), that her near choking on the umbilical cord was a symbolic reminder of the past life guilt and that a "higher" part of her had in some way chosen to be born this way to be with her mother again.

Often these archetypal "knowings" or flashes of deep insight will occur after a past life death when consciousness finds itself in some kind of intermediary realm. In this place between lives, called a *bardo* by Tibetans, we are often confronted by a supernatural figure, an angel or wise being dressed in white, who simply interprets the symbolic meaning of the life and death to the rememberer. For example, a woman who had remembered several rather selfish and materialistic past lives as a trader, potentate, and rich bourgeois, found herself confronted after death with a figure in white. The figure said simply: "You have been attached to that pattern of existence for too long." Immediately an image of working as a missionary nun in a leper colony in Africa flashed upon her. This was to be the next life she remembered; one where selfless service was greatly fulfilling and where material things counted for little. The fact that these profound insights come either at the moment of death or the moment of birth is not altogether surprising when we consider that these are the two major archetypal events in any person's life. When the complex touches upon birth and death it arouses an even deeper archetypal resonance of all past births and deaths and with it a greatly expanded form of consciousness, almost a supernatural omniscience. Not for nothing do the Tibetan Buddhists regard the moment of death as of utmost importance. It is here that karma may be either released or further intensified. Readers will notice from the cases cited throughout this book that I take great care to make the transitions of birth and death as conscious as possible.

Returning to our breakdown of the different levels or the aspects of the complex which Susan experienced during the session, we can see how her final reflections brought her very much back into her present life. She was able to recognize clearly that for as long as she could remember she had constantly worried about her mother, feeling somehow responsible for her. She was also able to identify that worry with her neck and her shoulders, as the place she carried anxiety in her body. Condensed in this awareness, then, was another aspect besides the existential, namely, the accumulated guilty memories of all the times she had failed her mother as a child in this life.

This last aspect I call the biographical level of the complex. This level is more typically what traditional psychotherapy concentrates on, and, to be sure, there is usually a rich array of infant, childhood, and adolescent associations in any complex. In Susan's case, however, we bypassed the biographical material and went directly to her past life memories. With other clients it is quite common for me to start with what is going on currently and then go into early childhood memories before reaching past life or perinatal memories. But there is no set order; the sequence of images depends on the symbolic resonance and associations between the images.

Complex, COEX, and the Lotus Wheel

From our analysis of Susan's session we can give a summary of six different aspects or levels that I have found to belong to any complex.

1. *The Existential Aspect:* The current reality situation: "my marriage and my mother."

2. *The Biographical Aspect:* Childhood and later memory traces: "always worrying about Mother since I was small."

3. *The Somatic Aspect:* Chronic postural rigidity: "taking it all in the neck."

4. *The Perinatal Aspect:* Birth trauma of cord wrapped around the neck: "Do I deserve to live?"

5. *The Past Life Aspect:* Suicidal guilt for neglecting a dying child: "It's all my fault, I deserve to die."

6. *The Archetypal Aspect:* Spiritual insight into karmic

debt, deep psychic connectedness with the mother: "I choose to take care of her."

Naturally this picture is not complete, as later sessions were to show, but within itself it was a remarkable opening to a complex that seemed to form a root metaphor in Susan's life. The guilty death by hanging was Susan's unconscious myth, the script she had always lived by without being fully cognizant of it.

The sequence in which the various aspects of Susan's complex came to consciousness—neck, past life, death, birth, current life—could be varied in any number of ways depending on the therapeutic approach taken. To make this clearer I want to propose that we imagine the multidimensional aspects of the complex in the form of a six-petaled lotus wheel. One benefit of this model is that there is no need for any particular order of priority on the lotus wheel any more than there is a need for a fixed starting point in any therapy session. In Susan's case we could have started and even remained with any one of these aspects and still have reached what I call the feeling core of the complex. A Reichian therapist might entirely have used body work, concentrating on the somatic aspect, while a primal therapist might have taken her directly into her birth experience, the perinatal aspect, and so on—each with equal success. Readers familiar with different therapy practices will easily identify which aspect or aspects of the complex particular schools of psychotherapy generally work with.

In addition to being designed to give equal weight to the ways different therapies approach a psychological complex, the petals of the lotus wheel overlap with each other to symbolize how all the aspects mirror or interface

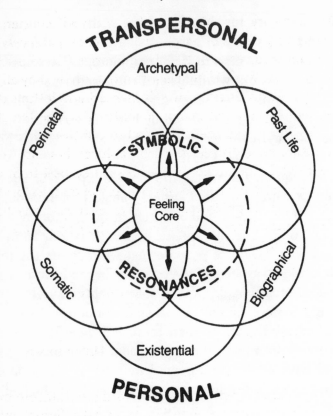

with all the others. This is fully in accordance with Grof's Chinese parables of the reflecting hall of mirrors and the refracting crystal. It also suggests the simultaneity or timelessness of the unconscious when it is encountered, a phenomenon both Jung and Freud were struck by. Freud once said, for example: "In the unconscious nothing can be brought to an end, nothing is past or forgotten."

Just how liberating I have personally found the lotus wheel image of the multidimensional psyche may be shown by a short digression. While working on early drafts of my casework for this book I found myself constantly referring to past life or existential or archetypal *levels* of the complex for each of the six categories I have distinguished. What was still not clear to me was how they all fit together. Slowly I found myself increasingly letting the levels develop into an image of strata or layers. But if I followed this image I felt impelled to put the existential on the top, beneath that the biographical, beneath that the perinatal. The archetypal level seemed best to fit on the bottom with the past life level on top of that. As for the somatic level, that didn't seem to fit at all, so I sandwiched it between the biographical level and the perinatal level. So I ended up with this:

1. Existential ⎫
2. Biographical ⎬ Personal Unconscious
3. Somatic ⎭
4. Perinatal ⎫
5. Past Life ⎬ Transpersonal Unconscious
6. Archetypal ⎭

It was neat and orderly, but it sat with me as uncomfortably as a huge piece of chocolate layer cake. Somehow it wouldn't digest.

Finally I realized I had been seduced by one of the dominant images of "depth" psychology, the idea that "deeper" is more fundamental, older is better ("arche" means ancient in Greek), etc. As a Jungian, I had tended to assimilate uncritically the geological metaphor of strata: analysis as a mining operation intent on excavating precious gems or metals buried in the psyche or else an archaeological dig for lost fragments of civilization, the gods beneath the complexes. It all became clear once I remembered that Jung as a boy had ambitions to be an archaeologist, while in his old age he was utterly absorbed in alchemy.

So instead of a "layered" image of the complex, I offer one of convergent circles dynamically radiating from a central nucleus and moving in and out of each other.

I have chosen the term "symbolic resonance"—a musical metaphor—to describe how the different aspects of the complex all share the same emotional quality and feeling tone images. I will return shortly to how the different aspects actually resonate.

Throughout this book I use Jung's term "complex" because it is practically a household word, but I could equally use a term coined by Stanislav Grof which even more accurately describes the same range of phenomena, namely, the COEX or "system of condensed experience." Strictly speaking, Jung's description of the complex did not include perinatal or past life aspects, even though he was fully aware of somatic and archetypal dimensions in addition to the other factors. Grof's basic definition of COEX is very close to Jung's description of the complex. In *Beyond the Brain*, Grof writes:

> A COEX system is a dynamic constellation of memories (and associated fantasy material) from different periods of the individual's life, with the common denominator of a strong emotional charge of the same quality, intense physical sensation of the same kind, or the fact that they share some other important elements.[5]

It is important to add how he supplements this definition from his own findings in LSD research. In the same place he says:

> It is not uncommon for a dynamic constellation to comprise material from several biographical periods, from biological

birth, and from certain areas from the transpersonal realm, such as memories of a past incarnation, animal identification, and mythological sequences.[6]

Clearly this refers to the same array of psychic experiences. COEX and complex could be used almost interchangeably, provided, as I propose, we expand the reference of the complex to include past life and perinatal memories. I will return to this in slightly more detail in the next chapter.

Symbolic Resonance: Cases of Loss and Separation

The images of hanging and choking which Susan carried in her neck from her past life and her birth were strongly charged with despair and guilt. Blaming herself, "taking it all in the neck," and feeling desperately responsible for her mother even if she couldn't articulate why, etc., all described the cluster of feelings that resonated symbolically in Susan's unconscious. Understanding the principle of symbolic resonance helps me to take my client swiftly from one aspect or level of the complex to another by using words, images, or feeling states as probes to explore the unconscious for its stories. This is how I look for the story *behind* the story, as I described my method in the last chapter.

The major pioneers in understanding the symbolic discourse of the unconscious were, of course, Freud and Jung. Freud worked initially with slips of the tongue and dream symbols while Jung observed from his clinical experiments how unusual word associations would reveal hidden stories. Therapists have grown more and more sophisticated in learning to read these symbols as this century has unfolded. Wilhelm Reich early learned to read the muscular holding patterns or the armoring of the body for its emotional attitudes. "Nobody loves me" or "Don't tell me what to do," the posture might say. Fritz Perls in his Gestalt therapy further refined our symbolic awareness of the somatic aspects within the complex.[7] Hypnotherapists have for a long time employed what is called "the affect bridge" to take clients into buried biographical aspects of a complex by giving suggestions such as, "Allow yourself to feel the anxiety until a much earlier story comes to mind."

So far as I can tell, Dr. Morris Netherton in his *Past Lives Therapy* was the first therapist to apply the Gestalt method of repeating symbolically resonant phrases as a stimulus to awaken perinatal and past lives memories. Perls had developed an acute ear in therapy for stock phrases or gestures that seemed to encapsulate the essence of the complex or, in his terminology, an incomplete gestalt—unfinished business. A phrase like "it sticks in my throat when . . ." will be used by Perls to enter swiftly and effectively into some major life drama about swallowed thoughts and emotions. Netherton has also clearly demonstrated how similar phrases resonate with birth trauma, conversations overheard in utero and past life dramas. In my own work I am indebted to his brilliant methods and teaching, which I had the good fortune to experience personally during my own early experiments while in Vermont.

To illustrate further how the principle of symbolic resonance can be used for uncovering unconscious aspects of a complex and, in particular, the past life aspect, I

THE MULTIDIMENSIONAL PSYCHE

want to describe extracts from three different cases in my own practice.

1. *Rick* was complaining to me in therapy about how miserable and lonely his life was now that his wife had left him. *"I've got to do it all alone"* was the phrase that kept recurring in one form or another.

"I want you to close your eyes and keep repeating 'I've got to do it all alone,'" I say to him. "Pay attention to your body and your feelings and just see where it takes you—in this life or any other."

My instruction is designed to give him full rein to go anywhere on the lotus wheel that the phrase may take him.

"I'm in my childhood, cleaning the house. My mother is dead and Father is at work. I'm eight years old. I've got to do it all alone."

Tears begin to well up in him as images from his lonely childhood come to mind. Next I instruct him to go to any other time when these words had strong meaning for him.

"I've got to do it alone," he says again. "It's not fair, I can't manage alone. I'm terrified. Who's going to help me?"

"Where are you?" I say.

"I'm inside my mother. It's her speaking. Father's away in the army. She's terrified of giving birth," he continues.

We pursue further in utero messages that he absorbed from his mother, helping him to be conscious of how her voice is still active in him.

"It's not fair. Why did he have to leave me? What am I going to do? There's no one here. I just can't face it. How am I going to manage?"

Then I say, "Go to any other life repeating the phrase 'I've got to do it alone.'"

Almost immediately Rick finds himself as the eight-year-old daughter of Russian peasants who have been massacred by cossacks. She is digging their grave in the hard earth as the only remaining survivor. Again, tears and bitterness. When it is over we move through the peasant child's life to its completion. It becomes clear that the eight-year-old Russian girl never recovers from the shock of finding her parents massacred. She lives alone for much of that life never marrying.

Rick is still carrying the frozen affect from that life, still repeating the miserable, lonely eking out of a life. It has, it seems, become a deep habitual response, a miserable way of being in the world that still rules his life today.

First the perinatal memory traces are reinforced in utero and, much later, as a child of eight, the memory is awakened in an emotional reverie of his dead mother while he struggles to clean the house all alone. Each experience only seemed to reconfirm an old residue of anguish and sorrow.

2. Another client from the days when I had just begun to use past life work was a young woman whom I will call *Barb*. Barb was not long out of college and suffered from extreme shyness combined with a strong attachment to her parents, whom she described as very overprotective. Her only explanation for their overprotectiveness was that she thought they felt guilty over some neglect of her when she was a small child. We had probed for many months in conventional analysis for any childhood story of being either neglected or abandoned. None surfaced. Then, in one session, as we were talking about ways she could meet new friends and overcome her shyness, I made a suggestion about her having a dress-up party. "Oh no!" she said, "I couldn't do that. People would think I'm crazy."

It suddenly struck me that she had quite often used that phrase, "They'll think I'm crazy," so I asked her to lie down, close her eyes, and repeat, "They'll think I'm crazy." She immediately became quite scared and her whole body tensed. Today I would recognize that we had touched the somatic level of the complex, but then I was simply puzzled that repeating a phrase she used habitually should suddenly frighten her. "I don't want to," she said, "I'm scared." A fleeting image came to my mind that she thought I was going to hurt her, so I reassured her and managed to persuade her, now in a state of some agitation, to lie down on the couch. She lay down and repeated the words, trembling and rigid as she did so.

> *"They'll think I'm crazy. They'll think I'm crazy." Then followed: "I mustn't do it. I can't help it. They'll think I'm crazy. No, don't touch me! DON'T TOUCH ME! They're taking me away. They've got this thing on me, I can't move my arms. Don't take me away! Don't! Please, don't! No, no, no!"*
>
> *She wept and sobbed and writhed on the couch in evident anguish for some time until finally she was able to tell the whole story:*
>
> *"I'm twelve years old. It seems like the early nineteenth century. My parents are kind enough but I have these fits and roll on the ground. They think I'm crazy. They don't know what to do. I can't stop the fits coming on. I'm afraid they'll think I'm crazy. They'll have me locked up. And that's what does happen. These men came and put me in this thing* (presumably a straitjacket) *and take me to an asylum. I never see my parents again. I die at eighteen years of a fever. What a terrible life."*

Nothing remotely like this had ever happened to Barb in her present life. We were clearly dealing with residual feelings and events from a past life. When the story was over she was able to see how she had been unconsciously dominated by a deep, irrational, and unfounded fear that her present parents would have her locked up. Her reticence in this life was a way of making sure that absolutely nothing in her behavior would provoke the judgment that she was crazy. Shyness thus became her chief defense against this unacknowledged fear. The words "crazy" and "I'll never see them again" were certainly charged with meaning and emotion for her, but in her case they did not appear to derive from her early childhood at all. By probing the symbolic resonance in these words, we were able to move swiftly into a region in her psyche where the fears made sense and were in proportion to the extremity of her feelings.

Barb's case is typical of how an expanded picture of the psyche can save us years of looking in the wrong places for the origins of a psychological problem. In the light of such experiences much of the psychoanalytic enterprise now strikes me as hopelessly restricted by its unquestioned dogma that everything *must* originate in early childhood. Rather like the early explorers who insisted that the Caribbean islands must be part of India, we can if we choose continue to fit our new discoveries into the familiar patterns of known psychoanalytic territory—call them phylogenetic traces, archetypal fantasies, or whatever—but the truth is slowly dawning on therapists of all persuasions that past lives constitute an unsuspected and incredibly rich new world of the psyche that has lain almost completely unexplored in the West until quite recently.

Acknowledging the past life level of the complex and, along with it, the perinatal levels has also led to another major shift in the recent practice of psychotherapy. By treating these fragments of stories *as if* they were real, the emphasis in therapy has moved away from the endless psychoanalytic *interpretation* of their meanings—therapy as an intellectual exercise punctuated with bursts of emotion—to the direct experiential reliving of a traumatic event buried in the unconscious. What is striking about so many sessions like Barb's is that interpretation is often completely redundant. The story explains itself. "Now I know why that fear has always been with me" a client will often say after such a session.

The wheel has come full circle in psychotherapy. From the cathartic cures of the nineteenth century and Freud's early emphasis on trauma many therapies followed Freud in moving away from the experiential to an interpretive or, as in behaviorism and psychiatry, to a manipulative approach to psychological illness. Now, thanks to Moreno, Perls, Janov, and all who have stressed the direct reexperience of trauma and attendant catharsis and also the larger visions of Stanislav Grof and Morris Netherton, experiential therapies are once more available to heal the psyche in all of its complex levels—or, following the lotus wheel, on all levels of the complex.

The Case of Sol: At the Wailing Wall of Jerusalem

My last case in this chapter is a particularly poignant example of how experiential exploration at more than one level of a complex can succeed dramatically where a single focused treatment has failed.

Sol was a very respected osteopath and healer in his late fifties. He had always been extremely conscious of his own health, being meticulous about diet and exercise. He had nevertheless suffered throughout his life from sinusitus, which had resisted every kind of conventional and alternative therapy. "I've cured every other ailment I've ever had," he said, "but this one has me licked. I can't seem to shake it." His reason for trying past life therapy was that during a recent tour of the Mediterranean he had gone to Jerusalem and, at a certain section of the famous Wailing Wall, had found himself weeping uncontrollably. He thought afterward that perhaps a past life memory had surfaced in part, but he could offer no further explanation.

I wondered, as I listened, what it might be. Jerusalem has a history of so many massacres and tragedies in its life history, ancient, medieval, and modern, that it could have been one of countless stories. However, I was not prepared for what came up or for the way it came up.

In listening to Sol's story no particular image or phrase came to me, so I had him lie down with his eyes closed, focus on his breathing and particularly his nasal area, and let himself go directly to the time when his sinusitus had originated. I half-expected him to go to a scene at the Wailing Wall, but instead he found himself in sandals and short corduroy pants walking along a damp forest path:

"I am nine years old. It is a summer camp in Michigan. There's half a dozen of us walking along together. It's been raining. I fell in the creek and that makes me even wetter. I'm miserable. I want to go home. I'm so cold I'm shivering."

Sol had indeed started to shiver as he lay on the couch, despite its being a hot summer day, and his eyes were showing signs of tearing. Clearly both the biographical and the somatic levels of his complex had been touched.

"Stay with your feelings and just say whatever comes to you," I urge.

"I want to go home. I'm so miserable. I'm so cold. I'll never see her again. I'll never see her again."

Sol begins to sob, tears and mucus streaming out of him. I hand him lots of tissues and say, "Who won't you see again?"

"It's my mother. She's very sick, in the hospital. She and

Dad put me here for the summer because he can't look after
me. She may die. I'll never see her again."
   "Do you tell anyone in the camp?" I asked.
   "No, I can't. I've got to be tough. I mustn't cry. But I feel so
unhappy."
   "So let yourself express what you couldn't let out then," I
say.

As with reliving any story, present or past life, it is
important to express the buried affects. It was becoming
apparent that Sol's sinuses were where he had been holding all the feelings his strong little nine-year-old ego so
stoically refused to allow to the surface. I let him unbur-
den more of his tears for a while and then said:

   "I want you to repeat 'I'll never see her again' and let the
words take you to any other story they have meaning for."
   "I'll never see him again! I'll never see him *again!"*
   With the change in this one word a whole new paroxysm of
sobbing burst out of Sol; deeper, older tears it seemed.
   "They've taken him. I'll never see him again! What am I
going to do? We could have done something. It's too late. We
abandoned him. I'm standing behind a large crowd. It's Jeru-
salem. I'm a man in a long robe. They've taken Jesus. I'll never
see him again. I'll never see him again!"
   From a distance this man sees events familiar to everyone:
Jesus being dragged to his death by crucifixion with common
thieves in ancient Jerusalem. Sol sees himself as a Roman who
has come to Jerusalem on commercial business for the Roman
imperial authorities. A chance hearing of Jesus preaching one
day has utterly changed his life and he has exchanged his
high rank for a local post that enables him to live perma-
nently near this remarkable teacher. He even marries a Jewish
woman and wants to convert to the Jewish faith so as to be
closer to Jesus. More than anything, seeing Jesus heal someone
one day makes a profound impression on him. "It awakens

*something in me," he says, almost ecstatically through his
tears. Sol tells of pieces of Jesus's message handed down to
this Roman merchant:*

*"We can learn to heal if we have faith and love . . . We are
all one . . . We must love one another . . ."*

*Simple and familiar words, to be sure, but they seem to
arise quite spontaneously from a deep place within Sol.*

*The rest of the Roman's story is commonplace—no special
revelations of how Jesus died and where his body was taken.
With crowds of others he keeps vigil until the body is taken
down. He never sees his teacher again. Later he bands together with other followers of Jesus and they study and worship together as a form of remembrance. Living as a merchant for many more years, the Roman convert finally dies of
natural causes at an old age somewhere in the countryside.
"The followers," he says, "are now scattered, their future
uncertain."*

Sol emerges from his story with great emotion. It has
been a true catharsis for him, a cleansing in the Greek
sense of that word. He recognizes the spiritual roots of his
vocation to be a healer and how this is entangled with a
penitent sense of responsibility toward his abandoned
master. From his remembering of his current childhood
and then his life as the Roman merchant, Sol knows deep
within him what it is to have been abandoned *and* to
abandon another dear to him. It is rare to experience both
sides of this very familiar complex in one session, but it has
brought with it a kind of completion. Just as Susan in our
earlier story carried an old karmic reminder to herself in
her neck, so Sol has carried one in his sinuses; a personal
grief and a resolve to heal the sick.

What was striking as we talked afterward was that he
had seen his mother again; she had not actually died in the

hospital but had recovered. The thought of losing her had, however, brought up an unhealed karmic level of the complex that remained too severe to release fully at the time of his childhood. So it had remained buried with his tears in Sol's sinuses.

Stories with such familiar historical events inevitably arouse skepticism. As a Christian and a healer today, Sol would naturally have reflected upon Jesus in this life and perhaps visiting the Wailing Wall had set off an unconscious fantasy during his stay. Certainly this is a possible interpretation, and it can hardly be denied that the great archetypal dramas of history and literature can provide a focus for us to identify with on many levels. We have all been Hamlet, Judas, or Camille at one time or another. As for the story of Jesus, meditations on his Passion and death, from the Stations of the Cross to Bach's *St. Matthew Passion,* abound in Christian devotional art, music, and literature.

But there was an ingenuous simplicity and unaffectedness about Sol's story that nevertheless rang true. Above all it was *his* story, *his* drama, and not one that any culture or creed had forced upon him. It gave him a deeply meaningful personal myth.

The ease of modern air travel and tourist services has made the experience of visiting the site of some past life event more and more common today. Numerous people have reported seeming past life memories that were spontaneously triggered by a specific visit to a foreign place. A woman from New York known to me recently visited Rome for the first time in her life and on the first day there threw away her map because she knew her way precisely around the old streets of Trastevere. It was as if she had been there before. Could this familiar experience of *déjà vu* be a fragment of a past life memory surfacing? I have often thought so, with such stories.

From the therapeutic viewpoint, Sol's story works as a vehicle for the abreaction and release of a buried aspect of a deeply entrenched complex; it also gives spiritual meaning to his vocation as a healer. I like to believe that his unconscious led him back to the old familiar place in Jerusalem to reconnect to a memory of a figure who was both human and, in a certain sense, an embodiment of a certain aspect of Sol's aspirations. From a Jungian perspective, it was an encounter with the Self, the divine image in every man and woman, which in Sol's case retained all the characteristics of a fully lived human experience.[8] Above all, it had profound psychological meaning for Sol himself, and left him with much food for meditation.

The Archetype of Abandonment: All Things Are But Loss

The agony of abandonment, separation, and loss is probably the second most common past life trauma that we all carry collectively as human beings—the first of course must surely be violent death. Instead of the three cases just described I could easily have substituted hundreds of others from my practice alone: babies left out to starve during famines, children separated from parents by raids, massacres, or slavery, pioneers cut off from their loved ones, heretics dragged off into dungeons, political dissidents who "disappear"—a train of human misery that continues unabated to this day in almost every known country. In so many workshops and private sessions I have sat silently and patiently passing the Kleenex while my client sobs and screams out his or her particular outrage and private loss. And usually there is no comfort, no rescue, no cavalry. What is lost is lost, it seems, forever.

Psychoanalysts, of course, identify the origins of such painful losses with the infant's separation from the mother, if not the very emergence from the womb and uterine bliss. Certainly many a session will weave in and out of such biographical memories stimulated by the symbolic resonance of phrases like "she's gone," "I'm all alone," etc., and the emotional release is likewise enormous. But from the holographic picture I am proposing I would maintain that there would always be past life experiences interfacing with childhood abandonment stories which will add another tremulous octave to what Matthew Arnold once called "the eternal note of sadness."

With loss comes grief and the necessary process of mourning. Often past life sessions like those described give a person the opportunity to finish some old piece of unfinished grief, fragments of which have surfaced in childhood, in the ending of love affairs, or in the loss of parents or loved ones. It is a good question as to how long we may need to grieve or whether there is a natural end. We can, like Hamlet, become addicted to our loss or else deny it entirely, like King Lear, and go crazy in the process. But certain spiritual and psychological authorities are in agreement that abandonment and loss can be our greatest teachers. "When the heart weeps for what it has lost, the spirit laughs for what it has found" runs a Sufi saying.

When Sol lost his master he underwent the beginnings of a process well known among the mystics, especially those of the Christian tradition. For commonly after a spiritual awakening like Sol's encounter with Jesus, there follows a honeymoon period of intense devotion and then a spiritual depression, what St. John of the Cross called a "dark night of the soul."[9] This is a period of emptiness and intense inner anguish in which there is no consolation. It is actually a period of inner cleansing from desire, attachment, and longing which may lead eventually to a different kind of spiritual consciousness and possibly end with some deep inner communion with the higher Self. The mystery of spiritual abandonment has been succinctly summarized by the German mystic and poet Angelus Silesius in this striking way:

> Abandonment ensnares God; but to abandon even God is an abandonment few ever comprehend.

This then is the archetypal or spiritual octave of abandonment that interfaces with the biographical and past life experience of loss. It is by no means an easy one to face but, when traversed, it can bring us to a deep sense of peace, of trust, and what might even be called faith.

CHAPTER 6

UNFINISHED SOUL BUSINESS: THE PSYCHOLOGY OF KARMA

Great is the power of memory, exceedingly great, oh my God, a spreading limitless room within me. Who can reach its uttermost depths?

Augustine, *Confessions*

To redeem those who lived in the past and to re-create all "it was" into a "thus I willed it"—that alone should I call redemption.

Nietzsche

Remembering is for those who have forgotten.

Plotinus

New Light on Childhood Trauma

In three of the cases I described in the last chapter—Susan's guilty attachment to her mother, Rick's fear of abandonment, Sol's chronic sinusitus—we once more found there to be a past life story behind the suffering each of them had experienced in their current life. Neither Susan nor Rick appeared to have experienced traumas in their early life which could account for the degree of the guilt and anxiety that each of them suffered. Sol, it is true, did come up with an early childhood memory of summer camp in this life which related to his blocked sinuses, yet there was nevertheless another layer to his particular pain which derived from his visions of a life at the time of Christ.

Such a small sample of cases is, of course, far from statistically significant from the perspective of research, but I cite them because they are representative of hundreds in my own files. Similar cases could without any doubt be paralleled by many thousands in the files of the growing number of established practitioners of past life therapy. The implications of these findings are indeed quite radical by the standards and received doctrines of Western psychology. They seem to show that *most psychological illness is inherited at a psychic level.* When I use the qualification *most* psychological illness I naturally leave open the possibility of genuine first time trauma in this life, but this seems more and more to account for only a tiny proportion of psychological disturbance.

More often than not, childhood traumas like Sol's turn out to be reruns of past life events. Specific incidents in childhood reactivate or "trigger" a latent past life story which belongs to the inherited or karmic level of the complex. The childhood incidents have a symbolic resonance with the specific past life trauma they trigger. Thus Sol's anticipated sorrow when he was a child that he might never see his mother again triggered an ancient past life memory of never seeing his beloved teacher again. This reopening of an old karmic wound was an opportunity for Sol as a child to relinquish his old grief, but circumstances were not propitious and the grief became even more deeply buried in his sinuses.

It is extremely common, as we shall see in detail in later chapters, for childhood sexual traumas also to have past life underlays. I have frequently found that the therapeutic exploration of a scene of childhood sexual abuse in this life will suddenly open up to some wretched past life scenario such as child prostitution, ritual deflowering, brother-sister or father-daughter incest, or else child rape in any number of settings ranging from the home to the battlefield.

Often, though by no means always, the reliving of a past life story of sexual abuse can prove to be considerably more painful and dramatic than the current life repetition. In many cases it appears that only the mildest interference in the current childhood is enough to evoke horrors that sometimes border, it seems, on madness.

The Cases of Melinda and Cindy

Melinda had consulted several therapists about her failure to form close relationships with men and her near frigidity when it came to sexual contact. For a period she had been in a lesbian relationship which helped her somewhat because her lover wanted companionship more than physical contact. Yet the root issue remained untouched. She reported a clear memory of sexual molestation at eleven years. A twelve-year-old boy from the neighborhood had enticed her into a disused garage and had fondled her genitally though he had not attempted penetration. Her retelling of the story was cold and detached; she seemed to hold herself clenched as she told it. Apparently she had talked about this event many times with her previous therapists and, though she had also beaten out her rage on pillows and mattresses, part of her was still holding unfinished anger.

When I invited her to lie down on a mattress to relive the event, her clenching became even more pronounced:

"I don't want to do this," she says, with markedly more anger in her voice now.

"Lie down anyway and keep repeating that phrase to whoever it applies to," I urge gently.

With her eyes closed, the following monologue emerges with very little prompting from me other than to direct her to repeat certain phrases and to exaggerate her bodily posture:

"I don't want to do this. I don't want to do this. Don't make me. DON'T MAKE ME. NO! NO! NO! You're hurting me. Get away."

She starts to kick, shake her head, and writhe. "Get away. Get away. No. Don't make me." For a while she continues this way, her body becoming more and more tense, her outrage more pronounced. I imagine that she must be reexperiencing the incident from her childhood. Then suddenly her words indicate that we have slipped into another lifetime:

"They're raping me. They're raping me. Help! Help! HELP! There are six or seven of them. They're soldiers. I'm in a barn. My arms are tied. It's Russia somewhere. I'm a peasant girl about eleven or twelve. God, it's awful. They don't stop . . . I don't want to do this. I don't want to be here. LEAVE ME ALONE. I'm not going to feel this. I won't feel this. I won't show them anything."

Her pelvic area is stiff, her legs taut, her head turns from side to side. I urge her to let these parts of the body speak and express what is going on with them.

"I'm not going to feel this, I'll never show you I like it" (pelvis and genitals).

"Don't touch me! Get away! I'll kill you! I hate you. I hate you. I'll kick you!" (legs).

"I'm not going to see this. It's not happening" (head).

For a while we work through this awful scene and I encourage her to let her legs kick, to let her genitals record exactly what they feel, and to allow her head to see and understand all of it. There is kicking and weeping and rage and terrible confusion as for a while her genitals register both pleasure and pain. Gradually, as these sensations and movements surge through her body, she seems to experience a huge releasing and letting go of the earlier clenchings, all of which culminate in a bout of intense sobbing and convulsive movements in her pelvis.

Suddenly she is no longer with the soldiers:

"I'm in that garage. I don't want him to touch me. I don't want to do this. Don't make me. I just freeze up, but he doesn't hurt me. He's quite gentle, but my thighs just go rigid and I'm not really there."

I urge her to breathe deeply and see the similarity to the earlier rape scene.

"Oh, yes!" she says. "My body was remembering something else. It was like a flashback, a nightmare, but I didn't want to see it."

As Melinda surveys the two stories and gives herself permission to really see them now, she has all kinds of spontaneous recognitions: how just being touched always leads to a kind of freezing, how she is always somehow not present in sex, how she has always had fantasies of wanting to kick men, and so on. In a later session she reclaimed more of the Russian girl's story: how she had become pregnant, raised the child, a boy, alone and had bitterly avoided contact with men from then onward, dying quite young from a wasting disease. The crucial events, however, were clearly locked into the rape scene at eleven or

twelve. Her unconscious compulsion laid down in the previous life had led her—unconsciously, of course—to repeat a similar but far less violent sexual trauma in this life.
The contemporary trauma served to reawaken the latent
past life level of the complex, fraught as it was with terror,
humiliation, and rage.

My second example, Cindy, had been in therapy for
quite a while, working on issues of deep emotional longing mixed with a fear of rejection. She wanted depend-
able love so much, she said, that it was like "being eaten
from inside," and she indicated her belly. She was also
tormented by a severe childhood nightmare of flashing
eyes and teeth in a dark corner of her childhood bedroom.
In her interview the two issues seemed unrelated, but
they were equally troubling to her. One well-meaning
therapist had urged her to image a monster in the dark
and then to befriend it, but somehow this ploy had not
lessened the residual terror.

Working on the assumption that the childhood night
terror might well be a past life flashback, I got her to find
herself back in her bed as that terrified child:

> "I'm standing in my bed, clinging to the railing. There are
> horrible yellow eyes in the corner and it looks like teeth.
> Mommy! Mommy! Please help me! They're trying to tear me
> up! Help me! Help me!"
>
> Her mother comes and hugs her, saying, "It's only a dream,
> go back to sleep." She lies down, but still the eyes are there in
> the corner. Still the terror in her child's body—especially in
> her belly.
>
> I direct her to look closely at the eyes and teeth and to stay
> with her feelings of terror, reminding her that her body as
> Cindy is safe and sound here in my office. I get her to repeat
> one phrase as she looks into the darkness:

*"They're going to tear me up! They're going to tear me up!
Oh, help! I'm running, I'm in a forest, it's almost dark.
They're coming after me! I'm a boy, about six years old.
They've caught me—it's a pack of wolfhounds! Help! HELP!
Their teeth . . ." (She screams and writhes violently.)
"They're tearing me up . . . Help me! Help me!"*

*After an agonizing five more minutes of screaming and
writhing, Cindy suddenly goes completely limp.*

*"It's all over. I'm above the body. They (the wolfhounds) are
all eating it. Ugh! They ripped out my guts, my neck, my
chest. Oh, it's awful! But I'm dead now, I don't feel anything."*

Cindy weeps for some time while I encourage her to
breathe and let go of as much of the trauma as is possible,
especially what is lodged in her belly. She realizes her
belly is where she has always carried all the terror from
this memory. I guide her to look back on the young boy's
life until then. He had been the young son of a peasant
woman who worked as a serving woman to a particularly
brutal feudal lord. On a cruel impulse the lord and his
cohorts had selected a human victim for their hunt one
day and had driven the boy into the woods for sport.
Although the mother had been helpless to prevent it, the
boy felt deeply betrayed by her and by her master. The
failure of Cindy's mother to rescue her from her night
terrors had unfortunately served only to reinforce an old
deep wound of betrayal, a wound which had become increasingly generalized in adult life and had lodged itself
symbolically in her stomach as a gnawing longing for trust
and protection.

The Compulsion to Repeat

"A complex arises," Jung once wrote, "where we have experienced a defeat in life." The stories of Melinda and Cindy and thousands of others raise a provocative new question: *"Which life?"* For as deeper experiential therapy uncovers more memories of past life trauma I believe we need to expand Jung's dictum to the extent of stating that a *complex arises where we have experienced a defeat in any life.* Freud's concept of *repetition compulsion—* the drive to repeat—for example, and Fritz Perls's notion of *unfinished business* can likewise be seen as dynamics across lives as well as within them. It is as though each of us is born with a portion of the unfinished business of humanity at large which it is our personal and karmic responsibility to complete in one way or another. Unless we bring to consciousness and detach ourselves from these latent compulsions, the past life content of our complexes will continue to drive us to repeat the circumstances and scenarios of old defeats, betrayals, losses, humiliations, violations, deprivations, injustices, and so on.

Some of the past life issues attached to a complex show such a high degree of moral and psychological complexity that they take considerable skill and patience to unravel, as later cases in this book show. But many issues derive from nothing more than the universal experience of fear and dread, as we saw with Melinda and Cindy. Trauma arising from such fear is a major component in many past life complexes.

Clinically, an irrational fear is called a *phobia.* Although many phobias do, indeed, arise in this life, it seems to be the case that almost everyone has some particular deep fear that will not be thus explained. Whether it be terror of spiders, wild animals, fire, water, heights, crowds, knives, machines, dark places, and so on, I have consistently found that behind the fear lies a specific and detailed story of past life trauma. So powerful are many of these inexplicable terrors that they will often drive a person to risk the very thing he or she most fears. It is as though they are trying to heal themselves apotropaically, warding off "evil," that is, by actually inviting it.

I treated, for example, an alcoholic client who had a terror of drowning. Yet this client would go out sailing on the high seas or else lash himself to a beacon during heavy storms so that waves crashed all about him. Was he trying to re-create some old story? His past lives did indeed reveal several stories of his own drownings. In one life in particular he had been a buccaneer and had shamefully murdered a whole crew of captured sailors by brutally drowning them. In his case the phobia was clearly exacerbated by guilt. I was also told by a colleague of a young adolescent boy with a fear of fire who would build himself huge fires in a fireplace and stare into them. Eventually in a kind of trance he saw himself and his parents burnt as heretics in the sixteenth century.

In my own cases I have records of all kinds of phobias that in similar ways reveal past life stories behind them. Animal terrors evoke memories of being thrown to wild beasts by the Romans, or by primitive tribes; such people often unconsciously attract aggression in certain animals around them. People remember deaths from poisonous insects, from spiders, snakes, sharks and more. Many who fear heights recall deaths from being thrown off cliffs, falling from planes in recent wars or simply falling accidents. Crowd fears frequently bring back memories of being crushed in a panic stampede or a riot. Accidents with industrial machines, murder by knives, suffocation in mines, landslides, gassing or simply smoke from fires have all been found to underlie specific fears.

A more complex kind of complaint than phobias are neurotic fears connected with physical and material survival. Eating disorders, such as anorexia nervosa and bulimia, often reveal old stories of starvation due to crop failure, famine, or disease. It may well be that newborn babies with colic are unconsciously and somatically rerunning old patterns of being too starved to assimilate food. Some cases reveal memories of tribal lives where women, children, and the elderly were left in the snow or in the desert to starve. Other stories reveal internment camps, concentration camps, or dungeons where dysentery or starvation took their toll and left tendencies to organic disturbance in the digestive functions. Many a client undergoing financial hardships with accompanying symptoms of depression will reveal from the unconscious stories of lives as a beggar, or as an orphan, or as some kind of outcast living on the fringes of human society.

When we are subject to such past life fears about material security we find ourselves either reliving them—out of work, deeply in debt, wasting away—or else obsessively compensating for that fear by an over-accumulation of food, money, or fat around our midriff. "I'll never be without again" is an underlying thought in such cases. Indeed, if there is a collective past life complex that many Americans seem to share, it is a fear of starvation. No country has more abundance in it, yet nowhere in the world are there more twenty-four-hour supermarkets, fast food chains, and so on. Of course, this is an ancestral pattern primarily deriving from European famines and the Depression of the Twenties, but more and more cases of starvation from World War II, particularly in concentration camps, are now surfacing in the unconscious in contemporary cases of anorexia and other eating disorders where the sufferers have no biological connection to the war.

One area where I have found repetition compulsion to be particularly strong is in adolescence, particularly among teenage boys. Reckless behavior such as drunken driving, drug abuse, playing with weapons, or going off on foolhardy expeditions all amount to a certain kind of unconscious flirtation with death. Although I have myself worked with relatively few adolescent boys, those I have treated are often carrying bitter past life memories of dying young and unglorious on the battlefield, of having somehow never finished their initiation into manhood. So they are either unconsciously rerunning old battlefield deaths with a deep residual devil-may-care attitude born of despair and defiance, or else they are trying to prove themselves unconsciously to elders they failed in past lives. Sometimes the shock of being in an actual accident where a close friend is killed may dimly bring the old memory to consciousness sufficiently to change things, but more often the old warrior stories will merely echo violently in the background of consciousness until the turmoil of adolescence passes and onlookers and parents heave a sigh of relief.

But it is not just adolescents who "act out" under the unconscious influence of past life compulsions; many an adult is driven to kinds of behavior or changes in life pattern by the residues of unfinished past life business. A man or woman in middle age may suddenly become intensely involved in some political cause, having shown little or no interest in politics in earlier life. What has been activated from the unconscious is a past life memory of having died around the age in question, powerless to combat political oppression. One client, for example, recalled taking an active part in the freedom bus rides in the sixties in the American South, which made considerable sense to him when he recalled an early nineteenth-century life as a cruel slave owner. Another client, a woman, remembered being a tribal chieftain who had failed to find food for his people during a famine and had died intensely sad and guilty. In this life the woman finds herself almost obsessively concerned with the marketing of food and with questions of economics.

Another intriguing area of past life compulsions concerns settling and voyaging. History is full of nomadic migrations, ocean and desert crossings, colonization, or else involuntary exiles. Many of them leave profound imprints on the psyche. For some, the failure to complete the crossing or being left behind during some mass migration to a new territory or continent may leave an unfinished urge to explore and settle in distant places. In my own case, I have the painful memory of once being an old man in a Huguenot family that fled from Catholic France to the Netherlands. Our family was seeking a passage to the Dutch settlements in the New World, but sickness overtook the old man and I remember him dying miserably by the roadside. The life that followed found me as a trapper exploring the Hudson Valley above New York City, a place to which I have been drawn back in my current life.

Sometimes a reverse movement may occur: a deep yearning to return to a country that we may have abandoned or from which we have been exiled in another lifetime. These patterns all belong to overall themes of separation and incompletion. In therapy we may need to voice words that were never said, image projects not completed, and re-image lovers, parents, and children we never saw again because of tragic deaths or premature separation. Often, when this is done, there is a surge of new energy or creative endeavor connected with certain countries, skills, or activities. It is the psyche picking up old threads once more, returning, completing, continuing.

Toward a Karmic View of the Complex

In India the psychophysical discipline known as Yoga has long recognized past life compulsions as a fundamental aspect of every individual's makeup. Everything that happens to us or which we initiate creates impressions within the mental stuff *(citta)* of the experiencer or doer in such a way that a disposition or tendency to repeat or reexperience the action is laid down. The good or evil acts we perform create what Yoga masters call karmic residues *(karmaskaya)*, literally the residues of past actions *(karma* = action).

A modern scholar of Indian philosophy, Dr. Karl H. Potter, has summarized the doctrine for us very clearly:

> This karmic residue has or is accompanied by dispositional tendencies *(samskara)* of more than one sort, including at least two kinds of traces *(vasana)*, one kind of which, if and when it is activated, produces a memory of the originating act, the other which, if and when it is activated, produces certain afflictions *(klesa)*. These *klesas* are erroneous conceptions which characterize the thinking of those engaged in purposive activity and it is they which are responsible for the

person being in bondage, that is, continually creating karmic residues.[1]

Vasanas in Sanskrit usage are analogous to the traces or fragrances left behind by perfume on a cloth or smoke from a fire, but in the context of past life memories this trace is conceived as psychic rather than physical. The klesas are the wounds or afflictions that are passed on from life to life in the form of negative and emotionally laden thoughts and attitudes. We have met many examples of these klesas in the various examples so far: "I'll never get enough," "It's all my fault," "It's not safe to risk my feelings," "I've always got to do it alone," "I'll get back at them," "My life is too short," "He/she is bound to hurt/leave/betray me," "I deserve to suffer," "I am not good enough/worthy," "No one could ever love me." It is the klesas which are aroused by identifying with the symbolic resonances that we have talked of.

Many other psychotherapies have, of course, identified such thoughts as these, calling them "negative laws," "patterning," "life scripts," "dominant myths," etc., but what has not been proposed until recently is that these scripts are actually inherited as part of our psychic makeup at birth. In the words of the celebrated Indologist Heinrich Zimmer, "These vasanas tend to cause samskaras, permanent scars that go from life to life."[2]

The samskara, then, is like psychic scar tissue, or like a "furrow in the psyche" (Zimmer) that leads us to precisely the repetition compulsion Freud observed. We repeat the same old failure one life after another; we are repeatedly attracted to lovers and spouses who hurt and betray us, or we end up with bosses and especially parents who bully and tyrannize us; we contract diseases and undergo pains that other bodies have suffered before and so on. Depressing as this picture may appear to some, I can find no better one to encompass the extraordinary variety and uniqueness of each person's allotment of what Hamlet called "the heart-ache and the thousand natural shocks that flesh is heir to" in any one lifetime.

In discussing the samskaras both Potter and Zimmer emphasize that they are dispositions, propensities, or "tendencies to act according to patterns established by reactions in the past" (Zimmer). The samskara is like a scratch on a phonograph record; every time the record is played, the needle jumps in the same place and there are the same predictable "clicks."

The closest the Western tradition of psychology has come to the Yogic notion of samskaras is Jung's theory of the archetypes of the collective unconscious. Rather than adopt Yogic terminology, he preferred his own theory that the archetypes are responsible for "psychic heredity" . . . such as predisposition to disease, traits of character, special gifts, and so on (see Appendix 2). He insisted that archetypes are simply formative principles, devoid of actual content, in contrast to the vasanas and samskaras.

"An archetype," Jung wrote, "is like a watercourse along which the water of life has formed for centuries, digging a deep channel for itself."[3]

At the time of Jung's death in 1961, both the world of professional psychology and the general public in the West were still skeptical, if not downright hostile, to the idea of past lives and reincarnation. The Bridey Murphy case had been effectively demolished, it seemed, in the late Fifties and Edgar Cayce's readings were still only known to a relatively small number of readers. Today, as Gallup polls, TV talk shows, and magazine articles amply

demonstrate, the climate surrounding the issue of reincarnation and past lives has markedly changed. There are
now thousands of past life memories accumulating in the
files of therapists and researchers in Europe and North
and South America.

As for prenatal memory, we now have the internation-
ally known work of Dr. Thomas Verney. Verney has gar-
nered the researchers of many experts around the world
who have demonstrated experimentally the existence of
in utero patterning laid down in the fetal consciousness.
Verney's important book, *The Secret Life of the Unborn
Child*, summarizes many of these findings. Interestingly,
more and more of his researchers who began with a
strictly medical and material standpoint are reporting
past life memories mixed in with in utero memories.

I believe that the samskara, which I propose to translate
as a past life or karmic complex, offers the missing key-
stone in the overarching bridge between Eastern and
Western psychologies. Conceptually a karmic complex
can be seen to lie midway between an archetype, which
has no personal memory traces, and a complex, which
derives directly from personal experience in this life. In
short, I would propose the following extension of Jung's
original terms:

	ARCHETYPE	SAMSKARA (Karmic Complex)	COMPLEX
Contents:	Mythological images; uni- versal forms	Past life memory traces (vasanas, klesas)	Current life memory traces

The immense importance of the samskara for understanding the structure and evolution of the nascent per-

sonality was seen clearly by Heinrich Zimmer in his unpublished meditations on the Sanskrit term samskara:

> Samskara is a rich and highly suggestive term. Its connotations cluster about a concept of "that which has been wrought, cultivated, brought to form." But this, in the case of the individual, is the personality—with all its characteristic adornments, scars, and quirks—which for years, indeed for lifetimes, has been in the process of concoction.[4]

With our characteristic bias in favor of material rather than spiritual causes, the West has long accepted the genetic inheritance of physical and temperamental traits, but lacking the sophistication of Eastern psychology and wary of the excesses of reincarnationalism we have shied away from the notion of psychic inheritance—the claims of astrology being seen as so much arbitrary nonsense. Yet now it would appear that the tide is turning. Increasingly, the evidence is that all the major complexes that structure our lives and determine our personal interactions are already laid down at birth and before. Even though the costumes, the scenery, and the stage set may be different in this lifetime, it is nevertheless a dimly familiar part that we act out, some old unfinished "play of passion" that we find ourselves drawn into by the archetypes and our karmic complexes. But once we bring this to awareness we may find that we need no longer stay stuck in the unconscious compulsion of the samskaras but that finally we can be the true director of our own destiny. What Nietzsche wished for—"thus I willed it"—is within our grasp with the help of our past life awareness.

Residual Shame: The Case of Leonard

Leonard was a young man in his late twenties who came into therapy with a number of issues around work and relationships. He had graduated from college a few years earlier with a major in engineering that he made little use of. Instead, he chose to live in a cabin in the woods and got by with odd carpentering jobs. These jobs were not very satisfying to him since he frequently felt put upon and pushed around by his bosses. Things were not much better in his personal life. He had had a number of brief relationships with women, all ending, so he recounted, with their dropping him.

All this contributed to a very poor image of himself and to a low-grade depression which tended to isolate him even more. He was stuck in one of those vicious circles where negativity seems to feed upon itself; a slough of despond into which we seem to sink further the more effort we make to pull ourselves out.

As I listened to his story I was struck by the overall social picture of his isolation from any community and almost a loathing of being part of any group or gathering. Having practiced psychotherapy for some years in a college town, I was accustomed to working with graduate students who were weaning themselves away from the comfortable containment in their old *alma mater* and avoiding being initiated into the not-so-cozy real world of work and adult responsibility. But Leonard's reactions were much more severe than these. He was actually resentful and bitter about a society that had, it seemed, done little more than fail to provide an instant career and a perfect mate! Clearly it was a waste of time to point out that most of his immediate contemporaries were also struggling along with part-time jobs and muddling through in relationships. Leonard's despair about his place in the world seemed to issue from more than his immediate circumstances, but from what I had no idea.

Whenever there is strong affect, the most helpful approach, I have found, is simply to exaggerate it so as to give it full expression. So I had Leonard lie down on the couch with his eyes closed and breathe deeply as if sighing. "Really let yourself go into all the sadness and bitterness," I instruct him. "See where it takes you." He does this for some time, heaving, shaking his head, and clenching his fists:

> "It's not fair," he says after a while, "It's not fair. Why did you do this to me?"
>
> I encourage him to name the person, and he adds the name "Sarah," his last girlfriend.
>
> "It's not fair, Sarah. Why did you do this to me? I really cared about you. You led me on. You didn't care at all about me. Why did you do it? Why? Why?"
>
> I urge him to keep repeating these phrases, to fully feel their import and let anything surface.
>
> "Why did you do it? In front of them all. I felt such a fool. What am I going to do?"
>
> "What's happening?" I ask, alerted by the phrase "in front of them all."
>
> "It's not Sarah anymore. It's this woman on a boat. A big boat. Like the Mississippi steamers. She is very well dressed. Kind of a hostess type . . . Why did you do it? You led me on. You didn't care at all. I feel such a fool."
>
> Now the tears are beginning to come and Leonard's fists are held, his face a grimace of torment and rage. Behind the pain of rejection by Sarah in his current life, the karmic level of the complex has started to emerge.

Leonard is remembering, it seems, the life of a young man on a river steamer in the American South in the early nineteenth century. He has established himself as a fairly successful gambler and has just had a brief affair with an attractive but far from monogamous soubrette. For all his worldly braggadocio, he is underneath quite shy with women and has naively opened himself up to one who has done little more than toy with his affections. Unable to win her back and feeling publicly shunned by her, he falls into a cycle of drinking and gambling from which he does not emerge. Picking a foolhardy fight with another more seasoned riverboat gambler, he is shot and dies from the bullet wound. Clearly there is a suicidal element in his provoking the other man and he dies bitter, resentful, and humiliated by the way this woman has publicly jilted him.

This first session brings a lot of emotional release and helps Leonard separate his current feelings about Sarah from the older, karmic complex of rejection and humiliation. He realizes that this old wound drives him to choose women that hurt and humiliate him because a part of him needs to replay the old story. As we go over the past life a second time, I encourage him to speak out some of his unexpressed rage at his riverboat lover:

"You bitch! I hate you! I HATE YOU! You really hurt me. You really didn't care about me. You are heartless and cruel. You just played with me. You just used me."

Yet the karmic wound is far from healed, as we learn in later sessions. The tragic riverboat life turns out to be one of several past lives in which a fatal repetition compulsion has produced one rejection after another, resulting in the unconscious negative thought or klesa that "women will always hurt/leave me." We work through these lives slowly and painfully.

One theme that keeps recurring strongly in Leonard's past life memories of rejection is that of abuse. "You just played with me. You just used me." These words have a particularly bitter ring to them, so in a later session, following the principle of symbolic resonance, I encourage Leonard to find himself in a life where this abuse happened *for the first time.*

This time the phrases themselves serve to focus all the bitterness and resentment that seemed to lie at the core of this deeply entrenched samskara or karmic complex. By having Leonard repeat the same words that express his hurt in the riverboat life—"You are heartless and cruel. You just played with me. You just used me"—we swiftly moved into the following past life story, which I have here summarized:

>   *Leonard finds himself as a young male slave in a small Greek town in the early days of the Roman Empire. His master is a wealthy but uncouth merchant who is generally disliked and feared in the town. It is this slave's particular fate to be forced into the role of the favored homosexual lover to this ugly merchant whom he hates. His miserable choice is either to submit to his master's sodomy or to be cruelly beaten. Choosing the slightly less painful alternative, the slave is to find yet another level to his humiliation. Word gets around the small town that he is the merchant's "boy" and for many years he finds himself taunted and ostracized by other slaves in the town who might otherwise have been his friends. The general disgust the townspeople feel for this lascivious merchant thus gets meted out to his unhappy slave.*
>   *The turning point in this cruel life comes when a garrison of Roman soldiers take over the town and, for reasons not*

clear through Leonard's remembering, imprison the merchant and confiscate his property. His several slaves are turned loose, not being held accountable for their master. But the favored slave whose life Leonard agonizingly reconstructs finds himself the object of loathing of all in the town. No one will feed or employ him and finally a group of younger men drive him with stones to the edge of the village, forcing him to leave.

Bruised, homeless, and utterly embittered at the townspeople and human society in general, the wretched slave wanders the dusty roads for months, begging. Eventually he finds himself work as a goatherd in the mountains. Here he lives out the remainder of his days ruminating over his grievances until death puts an end to his misery.

Here, then, lay all the karmic roots of Leonard's isolation from society, his feelings of rejection and bitterness, his distrust of bosses, and his fear of abuse in sexual relationships.

If there was one feeling that most fully expressed the sum of all these hurts and humiliations it is shame. Anthropologists have pointed out that shame is essentially a feeling of public disgrace; in this sense it is quite different from guilt, which is private and internalized. We can feel guilty when alone, but shame usually requires the presence and disapproval of our whole community or our peers. Hellenic Greece was certainly a shame culture rather than a guilt culture, so that the very public way in which, as the slave, Leonard remembered first rejection by the community for his sexual behavior and then actual ostracism were deeply wounding. In the light of this old memory trace, Leonard's compulsion to live in a hut in the woods seemed very understandable, as did his accompanying depression and failure to fit into any community.

The session was immensely salutary for Leonard. The connections between his current life and this one story were obvious to him. It was as if a large burden dropped from his psyche. He started, as we say, to lighten up. Leonard continued in therapy and explored other issues in his past lives. For a while the import of the Greek story receded into the background. Leonard's social life at this time was slowly beginning to open up. He moved back into town and started dating again. This time he carefully questioned his assumptions each time and avoided setting himself up for rejection. He made friends in the community and started to see himself quite differently.

In one of our later sessions he found himself in a past life in ancient China when he was the warlord of a small town struggling with invading Mongolian hordes. He was a valiant, even noble, leader of his people, incessantly involved in fighting, rebuilding, supplying, and organizing. He died exhausted in that life, having given his all to his people. Looking back on it he felt enormously empowered. "I gave my life to the community," he said. "It felt good." I urged him to hang on to that image of the powerful self at the living center of his community. It was a valuable counterbalance to the bitter and despairing ostracized slave in his psyche. Both were present in him, but a whole process of rebalancing and integration were clearly beginning in Leonard's life. It seemed a fitting conclusion to our work.

PART III
KEY ASPECTS OF PAST LIFE THERAPY

HEALING

I am not a mechanism, an assembly of various sections.
And it is not because the mechanism is working wrongly,
    that I am ill.
I am ill because of wounds to the soul, to the deep
    emotional self
and the wounds to the soul take a long, long time, only
    time can help
and patience, and a certain difficult repentance
long, difficult repentance, realisation of life's mistake, and
    the freeing oneself
from the endless repetition of the mistake
which mankind at large has chosen to sanctify.

                    D. H. Lawrence, *More Pansies*

CHAPTER 7

SUBTLE BODY, DENSE MIND: PAST LIVES AND PHYSICAL ILLS

Thinkers, listen, tell me what you know of that is not
    inside the soul?
Take a pitcher of water and set it down on the water—
now it has water inside and water outside.
We mustn't give it a name,
lest silly people start talking again about the body
    and the soul.

                Kabir, Sufi poet and mystic
                (translated by Robert Bly)

Every part of the body has a story to tell.
                Anna Halprin

The Body Remembers

In many of the cases we have looked at so far, my clients were suffering from prominent physical symptoms that turned out to be connected with a key event in their past life stories. In some cases we even started directly with the somatic complaint, allowing the body to tell its own story. In Susan's case (Chapter 5) we found that her rigid neck and shoulders carried memories of a guilty suicide from her past life as a Dutch painter; Gregory's impotence (Chapter 4) was bound up with the harrowing story of shame and castration from his life in the French court; Melinda's present sexual frigidity (Chapter 6) revealed a past life of child abuse and rape.

In all three cases the emotional issues central to the stories had become embedded in the particular part of the body that was wounded in the past life. The result was that the unresolved emotional distress for each of them had become unconsciously identified with the bodily trauma. Seen karmically it would seem to me that in such cases a physical predisposition for that part of the body to be hurt is passed on in association with the emotional content of the samskara, what I am calling the past life level of the complex.

However, this emotional association does not necessarily arise with all physical samskaras that are transmitted. Often the transmission is predominantly of a physical memory trace, the emotional and thought content being quite secondary. Mitchell's residual memories of leg injuries (Chapter 4) were of this kind, as are the many phobias listed in Chapter 6. What this suggests is an important distinction to be made between 1) past life physical traumas that are in some sense brought on by or which express an emotional conflict and 2) past life physical traumas that are largely accidental.

In the second category there will of course be emotions such as terror or grief to be handled with the help of cathartic release, but in these cases the emotions are almost entirely reactions to the physical accident itself. The young urchin's death remembered by Alice (Chapter 2) required only minimal catharsis, since the child had no strong attachments in that life and passed on no particular karmic issues. By contrast we have seen a number of cases in the first category where emotional issues are strongly attached to physical traumas in quite subtle ways: Sol's sinuses (Chapter 5) seemed to have imprinted in them all his unfinished karmic business about abandonment, while Jane's back and kidney problems (Chapter 4) reflected her ambivalence about work and marriage at a deep organic level.

I realize that I may already be stretching the credulity of my more skeptical readers with the idea of inherited *psychic* contents from past lives. To further propose that *physical* predispositions to illnesses, weaknesses, and accidents are also very specifically transmitted (quite apart from genetic inheritance) may seem doubly problematic. Perhaps it might help if I back up a little and sketch how psychotherapists and body workers currently regard psychosomatic matters.

As everyone knows, Western psychology and philosophy has for a long time tended to treat mind and body as two quite separate realms. There is no need for me to rehearse the history of this doctrine, which is usually called "mind-body dualism" or "Cartesian dualism" (after René Descartes), since it is easily found in every primer of philosophy. Its consequences are obvious to all: doctors and physiologists treat the body; psychologists and psychiatrists supposedly treat the mind. Universities have departments that reinforce these divisions so successfully that learned exchange between, say, a faculty of medicine and a faculty of psychology are quite rare events. Psychiatry, which theoretically should embrace both the medical and the psychological, has for a century or more been caught on the horns of this dualism and has progressively moved toward organic and biochemical explanations— some would say reductions—of everything to do with the mind. Indeed, many writers treat the mind and the brain as quite synonymous.[1]

Of late there have been new experiments using mental imagery in the treatment of diseases such as cancer. The widely known work of Drs. Carl and Stephanie Simonton and the recent practice of psychoneuroimmunology (PNI) are notable incidences.[2] The so-called holistic health movement also attempts to bridge the abyss of mind and body by referring to oriental systems of subtle energy or the power of thought forms. Yet the principles by which the body and mind interact are still understood very little and the role of imagination and imagery even less. There has been some progress in what used to be called psychosomatic medicine, but in general it has been a struggle against the prevailing tide of medical research where more and more refined surgical or pharmaceutical treatments are favored and where the role of either the conscious or the unconscious mind in physical complaints is hotly denied.

A physician turned psychoanalyst who swam against the tide his whole life and died in an American prison for his pains was Wilhelm Reich. He strongly believed that organic disease was a direct reflection of emotional disturbance and that as a consequence if we can cure the emotional dysfunction on an energetic level the body will come ultimately to heal itself.

I do not intend to go into the ramifications and controversy surrounding Reich's brilliant work except to mention a case reported by one of his followers that illustrates his principles perfectly and has obvious bearing on the somatic aspects of past life stories we have been discussing.

The analyst in question was the Australian Dr. Caron Kent who reports, in his book on Reichian treatment called *Man's Puzzled Body*,[3] the case of a young woman who consulted him with a severe curvature of the spine. She had already seen several specialists who claimed that the degeneration of her spine was much too advanced for surgery to be effective, telling her essentially that her condition was incurable. Dr. Kent learned that the curvature had arisen in childhood and that she had not been born with it. Since she had no childhood history of infection, injury, or disease, Kent wondered what could have brought on such severe symptoms.

In his effort to uncover the origin of the damage to the young woman's spine, he regressed her hypnotically back to the time of childhood when, apparently, she first experienced problems. In a trance state that sounds from his description like much of our past life work, Kent had the woman relive a traumatic scene. When the woman was a girl of six her father had been drunk a lot and had gone on violent rampages about the house, threatening his wife and children. On one horrible occasion he actually chased them all with an axe. In her regressed state the woman found herself as a six-year-old girl hiding in utter terror behind the wooden door of an outhouse while her father entered looking for her. As she relived the scene, she reproduced a crouched position on the couch leaning to one side—presumably to squeeze herself further behind the door. In order not to reveal herself, she also held her breath. Even though the father had failed to find her or hurt her, she had never fully released either her breath or the sheer terror of those appalling moments in which she crouched behind the door anticipating her father pulling her out and hacking her to death. Kent encouraged a full catharsis of the woman's terror and shock in reliving this totally forgotten scene. In doing so, the most amazing thing occurred. According to Kent, *the woman's spine straightened itself.* Apparently the emotional trauma had left the young girl physically frozen in the posture she had adopted to escape her father, an event later to be forgotten by the conscious mind. Kent afterward had her return to the spinal specialists she had consulted and they were all prepared to testify to the remarkable recovery.

Other striking but less severe examples of how emotional trauma can imprint itself on the body are given in D. J. West's authoritative work, *Psychical Research Today.* [4] West reproduces a photograph of a man's arm which shows strong indentations as from being bound by a rope. These marks appeared spontaneously much later when the man relived events of being captured and tied up. West also reports the similar case of a young woman where weals appeared on her body during a psychoanalytic session where she relived being beaten.

Hypnotherapists have long known that the skin surface is extremely sensitive and will frequently mirror emotional conflicts that can be healed by suggestion. But what Kent's case of the spinal curvature demonstrates is that imprints can be made at a much deeper organic level.

The Varieties of Somatic Inheritance

What Caron Kent and other Reichian therapists have consistently found about emotional trauma imprinting itself on muscular structures and various organs and systems of the body has been confirmed over and over in my own practice, but with the difference that many of the physical disturbances turn out to have a past life origin. Morris Netherton's ground-breaking book *Past Lives Therapy* is remarkable in that the majority of the cases he describes involved serious physical complaints: ulcers, epilepsy, migraine, incipient cancer. My own findings fully confirm Netherton's pioneer work. A surprising number of physical complaints do indeed have a past life story behind them which, when reenacted cathartically, can lead to substantial relief and often to quite rapid recovery. Some short summaries of the physical problems that I have found amenable to past life treatment may give an idea of the kinds of issues that many of us carry in a somatic form:

—A young woman who had suffered from ulcerative colitis relived the life of an eight-year-old Dutch girl rounded up and shot at a mass grave by Nazi soldiers. The colitis was an expression of the residual terror during the girl's last moments awaiting execution;

—A man with chronic back pain relived an agonizing death pinned under a wagon with a broken back; the pain substantially lessened after the session;

—A woman with eye problems and asthma remembered the life of a medieval monk accused of leading a whole village into heretical beliefs. The monk's punishment was to watch the whole village be burned alive before him, his eyes watering and his lungs heaving at the smoke from the burning flesh;

—A man with epilepsy relived a terrible battlefield death in which he was painfully dismembered; some of his death agonies appeared to be mirrored in the pattern of his epileptic seizures;

—A man with compulsive handwashing behavior found himself as an eighteenth-century surgeon who realized that many of his patients had died from unsterile conditions; he was left trying to clean the infection from his hands and was later committed to a mental asylum;

—A woman's chronic migraine disappeared after reliving the agony of a young girl of seven whose father beat her over the head with an iron bar until she died.

(In addition to these, I could add numerous examples of sexual problems connected to past life traumas, but since they are quite common I have reserved a whole chapter for them. See Chapter 8.)

Every part of the body, it would seem, has in one person or another revealed some old accident or wound. But the past life traumas always have a specific and not general relationship to the current physical problem. In other words, not all migraines derive from head wounds or all throat problems from strangling. A similar throat complaint in several people may carry quite different stories from those people. In one it may be a death from a beheading, in another a suffocation death, while someone else may remember having been hanged. In different people a painful chest or pains in the heart region will bring up memory traces of all kinds of stabbings, gun wounds, lances, arrows, shrapnel, etc. Sore legs and arms remember being broken in accidents or war, crushed by fallen trees, shattered by torture, crucifixion, or the rack, or else ripped off by wild animals. A weak or sensitive belly area may recall cuts, slashings, and disembowelings or else starvation or poisoning. Sensitive feet and hands have in past lives been subjected to every kind of accident and mutilation, to say nothing of performing horrible acts on others.

So much unconscious past life material lies just below the surface in certain regions of the body that inevitably body work of one kind or another is bound to bring it up. Many of my clients come from rolfing sessions, which entail deep tissue massage, reporting fragments of past lives arising as certain painful areas of musculature are restructured. In my own case, I vividly remember screaming in pain as the muscles of my butt were being worked upon in rolfing. While my rolfer was working on this very tight area I immediately got an image of a schoolmaster who had beaten me when I was ten years old in this life. The rolfer noted how much looser the area was after my screaming and repeated the manipulation! It was still painful and I yelled again, only this time I saw myself as a Celtic warrior wounded in the buttocks.

Unfortunately, because of the persistent Cartesian division of problems into either the bodily or the psychological, most rolfers, massage specialists, and body workers are not trained to handle emotional material when it releases somatically; likewise, most psychotherapists have no expertise in manipulating or treating the body. More and more, it seems to me, professional therapists will need to learn from each other, particularly by concentrating on the content of the images that the body produces when they focus on or massage a particular body area. Nevertheless, there are some signs of change. Remarkable advances in this area have already been made. Skilled innovators like Anna Halprin in California and Ilana Rubenfeld in New York City are making body work more conscious.

A similar body-mind problem also exists with intensive

meditation practices like Zen or vipassana. Even though there is no physical manipulation or touching in such meditation, one side effect of long and repeated sitting sessions is that the muscular holding patterns—what Wilhelm Reich called armoring—start to break down spontaneously. Once, after sitting regularly at a Buddhist retreat, I had the painful experience of my unconsciously hunched shoulders slowly dropping an inch or more. Strange things were also happening to my breathing. By keeping my awareness focused right in the pain and not detaching from it, eventually I found myself reliving an agonizing death by crucifixion as a young twelve-year-old girl, a persecuted Christian in early Rome. My breathing was involved because the diaphragm slowly collapses with crucifixion and it is only possible to breathe by pushing up from the legs. My death as the girl came when her legs were broken and suffocation ensued. Similarly, a client of mine, who practiced Zen, found himself having severe heart pains in his practice. His teachers simply instructed him to stay with the awareness of the pain and eventually a scene of a frightful Near Eastern massacre during the Crusades emerged in which he and thousands were being put to death and mutilated by sword and fire. Unable to complete the vision by himself in meditation he sought me out and we finished the story, in which, as a young man, he had been stabbed in the chest and then burned.

Not every meditation practitioner is lucky enough to find a therapist to help when such images occur. Some beginners give up meditation, fearing they are on the verge of mental breakdown. My experience leads me to believe that this often frightening material represents the somatic eruption from the past life level of their complexes, which are breaking down the more they sit and let go of ego control.

The Case of Edith: A Russian Anarchist's Untimely Death

Increasingly, in practicing psychotherapy from a past life perspective, I am convinced that the likelihood of cure depends on whether or not I am able to guide my client to the crucial or key story from his or her past lives. My experience indicates that if we can reach such a story in the early sessions, cure will be correspondingly swift, but if we miss it we may take a long time meandering around stories and issues that are essentially secondary before we reach the core issue. Naturally, I would be the first to admit that there are as many misses as hits in my probing for key past life stories, so in recounting the following two cases I must confess them to be exceptional rather than the rule. Nevertheless, I hope the fact that in the following cases Edith and Arlette did find swift and enduring cures will encourage others as much as it has encouraged me regarding the extraordinary effectiveness of past life reenactment as a therapeutic tool.

For some time Edith had been the client of a colleague of mine who is both a Jungian analyst and a physician with considerable knowledge of alternative healing practices. Edith was a dancer in her late twenties who was suffering from the poorly understood disease lupus erythematosus. Lupus is a noninfectious disease of the immune system which produces a multitude of symptoms, including inflammation and cell damage. Heart, joint, and kidney disease are also common to it. According to one authority, "the disease may be suddenly triggered by certain drugs or foreign proteins, exposure to ultraviolet radiation, or psychic trauma."[5] It is therefore somewhat of a mystery and although Edith's case was not severe or life-threatening, my colleague, who was treating her, had become somewhat pessimistic about her chances of recovery.

In Edith's case the course of the disease had taken the form of painful stiffness in all her joints which in many ways resembled arthritis. When I met her, the slow spread of the infirmity through her limbs had already become a serious threat to the pursuit of her career. The occasion when I worked with Edith was a workshop devoted not to past life therapy but to what I call the "warrior within." The workshop's purpose is to encourage people to contact first their anger, then images of fighting and assertiveness, and eventually to feel the power of the archetypal warrior within them (see also Chapter 8). To this end I use a variety of physical and imaginal exercises to stimulate both a somatic and a visionary awareness of these difficult qualities most of us tend to fear or suppress. In one exercise in the workshop Edith attended I used a number of musical passages drawn from the works of Holst and Shostakovich designed to evoke from the unconscious images and feelings connected with war.

When the music was over, participants recorded their experiences in drawing or writing. Edith was unable to do either of these things, seemingly stunned, or as if in a state of shock after the music. I invited her to work on what she had experienced and she agreed, lying down on the carpet in the middle of our small workshop group. "Close your eyes and simply find yourself at any part that is vivid for you," I instructed her. Immediately the whole of her body began trembling violently and tears welled up in her eyes.

> *"Where are you?" I ask.*
> *"I don't know. I think I've died. I know I've died. I don't know what's happened."*
> *"Repeat those last words," I say.*
> *"I don't know what happened."*
> *"What went wrong?"*
> *Her body begins to twitch and convulse and she writhes from side to side. "I know what went wrong. The bomb went off too soon. I'm dying. Oh, the pain. Oh! Oh! Oh! My limbs . . . It's black. I'm not there."*

I recognized that we were in a death experience of some violence in which, as the victim of a bomb, she kept losing consciousness. Edith was in fact reliving all the symptoms of severe shock at an explosion and from the way her body reacted it appeared that, whoever the past life personality was, he or she was horribly maimed. From many such experiences I know that the body needs to reproduce the whole of the event for it to be released and that, painful as it is, the victim must not become unconscious. I asked her to go back and relive the events leading up to the explosion.

> *"I'm with a group of young men," she says. "I'm about nineteen, a man. It's Russia. We're going to kill them. We hate them. They killed my father! THEY KILLED MY FATHER! . . . Several of our group have been killed, but we go on fighting. No more of this tyranny. It's time to fight back."*

Edith rages for a while and slowly I am able to piece together parts of her story. She is reenacting the last hours of a young Russian anarchist in a large Russian city (Petrograd?) where the palace guards have been brutally sup-

pressing food riots by the poor. It is winter. The young
man's father has just been cut down a few days ago in the
last of the riots and he is part of a group of young anar-
chists whose main aim is to avenge the people and sow
chaos among the rulers. He and his comrades plan an
assault on the palace barracks with homemade bombs. It
is night. They arrive at the various concealed vantage
points near the barracks, carefully evading the guards at
the gates.

> *"I'm underneath the wall. The bomb's beneath my coat.
> I've just got to light the fuse . . . There, it's done . . . AAH!
> AAH! AAH!"*
> *Edith again screams and convulses. We are again at the
> scene we started from.*
> *"The pain. The pain . . . Oh, no! It went off. It's black. I'm
> not there."*
> *"Where are you?" I ask.*
> *"I don't know. It's all black. I'm not there. I don't know
> where I am. But my body hurts. Oh! Oh!"*

Edith continues to groan as her body writhes from side
to side on the carpet. It is a state of utter terror, agony,
confusion. Her body is suffering from what seems to be
appalling pain. Yet consciously she doesn't seem to be in
it. Is the young anarchist dead? Or has he fainted? I keep
urging her to get an impression of the situation no matter
how it comes.

> *"It's black. It's black. Oh, I'm high above it. I'm not in the
> body."*
> *"Go back down and see it," I instruct.*
> *Suddenly she bursts into tears, almost screaming.*
> *"Oh no, no, no! I don't want to see. I can't bear to see. No!
> No!"*

Clearly she is already seeing something, so I urge her to let herself see it, however distressing.

"It's my body. It has no arms and legs. The bomb blew them off. Oh! Oh! Oh!"

As she says this, her body on the carpet is still convulsing and writhing, which I realize may be a clue to a painfully unfinished piece of the story.

"I want you to go back into the body and see if it is in fact dead," I say.

"Oh no! It is not. I'm just lying here, slowly dying, knowing my arms and legs will never work again."

"Be aware of your last words as you are dying and go to the point where your heart finally stops beating," I say.

"My arms and legs will never work again. Oh no!"

Edith weeps bitterly as she realizes that this is the most painful thought that lies behind her fear of progressive degeneration from lupus.

I guide her to be very precisely aware of the last few seconds of being in that maimed body. "Were there any other thoughts you had been holding in your arms and legs before you left them?" I ask.

"Yes. I wanted to kill them. I wanted them to suffer like my father." *She begins to cry.* "But now I'm hurting."

"Are you willing to let go of your anger at them?"

"Yes, yes. I am."

"So let go of the anger and let go of all the pain and tell me when you are finally out of your body."

Edith takes a deep breath and her whole body goes limp. There is an appreciable drop in tension around the room, since her body has continued to writhe and convulse throughout this whole agonizing scene.

To reinforce her awareness of what has happened I propose two verbal affirmations to her to counter all the pain and negativity. This is what I have her repeat:

"These arms and legs are strong and healthy and can work for me perfectly."

To help her even further I have everyone in the circle simply lay hands on her arms and legs to bring her fully back into her body here and now.

Edith sits up and opens her eyes. "There's no pain! It's all over. I understand it all," she says and beams at everyone around her.

It had been a harrowing and almost unbearably intense session. By now the past life origins of Edith's joint pains were clear to us all. The young anarchist had died in terrible agony mixed with angry thoughts of vengeance that had all become imprinted psychically on the limbs. Because of the explosion he had gone unconscious near the end, but the body had nevertheless registered every detail of the final moments. It was my task first to make the body conscious of its trauma so it could be fully released cathartically and then to help Edith be aware of the anger that she, as the anarchist, had turned against herself with the negative thought, "My arms and legs will never work again."

The session was a turning point in Edith's therapy. I saw her once more six months later when she informed me that all the joint pains were gone and she was beginning to dance again. The lupus was in remission. The one session had opened up all kinds of things for her regarding her anger and fear of self-assertion in the world. She had, it seemed, regained the youthful energy of the anarchist which had been cut off so prematurely. Life for Edith was beginning again.

The Case of Arlette: An Opera Singer with Stage Fright

In Edith's case most of the residual content of her past life trauma derived from the physical shock of her dismemberment when the bomb had exploded. This is what I earlier called the accidental category of physical karma. The healing process involved releasing and disidentifying the physical samskaras that had been passed on to her present body. Although there was also a degree of emotional karma in the form of the anger which coincided with the accident, it was secondary and did not obstruct the cathartic process of the release.

When the emotional content of the past life scenario associated with physical violence or death is more convoluted the therapeutic release will accordingly be more involved. Not just the bodily trauma, but highly complex feelings and thoughts revolving around guilt, failure, humiliation, self-disgust, etc., may need to be brought to the surface, expressed, and relinquished. In these instances, the physical trauma will be secondary, though by no means less painfully present, but the part or parts of the body will have a more metaphorical or symbolic meaning.

For example, a woman physician's assistant who had been in a considerable power struggle with her superiors in the hospital where she worked had had stomach problems over the years. The crucial past life that surfaced for her was that of a medieval peasant dispossessed of his land who sought revenge on his feudal overlords. Having entered the castle with an intent to murder the lord, the peasant is apprehended, disemboweled, and left to die wretchedly. Coinciding with the physical release that took place in this woman's stomach as she relived the death was the symbolic realization that in both the past life and the present she had "lost her guts," which is to say her power. Soon after the session she had it out with her superior, resigned her job, and set up a private practice. She thus took back her power and strengthened a weak area in her solar plexus, which in the Yoga system of the chakras, or psychic energy centers, corresponds to the issues of personal power.

A much more complex but equally dramatic case where the emotional content was uppermost among the physical samskaras was that of Arlette. Arlette was a highly attractive singer who consulted me once in Montreal. In her adolescence she had displayed a voice of such exceptional beauty that her parents and teachers had all urged her to take up singing professionally. She underwent voice training and performed in an occasional concert, but she shied away from opera, the career that all agreed she was most suited to.

"Somehow," as she explained to me, "I never felt ready." Marriage, children, and the running of a small business came along and offered her substantial reasons— or excuses—for not fulfilling her talent. Still encouraged by friends and family, she continued voice lessons and recitals and on several occasions went to audition for major roles in opera. But whenever she auditioned she would have a throat seizure and sing at a feeble echo of her true ability. Once meeting a well-known opera impresario at a private home she had the opportunity of singing for him, but she was so overcome that she could not bring herself to sing at all.

"Overcome by what?" I asked her in our initial interview.

"By fear," she replied. "Fear that I'll fail, that it's not safe . . . Most of all that it's not safe. But also that I'll disappoint them. When I see that selection panel, they're like judges. I know I'll disappoint them. It's humiliating. I know I'm just not ready."

As is characteristic of any complex, there were several interwoven and emotionally laden themes right here. And at the core of all these fears was that most sensitive and most expressive organ of human feeling, the voice box. What was it about failure, judges, and disappointment that had accumulated in this most precious possession of hers?

I invited her to lie down, close her eyes, and explore these feelings, starting with the phrase "I'm not ready," and breathe in such a way as to open her throat somewhat. What came first was a whole stream of childhood memories:

"I'm not ready. I'm too young for my younger brothers. I don't want to go on the plane. I'm too young. I'm not ready . . . A man is feeling me up. I'm too young, I'm not ready . . . Now at school it's the same thing. I'm teacher's pet, but I'm not ready. I'll have to disappoint her. It's so humiliating . . . Now I'm with my father. I'm a bad girl. I've disappointed him. I'm a bad girl to disappoint him . . . I won't let it penetrate. I'm not going to feel anything. I'm flying, I want to soar, but it's not safe to soar. I want the bird to take me up.

As this confused but powerful stream of words and feelings began to emerge from Arlette's unconscious, certain images began to strike me: disappointing her father, teachers, elders; being too young; penetration; wanting to

soar. I start to suspect some premature sexual initiation
that led to a shameful exposure. The image of the bird
suggests the unfettered feelings that want to release but
cannot. Further probing of the childhood psyche does not
reveal any deeply shameful incident, but rather what
seemed to be secondary awakenings, of an older shame,
an older humiliation.

"Keep repeating what you feel about disappointing
him," I say, "and just let any story emerge from this life or
another."

*"I don't want to disappoint him. I'm very bad (repeated
several times). I'm very bad . . . Oh, I'm seeing a farm . . .
barn doors. I mustn't disappoint him. I see him now. He's an
old man with a white beard. He's my grandfather. (She cries.)
I love him so much but I've got to leave. It's humiliating him.
I'm pregnant. I'm only eighteen, but I've got to leave. I'm too
young. But I've got to leave. I'm not ready to leave, I'm just
not ready."*

*It is Amish country. Arlette finds herself in a blue dress,
with blue bonnet, near a barn with pastures. There are birds
soaring above. But she cannot or is not allowed to leave, for in
the next scene that surfaces she is being publicly shamed by a
tribunal of Amish elders.*

*"I'm totally humiliated. All these men. It's so unfair. It's
just a man's world. I have no power. Oh, no! (Her body tenses
up.) It's somewhere else. It's dark. They're raping me. No! No!
(writhing in anguish) I have to close off. No, you can't reach
me. I don't want to feel it. I'm too young. They have all the
power. I just don't want to be here. I want to absent myself. I
DON'T WANT TO BE HERE.*

At this point all visual images cease for a time even
though Arlette's body continues to writhe in torment. She
has, in the Amish woman's words, absented herself, which
means that consciousness has split in two, dissociating

from the body in some kind of faint. It is a natural defense against registering any more of the unbearable shame and torment. But just as we saw previously with Edith, when consciousness vacates the body, as it were, *the body is left to carry the thoughts and emotions entirely unconsciously.*

So with Arlette my first course is to help her body become fully aware of all the conflicting sensations of pain and pleasure it is feeling as well as the complex mixture of humiliation, loathing, and rage she feels for these cruelly abusive puritans. Since it is not just her body but her self-respect as a woman that is here assaulted, it is crucial for her to express the thoughts she was unable to utter at the moment of fainting, thoughts that are, not surprisingly, *stuck in her throat.*

"Tell them now what you think of them," I urge. "They cannot hurt you any longer."

"You're despicable! You brutes! You hypocrites! You just took advantage of me. It's you that should be ashamed. You have no right to do this to me just because I'm pregnant. I'm not 'fallen.' I am a woman. I have dignity and pride. Don't you ever touch me again."

Arlette's face is now flushed, her lower body relaxed, and her chest expanded as she takes power and energy from these words, words that have lain dormant in her throat for so long.

"My throat is open. My chest hurts. So vulnerable! (There are tears in her eyes.) They hurt me so much. There was nothing I could do."

Arlette weeps and her chest heaves.

There is clearly a great deal of emotion surfacing from

this terrible memory. I am struck, too, by the predominant feeling of helplessness, powerlessness, and by the fact that the recurrent phrase that we started with earlier, "I'm not ready," has only been briefly voiced. It does not seem entirely to belong to the tragic Amish story. Knowing from past experience that several past life scenarios may cluster around one theme or one part of the body, I say to her:

"Repeat the words 'There was nothing I could do, I wasn't ready' and let them take you into any other story that they bring up."

As Arlette begins to repeat these phrases, her head tilts back and the quality of her voice is raspy and hoarse:

"There was nothing I could do. I wasn't ready. It's so sad . . . so sad. I wasn't ready. I've disappointed them."

"Where are you? What's happening?" I ask.

"I'm lying on my back on the ground. There are white horses around me. I've fallen. There's something piercing my chest . . . and my throat! I can't talk. It's so sad. I'm a young warrior leader. It's an ancient warrior tribe. They have primed me to be the new warlord, taught me everything they knew. I've disappointed them! I've been struck down in the first battle. I CAN'T TALK! (She almost chokes.) THERE ARE ARROWS THROUGH MY THROAT AND CHEST! There's nothing I can do. I'm dying and I can't even tell them. It's as though I was their 'star' and I failed them. I just wasn't ready. I was too young. They're all around me with their spears pointed down. I'm dying and I can't talk to them. It's so sad. All their love and hope . . ."

For a while Arlette laments the futility and waste of this young man's life. Then I suggest that she now tell her warrior teachers what she feels toward them and has not been able to express:

"I'm so sorry I disappointed you. I wasn't ready. I wanted

so much to be everything you trained me for. You gave me all your love and hope but I failed you."

In her vision as the young warrior, Arlette feels herself rising above the body and she soars toward the sky like a hawk. "They heard me. They don't blame me. They understand."

I give Arlette some affirmations to help heal the humiliation of the first life and the anguish of the second:

"I express my strength and dignity as a woman."
"I let go of old pain and humiliation from the past."
"I no longer need to fear that I will disappoint my elders."
"I am ready to be the star pupil. I can soar now."
"It's safe to be vulnerable when I sing."

As we look at these two past life reenactments it is not hard to see how such unhappy stories had left Arlette with the karmic traces or samskaras of total lack of self-confidence when it came to asserting or expressing herself in front of a group, especially a group of men. Not surprisingly a panel of judges at an opera audition recalled in her unconscious the past life memories of abuse by the Amish elders, of disappointing her grandfather, and the feeling that she had failed her warrior mentors as the young warlord in the other past life. In both stories her throat was affected. In the Amish life it had held unexpressed thoughts, while in the warrior life the pain of that fatal arrow and the frustration of disappointing her elders were lodged there.

Equally complex were the feelings held in Arlette's genitals. Just as there was more than one story lodged in her throat, so too there was more than one in her genitals regarding her sexual self-expression. This was also contributing to her difficulty in performing.

Without going into so much detail as the stories already described, the salient facts about the next past life that surfaced in a later session can be summarized as follows:

Arlette finds herself as a pregnant black slave somewhere in the American South. She is beaten to death and abandoned by the very white master who has gotten her pregnant. She dies broken and alone with a great deal of shame in the midst of labor brought on by the beating. Behind this wretched death are the thoughts "I had no right to him. I brought it on myself. I loved him so much."

Going back earlier in the story, it appears that she was a very beautiful young black woman who willingly sleeps with her white master because of the special status it gives—she admits to being extremely vain—and a chance at having a white man's child means that she would no longer be truly black herself. The white master has two sides to his character and swings from an indulgent lover to an enraged killer when she is pregnant.

This story revealed another kind of fear that Arlette carried with her when it came to performing in front of men: a fear that her sexuality would be too alluring and would get her into trouble. Once more, when she saw clearly how these fears belonged to a story that no longer had any currency and that she need no longer punish herself for her good looks, she experienced huge relief and a new spirit of self-confidence.

After only a few sessions Arlette told me that her voice felt and sounded better than ever. Some weeks later at a major audition she amazed herself and a whole panel of men and women by "soaring" as she never had before in front of a highly demanding audience. She was awarded the leading role. The career she was obviously born for was finally launched.

Subtle Body Language

The successful outcome of my work with both Edith and Arlette naturally has as much to do with factors other than just our past life work. Both were clearly at a stage where their unconscious conflicts were "ripe" for this kind of work. Edith's previous work with her therapist meant that this material must have been very close to the threshold of consciousness for the work to evoke the visions she had. Arlette had set up auditions before she consulted me, so our work was a kind of last-ditch challenge to her unconscious. In both instances the internal pressure was intense. The symbolic content in both their symptoms was crying out to be heard so that my job with each of them was mainly to let the body tell its story.

I certainly don't claim past life work as a miracle cure for all physical diseases, but I do suggest that very often an illness may conceal an old "defeat in life" in symbolic language. One of the most important discoveries of Stanislav Grof's LSD therapy and deep experiential therapy is that physical traumas in this life—birth, automobile accidents, major surgery, etc.—leave huge scars in the psyche in the form of unconscious memories. What past life work seems to demonstrate further is that some of these scars have several layers to them. It is not uncommon in exploring an afflicted region of the body for a client to relive first surgery in this life, then several past life wounds to the same part of the body; for instance, during one session a woman client moved spontaneously from reliving a hysterectomy in a hospital to finding herself a victim of a primitive blood sacrifice with her belly being cut open.

But apart from the obvious consequences if we accept

the possibility of inherited structures associated with past life trauma—a weak stomach may carry past life memories of poisoning, starvation, dysentery, for instance— more significant, psychologically, are the physical samskaras with an emotional content. When, for example, strong traces of guilt are associated with parts of the body, they are harder to dislodge and may entail what D. H. Lawrence called "long difficult repentance." As we shall see in the longer cases described in Part IV, where there are several lives of alternating victimization and revenge, the psyche may often unconsciously be inviting repeated self-punishment to a certain area of the body. Hunched shoulders may contain several layers of past life stories where there were repeated beatings and brutality to others, the same soul apparently having been both slavemaster and slave, persecutor and victim several times over. Escape from the spiral of self-recrimination is not always easy, as extended cases will demonstrate.

In many cases where a crucial story is liberated from the body, I have witnessed extraordinary releases of energy in the form of shaking, tingling, heat, flushing, and even strange odors. In yoga these are called *kriyas,* in Reichian therapy, streaming. Modern physiology has no explanation for them or even ways of recording them to date. For a fuller understanding of what is occurring I have turned increasingly to Eastern systems such as Kundalini Yoga and acupuncture which acknowledge flows of subtle energy through the nonphysical vehicle called the subtle body. Heinrich Zimmer has summarized the Yoga teaching as follows:

Within the gross body which suffers dissolution after death, every living being possesses an inner subtle body, which is formed of sense faculties, vital breaths, and inner organs. This is the body that goes on and on, from birth to birth, as the basis and vehicle for the reincarnated personality. It departs from the sheath of the gross body at the time of death, and then determines the nature of the new existence; for within it are left the traces—like the furrows and scars—of all the perceptions, acts, desires, and movements of will of the past, all the propensities and trends, the heritages of habits and inclinations, and the particular readiness to react this way or that, or not at all.[6]

In addition, the nonphysical energy cocoon is endowed with spherical centers called chakras that can often be blocked for emotional and karmic reasons, according to this theory.

What I have noticed repeatedly is that the past life injuries often seem to correspond symbolically to the yogic interpretation of the meaning of certain of these subtle centers. Clients like Arlette who have neck and throat problems could be said to have deficient or karmically afflicted throat chakras. Yoga theory would predict past lives of failure to express the self, abuse of the power of words, hypocrisy, lying, etc. Similarly, persons who have heart problems, memories of chest stabbings or shootings may remember failures of generosity, mean-spiritedness, despair, lack of expressing true feelings; the heart chakra may be closed up and needs to be reopened.

Jung's genius in interpreting symbols was to see that every symbolic expression is dual. A symbol points backward to an origin in the past and forward to potential future change. Images of physical wounds in both dreams and past lives display this Janus-like aspect. Tragic as a memory of being starved to death or a knife in the belly is, it can reveal a chakra region to be opened up creatively in the future. What is needed is first to release the old pain cathartically, then to let go and reverse the old emotional pattern (e.g., Arlette's "I'm afraid I'll disappoint you" changes into "I'm happy to please you [with my singing/ love]") and finally to remain especially open to this area of vulnerability and not close it off again. In this way, our wounds become our strengths. They make us tolerant of the woundedness of others and constantly remind us of our own human frailties. These are what in the East would be called the lessons of karma.

CHAPTER 8

EROS ABUSED: THE PAST LIFE ROOTS OF SEXUAL AND REPRODUCTIVE PROBLEMS

When our personal worlds are rediscovered and allowed
to reconstitute themselves, we first discover a shambles.
Bodies half dead; genitals dissociated from heart; heart
severed from head; heads dissociated from genitals . . .

R. D. Laing, *The Present Situation*

The aim of psychoanalysis—still unfulfilled, and still only
half conscious—is to return our souls to our bodies, to
return ourselves to ourselves, and thus to overcome the
human state of self-alienation.

Norman O. Brown, *Life Against Death*

Our Bodies, Our Past Life Selves

Medical and psychotherapy practices today are full of
women with every kind of sexual and gynecological problem: infertility, ovarian cysts, dysmenorrhea, frigidity,

uterine and breast cancers, and more. Perhaps this has always been the sad lot of women, but my impression is that such complaints have increased in recent years. We are fortunate that in response to these many woes the medical profession has made many impressive advances in diagnosis and treatment. The origin of most of these conditions remains a mystery.

Many women seek out psychotherapy as an accompaniment to medical treatment and sometimes as an alternative to it because they intuitively sense—the word sense is very appropriate—that these matters arise from conflicts that are somehow bound up with their most deeply held —and sometimes withheld—feelings about themselves as women. Like D. H. Lawrence, who had the awesome courage to look at his total being as he was dying of tuberculosis, many of these women seem to know that they are ill "because of wounds to the soul, to the deep emotional self." In this case, to their sexual and feminine self.

In this chapter I will focus on problems that are specific to women's sexuality and are connected to the subject of childbearing. Not that men do not have sexual problems —we have already cited the case of Gregory's impotence in Chapter 4—but men do not menstruate, nor do they bear children. A woman's emotional as well as her physical constitution is fundamentally different from a man's by nature of this simple fact. That many women have achieved equal status with men in what used to be "a man's world" should not be allowed to obscure this fact. If anything, contemporary women are under far greater psychological pressure than earlier generations because they must now perform in an often hostile work world dominated by masculine values and at the same time not lose contact with the hallowed core of their feminine nature.

While it seems to me indisputable that at one level many of the sexual and gynecological problems that women are suffering from today are directly related to this intense conflict of inner values and self-identity, I believe there is still another level to these problems. From treating a sizable number of these cases from a past life perspective I have come to identify a common unconscious denominator at work, karmicly speaking—what I might call an archetype of the wounded feminine. This archetype is, I believe, commonly, or should I say symbolically, mirrored in the sexual and gynecological dysfunctions of certain women. What they are painfully and often embarrassingly manifesting at an organic or deep emotional level is no less than the psychic accumulation of the hatred and fear of the feminine that has fueled much of Western culture for over two thousand years.

Feminist writer Susan Griffin in her brilliant work *Woman and Nature* sees at the center of our culture a harsh patriarchal suppression of the feminine which is reflected jointly in the exploitation of nature in the name of science and the conquest and suppression of the body in the name of the spirit, conceived predominantly as masculine. Her poetic vision fully accords with all my findings from past life work. Given that we all, as men or women, carry in our unconscious mind the samskaras of previous lives within Western civilization *as both sexes*, none of us is without some degree of the psychically inherited misogyny, the wounded feminine archetype, that pervades our culture. Surprising as it may seem, it is not just women who recall past lives of violence where they have been raped or otherwise sexually abused. Many men, myself included, have come up with vivid memories of lives as women undergoing precisely the same horrors. My own humiliating memory of a young girl's rape, mutilation, and death came to light during rolfing work (i.e., deep tissue massage) on my groin area. As we shall see later in this chapter, women remember past lives in which they are men on the battlefield, finding themselves perpetuating the very same atrocities often with unashamed relish. From this archetype with its two poles —active and passive—none of us is entirely free.

When it comes to searching for the individual stories behind the specific sexual and gynecological problems that my women clients bring into therapy, my method is precisely the same as for other physical symptoms. When there is a physical symptom, I simply ask my woman client to direct her awareness to the specific area of the pain, whether it is a growth or some organic dysfunction and then describe exactly what it feels like. Or else I might ask her to focus on the predominant emotions surrounding whatever sexual or childbearing issue seems to be in question. Then we follow whatever images, associated feelings, or sensations belong to the complex until some kind of scene begins to emerge from the unconscious.

Since a woman's genitals are not, generally speaking, a place of accidental wounding but instead the locus of the most intimate of feeling states, the stories that arise are usually quite specific and emotionally complex in their content, frequently requiring painstaking unraveling for the full catharsis and healing to take place. A number of short summaries of gynecological and sexual problems that I have worked with will give some idea of what is entailed.

—*A young woman in her late twenties felt terribly inhibited around her sexuality. She felt herself to be unattractive to men and that she would be rejected by them. She had been slightly overweight since she was thirteen and carried from somewhere she couldn't identify the thought that she might turn into a slut. Her crucial past life story threw much light on all of this. She finds herself as a very pretty young woman taking care of her father, her mother having died many years previously. Her father forces her into an incestuous relationship with him and she bears two children by him. She is tormented by deeply conflicted feelings of disgust and pleasure. She tries to break out of this emotional hell by frequenting a local tavern and seducing anonymous men. Finally, one man whom she both seduces and taunts, murders her with an axe.*

In another past life in the American antebellum South her husband has affairs while she is pregnant, leaving her feeling abandoned and ugly. It was not hard for her to realize how these old unconscious dramas inhibited her current relationships with men.

—*A middle-aged woman in one of our workshops had successfully borne three children but had suffered terrible premenstrual cramps. In exploring the pains, she relived a fatal childbirth scenario as an African woman. In the midst of an extremely difficult labor her very clumsy mate attempts to help with the delivery. The presentation of the baby is breech. In his ignorance and clumsiness, the husband decapitates the child. The woman dies in terrible pain. The memory apparently imprinted for future lives in the region of her uterus was to be triggered each time she menstruated.*

—*A woman in her thirties reported in a workshop that she had experienced no less than three surgical operations in her abdominal region: for a ruptured appendix, for an ectopic pregnancy, and for the removal of a uterine cyst. In each case the operations coincided with difficulties in relationships*

*with particular men. Among her past lives, she relived one as
a young girl who is raped by her father. Later, as that adolescent, she becomes pregnant and her father is horribly abusive
to her, beating her and kicking her in the belly. Thrown out
by him, she becomes destitute, dying of pneumonia not long
after. Evidently the whole issue of pregnancy was deeply
fraught with ambivalence for this woman, an ambivalence
manifested by genital and abdominal complaints that arose
every time she became close to a man.*

*—A young woman graduate student came into therapy
briefly with no particular physical complaint, but a deep
resistance to the very idea of having children. During the
interview she expressed unwillingness to even discuss the
matter, but it was apparent that she was holding back a huge
amount of emotion when certain issues connected with this
were touched. On going into the rising feeling she finds herself (in a past life) as a prostitute with an unwanted baby, in a
state of what is probably postpartum depression. The father
has disappeared, never to return. Half-crazed and in despair,
she kills the baby by throwing it against the wall. To her
depression is added debilitating sickness. Finally, guilty, for-
lorn, and exhausted she dies in the squalid brothel, her last
thoughts being "I don't care about anything, I don't deserve
to have children." It is not hard to see how the unfinished
feelings of guilt totally blocked this young woman's desire to
be a mother today.*

For the first two women, their abdominal and genital
regions were in effect screaming messages of pain from
unfinished past life stories: "Don't touch me!" "You're
hurting me!" "You're killing me!" "I hate you!" "Leave me
alone!" The young woman who didn't want children was
luckier in some respects in that her body was not drama-
tizing such crippling old wounds. But for her the guilt of
killing her unwanted children had led her to uncon-

sciously close down the whole childbearing part of her being.

Therapeutic work with these issues is not easy and is by no means always successful, but where my clients have the courage and patience to allow psychic exploration of these sensitive and intimate areas, glimpses of some buried drama will always emerge. When we have probed the imagery behind uterine fibroids, growths, tumors, severe menstrual dysfunction, or the inability to conceive, similarly gruesome stories have been uncovered: arrested pregnancy, enforced abortion, child sacrifice, or else other unspeakable sexual tortures or mutilations. Lest anyone have sentimental fantasies about the good old days of matriarchal ascendancies, my files have numbers of memories of child sacrifice to the Goddess and not a few descriptions of tribes where women's genitals were ritually removed by priestesses as an offering to the Great Mother. I need hardly stress how the residual guilt, shame, rage, and helpless terror embedded in such memories can play untold unconscious havoc with a woman's genital functioning and sensitivity. Thus a karmic complex can have a continued presence in a modern woman's unconscious psyche.

The Case of Eliza

Perhaps because it resonates with my own memories of past life as a woman I find I can imagine no more painful event than for a woman to lose a child she has carried close to her heart for nine months. In offering comfort to the few women clients whose karma it was to suffer such a loss, I have on those occasions wished I were a psychic who could bring solace from "the other side." But I am no such thing and must therefore stick to the particular lathe I have built: past life work with the unconscious. The case of Eliza was, however, one occasion where my work was able to bring some measure of relief and understanding to a bereaved young mother.

Eliza was happily married and in her mid-twenties when she became pregnant for the first time. The pregnancy was uncomplicated until at six months or so she developed severe pain in one of her ovaries. A cyst was discovered and the affected ovary was surgically removed. (Earlier she had had a cyst removed from her left breast.) When the baby, a little girl, was born she was found to have a deformed heart and she died in the hospital after several weeks of intensive care.

Although it was uncertain whether the ovariectomy had directly contributed to the baby's heart condition, for Eliza the trauma of the surgery followed by the eventual loss of her baby had understandably become strongly associated emotionally. Psychologically speaking, the impact of these events had all become assimilated into the same complex. Whatever feelings Eliza had previously had about having children and being a mother, it was now impossible to separate them from the unhappy experiences of the previous year.

In accordance with my practice of trusting the unconscious to take the client to wherever he or she needs to go, using little more than images or phrases, I have Eliza lie down and close her eyes. She has just told me her story in detail and one of her asides was that she has always had a horror of knives. I make a note of this phobia, wondering silently what past life story might belong to this, but I encourage her mostly to focus on her recent experience.

It seems obvious to me that pregnancy and the loss of her baby is where the strongest emotional charge lies; no point in digging for further traumas until what is conscious has been approached.

As it happens, Eliza is familiar with the technique of rebirthing breathing which I have used myself a great deal in my practice. Since this technique is so powerful in releasing trauma of all kinds, I have Eliza breathe in the way she has learned and instruct her to allow anything at all to come to the surface. Before long she begins to turn her head from side to side as if struggling in some way and the following words emerge:

> *"There's blood. Blood. He's dressed in yellow. It's the doctor. No, I don't want to. Please don't cut me. Please don't cut me. It hurts. I can't move. DON'T CUT ME. PLEASE DON'T CUT ME. I can't move. There's nothing I can do. He's cutting me."*

Hypnotherapists have long known that anesthesia does not affect the unconscious mind. Although the conscious mind "goes to sleep" or floats off into some pleasant disembodied fantasy, the unconscious nevertheless records every detail of surgery—including, I regret to say, the asides, bad jokes, and dire predictions of many surgeons. So, I am not altogether surprised to hear Eliza's unconscious self reliving the trauma of her ovariectomy. But what I am listening for is the particular way her unconscious self is reacting to the events:

> *"He's cutting me. It's downward. My baby's in there. DON'T HURT MY BABY! PLEASE DON'T HURT MY BABY! He's asking the nurses something. He's cutting again. Oh, my ovary! He says it's exploded—ruptured. He's cutting it out. He's cleaning my other ovary. I've lost my ovary. I can't move.*

There's nothing I can do. What's happened to me? I'm neutered. I can't have a baby. I'm not a woman anymore. Nurse, tell me it's okay."

There is no question that all surgery is traumatic at the unconscious level at which the body records impressions; Eliza's reaction to being cut, losing her ovary, and the possible threat to her baby are what we might predict for any woman undergoing such an operation. Yet in certain ways Eliza's unconscious self is overreacting: "Don't cut me" immediately reminds me of her phobia of knives, while her helplessness and the fear that she will no longer be a woman all seem to run deeper.

We spend much of our session reliving the operation to allow Eliza to consciously experience the trauma her body went through and let go of it with full catharsis, full emotional expression. But the terror of the knife and her feelings about herself as a woman remain unresolved. I have her repeat the phrases that strike me as still heavily charged and I add the instruction: "Let your unconscious take you to any other story when something like this happened. Repeat the phrase 'Please don't cut me.'"

This is an abbreviated transcript of what followed:

"Please don't cut me. Please don't cut me. PLEASE DON'T CUT ME! I can't move. They've drugged me. There's nothing I can do . . . It's a barn, a haystack. He's cutting me. It's a man in pants. Blue lace. There's another man. I'm pregnant. I don't want to die. It seems to be the seventeenth century. They're trying to help me. It's a terrible birth. They're doing a cesarean . . . My arms are tied above me to part of the barn. I'm partly dressed. There's nothing I can do. There's blood, lots of blood from my abdomen . . . The baby, it's dead. (She weeps.) I'm dying. I don't want to die. I'm slipping out of existence. I'm leaving . . . I see my body from outside. I'm

not there anymore. It's a young woman. The man was my brother. He tried to save me. The baby's dead. It was stillborn. There was nothing I could do. It's not safe to have a child. It's not safe."

Once more we take time to fully release all the pain and sadness of this story—only this time these are apparently traumas that belong to a young woman from the past, one of Eliza's past life personalities. It becomes clear to us as we work how deeply this seventeenth-century woman's distress has seeped into Eliza's recent painful experience with pregnancy. Conscious of this, Eliza is now able to differentiate this other source of fear and begins to feel less dominated by it. She still needs to let go of the negative thought that it's not safe to have a child. To this end I suggest some affirmations for her to take away with her. It has been a huge piece of unburdening for one session.

Deep psychosomatic wounds of this nature rarely heal in one or two sessions, nor is there usually one single past life behind such traumas; if anything, major symptoms like Eliza's ovarian and mammary cysts are multiply determined. In past life terms they are often part of a repeating pattern. So it turned out in our subsequent work, which I will recount somewhat more briefly.

In a later session we explored further the region of the painful ovary:

Eliza now found herself as a servant girl in a village in the northern Sahara Desert. The historical period is not clear but seems quite recent. At fourteen years of age this girl is molested by soldiers who want sex with her. She tells them they are disgusting. One reacts by beating her brutally, and then, when she has collapsed, kicks her in the back with his heavy boots. Her kidneys and ovaries are badly damaged, leaving her in chronic pain for much of that life. She lives mostly alone from then on, the dominant thoughts she ruminates on being, "I'm afraid of men; they hurt me. I don't want them to touch me. I'd rather live alone."

Her ovary becomes the focal point of the hurt and humiliation of these events. This trauma is transmitted as a physical samskara that reemerges during her pregnancy in this life.

After this particularly grim memory had surfaced and we seemed finished with the other life of the failed cesarean, I propose to Eliza's unconscious that it produce a life when she had successfully born children. She quickly found herself as a blond woman in the Midwest in America in the last century—with six children! This felt good to her so I encouraged her to meditate on this healthy second other self.

But not all the traumatic past lives were done with. Her afflicted breast started to give her pain and images of knives and bloody hands came to her spontaneously in the course of our work. What we found behind these occurrences were two grisly memories of human sacrifice. In one she is an Aztec man who is captured and is beheaded while in another she is a female in her fifties, the victim of a medieval satanic ritual of some kind; the time is unknown. She is raped and horribly mutilated. Again the knives. This time we seem to have reached the full horror for in the remembered death her whole body is sliced open and her breasts cut off. Here was the somatic image behind the cyst in her breast as well as the pain in her ovaries. This and the cesarean memory were the source of her terror during surgery.

Had Eliza always been a victim in her past lives? It seems not, for in the next past life scene to emerge after these bloody images had been worked through, Eliza finds herself as a soldier in the trenches in World War I. "I shouldn't have done it. I shouldn't have done it," the soldier laments. He is standing over the bloody corpse of a young enemy soldier that he has just bayoneted in the stomach. It appears that he had already used his bayonet to kill on many occasions but that on this occasion something snaps in him. He goes on to survive the war but is forever tormented by unexpressed remorse for all the killing. He develops arthritis in his hands, legs, and back. When asked about these afflictions, this male personality in Eliza admits that it was because he had come to hate himself for all the killings.

A conundrum that frequently presents itself in past lives is this: Are we first of all the victim or are we first of all the killer? Since in linear historical time the World War I soldier's life came *after* the other bloody deaths, it can hardly be the karmic cause. But in the unconscious, "before" and "after" do not have the same meaning as in waking time. To the unconscious all lives are perpetually present. The karmic swing of action and reaction is more like a vast river whose currents, eddying back and forth, rebound from one bank to another. When a soul has suffered horribly at human hands—be it by knives, fire, water, or whatever—a deep imprint of the means that inflicted the pain is left.

Almost invariably a victim's thoughts like "How could he do this to me?" or "I'll get back at him" produce violent images of causing that pain to another. Or else the torturer becomes deeply identified with his victim's agonies to the extent of secretly imaging how it hurts. So in the play of lives the victim turns persecutor or the torturer, in his constant infliction of pain, needs to suffer the very thing he inflicts. A profound and disquieting identity of opposites exists in all complexes of violence and oppression: the master in one life becomes a slave in the next; the revolutionary becomes the new tyrant. Stanislav Grof too has observed this in his LSD therapy sessions:

> On a deep level, the emotional state of the sadistic torturer is similar to that of the tortured, and the raging drive of the murderer fuses with the anguish of the dying victim.[1]

The moment on the World War I battlefield when the soldier saw the agony of his dying enemy was for Eliza a profoundly important one. It was what James Joyce called an epiphany, a moment of revelatory insight, a knowing beyond the immediate act that opens out toward some larger spiritual meaning—in this instance the mystical identity between the victim and the slayer. Such epiphanies actually transcend individual past life experiences, taking them to the archetypal level I sketched in the lotus diagram in Chapter 5. Potentially, meditating on any of her past lives involving violence could have brought such an insight, but for Eliza it came through this soldier in the trenches. This memory actually marked the end of a cycle of violent lives for her. Her subsequent work focused more on relationships and unresolved issues about her own birth. The painful exorcism of these ancient samskaras that had embedded themselves in her reproductive organs was over and the sad death of her child could now be seen from a whole other perspective.

Rape, Revenge, and the Karma of Violence

I described earlier the two rather different cases of Melinda and Arlette whose past life rape memories had deeply disrupted current sexual and creative fulfillment. With Melinda (Chapter 6) the horror of rape by soldiers, reawakened by abuse as an adolescent, had left her close to frigid in her sexuality. Arlette's career as an opera singer was primarily blocked in her throat (Chapter 7), but a genital memory of being shamed and raped during pregnancy had deeply undermined her self-confidence and self-assertion in front of men.

Particularly important in healing past life rape memories is regaining full consciousness and sensitivity in the genital area, when it has become numbed by the trauma. The approach of Reichian and Gestalt therapists in giving the body permission to speak is particularly valuable here when combined with Morris Netherton's key observation of how consciousness splits and detaches from physical trauma in a past life memory. To emphasize how this phenomenon underlies the problems of frigidity and anorgasmy I want to cite once more part of Melinda's story. In the middle of her rape memory her pelvic area becomes stiff and her legs taut. What her body language is expressing of the past life personality's conflict is absolutely crucial:

> I'm not going to feel this. I'll never show you I like it [pelvis and genitals].
> Don't touch me. Get away. I'll kill you. I'll kick you [legs].
> I'm not going to see this. It's not happening [head].

Her head, body, and feelings are all at terrible odds with each other. One part of her genitals initially feels pleasure—which her consciousness is ashamed of—but in no time it changes into excruciating pain which naturally she does not want to feel, accompanied by rage which she can barely express. And so this terrible confusion of feelings, thoughts, and sensations all becomes numbed and buried. Doomed to lie in the unconscious as a samskara which must one day surface karmicly, this old trauma has a devastating effect on Melinda's capacity for sexual intimacy and pleasure.

One further short example of what a debilitating effect past life genital trauma can have on current sexual activity and genital sensitivity is the case of Gwen:

> —*Gwen was a young woman who suffered from an embarrassing fear of sexual penetration that was ruining her relationships with men. She was also terrified of being alone and had an irrational fear that she would never have children. First of all, she relived a humiliating and painful hospital memory of urethral penetration for a bladder dysfunction as a child of six in her current life. What this triggered was a past life memory of being a peasant woman who has stolen a baby when she finds herself to be barren. The community arrests her, cauterizes her genitals with a hot iron, and then incarcerates her for the rest of her life in a pit on the edge of the town, throwing her the minimum of food from time to time. This ghastly story lay behind her sensitivity to sexual contact, getting pregnant, and being alone.*

On a linear historical level, karma appears to be cumulative. The barbarities which (mostly) men have committed on women throughout history, but particularly during Western imperial, colonial, Christian history, all sit fraught with agonizing guilt in the collective unconscious.

Jung, in his pessimistic work *The Undiscovered Self,* reminds us of these grim facts when he comments that in the collective unconscious "nothing has finally disappeared and nothing has been made good" and that "none of us stands outside humanity's blackest shadow."[2] From witch burnings to concentration camps to the "disappeared" of South America today the record is far from savory and it is a considerable work of consciousness to detach ourselves from the collective inner compulsion of these old cruelties and not sanction new ones.

Some women—and men as well—seem to have a larger share of sexual violence to deal with than others. In Jung's terms, they would be seen as potentially bringing greater consciousness to humanity by owning a larger piece of that black collective shadow he talked of. But for the children of horribly abused mothers and fathers it is hard to break out of the endless downward spiral of violence begetting more violence. As is well known, adult child abusers almost always themselves have been abused as children; or, as W. H. Auden wrote one gloomy day in 1939: "those to whom evil is done do evil in return."

Though I haven't worked in social work agencies where such conditions are commonplace, I frequently hear similar horror stories of endless beatings, seductions, and other mental and physical cruelties to children from my clients:

> *An attractive middle-class woman in her forties whom I shall call Yvonne had been sexually molested by her father since she was three. By seven years he was forcing her to perform oral sex with him in a closet. This continued for years. She was too terrified to speak out. At eleven years, she finally told her mother, who refused to believe her. Her father had the perverse satisfaction of beating her "for lying." "It's*

total hell," she reports in reliving this. At fourteen, during a painful menstrual period, two men and a woman drugged her with Valium, tied a light cord around her neck, and forced her into oral sex. From then onward her period would always be accompanied by neck pain.

Pregnant at eighteen, Yvonne drops out of high school into a wretched marriage, her father telling her she is white trash. In her twenties she gets sucked into a violent drug-dealing scene where one man is murdered and she narrowly escapes being shot in an ambush. Sometime later her house burns down with all her personal possessions. Her sex life has, not surprisingly, always been anorgasmic. But an added misery is the discovery that she has both breast and cervical cancer and, later, a heart condition. She also has chronic back problems.

Although I was only able to do a few sessions with her, the karmic complexes behind all this violence and sickness emerged surprisingly swiftly. The first somatic symptom to surface was choking, back at seven years in that closet. Her body needed to expectorate the memories of fellatio with her father. From there the symbolic resonance connected with choking took her into her birth trauma with the cord around her neck and thence into a memory of being hanged for manslaughter as a man in the sixteenth century.

As her back and neck contorted while she lay reliving her death, she flashed into the whole bloody story. As this man, she had been a buccaneer of sorts who had developed considerable blood lust from all the boarding parties. Images of mutilations such as castration and the hacking off of limbs came to her as she surveyed these bloody forays. There was also a subservient homosexual relationship to the captain of the ship who forced oral sex upon him. Eventually he kills the bully and jumps ship, ending up as a very clumsy abortionist in a seaport. He is totally merciless, taking pleasure in being an exterminator.

*The next life to surface is that of a nun who is raped and
sexually tortured by marauding soldiers—her breasts and
vagina are mutilated before she dies. In the third life she
finds herself as a ruthless western gunfighter enamored of
women and violence. The gunfighter is shot in the face by a
woman he has abused and dies. It was not difficult for Yvonne
to recognize and own how she still carried the scars of these
past lives and how they had unconsciously activated all the
various illnesses and traumas—sexual abuse, neck problems,
cancer, murder threats, etc. She realized that in her guilt for
past violence she had in a certain sense invited it upon herself
as punishment. I encouraged her to image once more all those
she had brutalized as the pirate and ask their forgiveness.
This she did with tears welling in her eyes. When it came time
to ask forgiveness of the aborted children, she suddenly burst
out laughing: "I think I've paid for that one," she said. "I once
felt an inexplicable urge to get a job driving a school bus. I
hated every moment of it, but I knew I had to do it somehow. I
stuck it for three years and one day I knew it was enough.
Now I understand!"*

In more ways than one, we agreed, Yvonne had done a
lot to balance or equalize the violent karmic imprint she
was born with. I suggested that it was now time to start
loving and honoring her body as a temple of the holy spirit
—not as a karmic battlefield.

Reowning Power: The Case of Hildegard

Lastly, the case of Hildegard, who consulted me briefly
after a workshop in which past life rape memories surfaced very vividly for her. She had been working with a
therapist for some time about sexual interference as a
child. She had a lot of fear about sex and had come to the

workshop because of a hunch that it didn't all stem from childhood abuse. There had been few relationships in her life and she had always had the thought that somehow being a girl was a punishment. She always seemed to find it hard to find her power, she said. Her main somatic complaints were two: her back, which she had hurt badly as a child, and recurrent uterine fibroids.

Possibly because she had already worked on her childhood sexual issues, we bypassed these to go directly to a past life as a medieval woman who is brutally raped by three soldiers, with her belly and vagina ripped open by her assailants:

"Why did they do that? Where do I go now? Who is going to want me?" she cries out in her agony and despair. And then the thought we have already encountered often in such scenes: "I don't want to feel it [down there]. I don't want to feel it."

This thought, as we have seen, imprints itself upon the wounded area and lays down the karmic pattern for future lives. And even as she says this, flashes of a different battlefield scene from a past life as a soldier are trying to break through. But I urge her to focus on the wound she is trying so desperately to forget. As we complete the story, it emerges that she does not die but is taken half alive to a nearby convent and helped to recover, though she remains crippled for life by her wounds.

We work for a while on cleaning out the violent impressions left by the rape, among which is the sharp sensation of one of the rapists' knees digging painfully into her chest. The chest, it seems, is a point of symbolic resonance, for suddenly Hildegard is no longer the woman but the soldier she caught a glimpse of earlier:

"It's in my chest (breathing labored). I can't get up. It's a spear. I'm on the ground, pinned down. I fell from my horse. My leg . . . It's pierced. I can't move. My neck's twisted, my head's been trampled. I'm dying. There's blood in my mouth and stomach . . . Flies all over my face and chest. I'm stubborn and strong. I'm only leaving because I have to. I had a fine strong body . . . I may never be a man again . . . It's all over."

Then as he looks back over his life as a soldier, remorse at his own brutality comes to mind:

"I wasn't kind to women. I killed and raped women. It made me feel strong. I don't deserve to be a man again."

I direct Hildegard to explore any other lives in the vein of being cruel to women and first she sees one as a very primitive tribesman who brutalizes his wife and is eventually murdered by her brother. Then she finds herself in the very powerful body of a Roman commander turned patrician.

This character is cruel and self-centered. He kills a friendly rival in a chariot race and feels no remorse, seeming to enjoy his power over his slaves and his wife. To compensate for the hardness of both heart and body he spends more and more time in drunken debauches with young women. Boldly thinking he can have anything he wants, he openly commits adultery with a well-placed man's wife. He is obsessed by his lust for her. She grows more and more fearful of her husband. But finally his throat is cut in a public steambath. He dies furious with the woman, whom he blames for the betrayal. It is an ugly and selfish life. In retrospect this character realizes that what he was searching for in all these women was the affection and tenderness he couldn't find in himself.

From one brutalized life as a rape victim, Hildegard's unconscious had shown her no less than three violent

male past life selves. Was she still compensating in this life
for their violence and callousness? Had she had more lives
as a man than a woman, as some psychics allege is the case
for certain souls?

What is certain is that Hildegard experienced a deep
unconscious shame about the cruelties of these male figures that had kept her in an arrested state as a woman. No
wonder, with such strong male figures in her psyche, she
felt that being a girl had been a kind of punishment. In
fact, she was punishing herself. Not only did she feel she
no longer deserved to be a male—as if she had abused the
right—but, more importantly, she felt deep down that she
did not deserve to allow the masculine in herself in this
life to manifest, for fear of its old, brutal habits. So she was,
in fact, unconsciously cutting herself off from the real
source of her own power.

From his extensive studies of secondary personalities in
women's dreams, Jung identified the recurrent male figure in women's dreams as archetypal, calling him the
animus.[3] A strong, uncomplicated animus in a woman will
allow her to go out into the world with gusto and energy,
taking the rough and tumble of male competition with
resilience, humor, and pride. But when the animus in a
woman feels secretly ashamed of himself, as with Hildegard, or deeply guilty, as with Yvonne, he will either fail to
assert himself, hanging back from full involvement in life,
or else unconsciously invite catastrophe and attack to confirm his lack of self-worth or self-assertion.

A vivid example of a wounded animus figure in a woman's past life memories was that of a rather shy but highly
creative woman called Ellen who had chosen to work
quietly out of her home as a graphic designer rather than

risk the cut and thrust of the big advertising firms in the city.

In a harrowing past life memory Ellen relived the life of a shy adolescent woodsman who refuses to be part of an orgiastic gang rape with some older men. In their contempt for him, they castrate him and he retreats from the world for life into a lonely log cabin. In this young woman the wounded male or animus in her was symbolically still fearful of being made impotent once more by a harsh male world. I am glad to report that relinquishing that awful memory gave her renewed strength to go back into the world.

In the cases of Eliza, Yvonne, and Hildegard there was a point of reversal from the female victim to the brutal male figure. In each instance there was work to do with these masculine personalities who lived in them. Eliza's was quite healthy, but the pirate in Yvonne and the patrician in Hildegard had been largely disowned.

Often I find it necessary to have women—and men— really yell and scream when they are victimized by rape, torture, or unjust brutality. Simply by contacting that buried rage, an image of a warrior or a fighter will often emerge. In archetypal terms, and in astrological language, this figure is Mars, the energy of the fight, confrontation, and healthy combative defense—whether for one's loved one, one's community, or one's opinions. But the Martian function has, as I remarked earlier, gotten so out of control in our aggressive culture that the first image to surface may be far from healthy, as these examples show. Feminist therapists are right, it seems to me, to encourage anger at the patriarchal abuses in our society, but, as many outsiders suspect, in their righteous indignation—and there is no shortage of abuses in the last three thousand years—such therapists often fail to look at that character in themselves that fuels that rage. Not just the victim, but the bully and the rapist in all of us also are in need of healing and forgiveness. Men are not the only ones who must deal with this particularly pernicious shadow.

Past life therapy raises—though it is unable to answer—the question of to what degree any woman has a predominance of male lives beneath her female identity. And, conversely, how many female lives a man carries within him. Whatever the answer, there is a huge challenge for both men and women to encounter and make creative use of these other sex characters in each of us. From past life work a woman may gain all kinds of insights into the wielding—or the abuse—of power, while a man may have a lot to learn about tenderness, sacrifice, and solicitude from the inner woman of his past lives. It is challenging but rewarding work, even though at a somatic level we may have to face the sad physical effects of our failure as a culture to fully honor the feminine, as body, as earth, as mother.

CHAPTER 9

THE MANY LIVES
OF THE SOUL

Man is a plural being. When we speak of ourselves ordinarily, we speak of "I". We say "I did this" "I think this" "I want to do this"—but this is a mistake. There is no such "I" or rather there are hundreds, thousands of little "I"s in every one of us. We are divided in ourselves but we cannot recognize the plurality of our being except by observation and study.

> Gurdjieff,
> "Man Is a Plural Being" (1922)[1]

It is, in particular, the phenomena of somnambulism, double consciousness, split personality, etc. . . . . that have enabled us to accept the possibility of a plurality of personalities in one and the same individual.

> C. G. Jung,
> *Psychological Types* (1921)

. . . most important is Jung's idea that *every personality is essentially multiple* . . . Multiple personality is human nature.

> James Hillman,
> "Archetypal Theory" (1978)[2]

Other Lives, Other Selves

Even though the term "complex" has settled into popular psychological parlance for decades now, most people tend to resist the notion that personality is multiple. This may be understandable in the light of rather sensational stories like *The Three Faces of Eve* or Hollywood thrillers like *The Exorcist* or *The Entity*. Our resistance to the notion is also partly because the term "multiple personality" has been almost entirely used as a clinical label for a state of severe personality dissociation or splitting that borders on madness.

Schizophrenia, although mistakenly confused with a split or multiple personality disorder, is a condition where many voices or imaginary selves attempt to influence and undermine the sufferer's sense of an integrated personality or ego identity. (Actually, the main difference, clinically speaking, between schizophrenia and multiple personality is that in the latter case, the separate personality forms are strictly compartmentalized, each claiming ignorance of the other. A schizophrenic, by contrast, is fully and devastatingly aware much of the time that he or she has many voices or selves within but controls none of them.)

But regardless of which mental disturbance we are talking of, the term "multiple" retains frightening associations as compared to the more benign name "complex." So while we may feel perfectly comfortable talking to a stranger at a cocktail party about our "money complex," for instance, most people would think twice about saying: "I'm worried about money: the monk in me keeps urging me to take a vow of poverty!"

Work with inner figures, however we identify their origin, is a challenge. We need to become aware of precisely how *their* thoughts, feelings, and stories unconsciously influence *our* thoughts, feelings, and behavior in daily life, and then to seek to alter that influence.

In actual fact, it is not nearly as hard as we might think to identify one or another of the many selves, likable or loathsome, that hover in the wings of our inner psychic stage. From time to time one manages to upstage the principal actor, our ego, and steal the show. "I was beside myself," we say afterward, or, "I don't know what got into me," or "Those words just popped into my mouth." In this fleeting instant we have witnessed, albeit a little confusedly, another self momentarily nudging the ego self aside. Some of us hear these other selves nagging constantly in one or other of our ears. But it is a mistake to think, as some popular psychologies claim, that they are just parental voices we have internalized from childhood. Some of the characters jostling for prominence would have thoroughly shocked the nice expectations of our parents!

Of course, identifying these inner characters provokes a great deal of unease and resistance in us. A part of the fear of not being masters in our own house is the realization that to admit that I have a whole cast of characters jostling and fighting to win center stage puts me on the same continuum that does indeed include schizophrenia and multiple personality.

But no one says we should give way to the persistent and obsessive demands of our other selves. The first task is to recognize them; the second is to come to terms with them, as a king might need to pacify and listen seriously to rebellious subjects that he has carelessly neglected. Whereas more repression only creates worse foes, sympathetic negotiation may restore strength and harmony within the kingdom if properly pursued.

To be afraid of the multiplicity of the psyche—in its manifestation as many lives, many selves, the abnormal extremes aside—is in the end to be afraid of the psyche itself. The fact that many people find the very idea of an inner world and other selves both disturbing and distasteful is, alas, a sad commentary on how very unpsychological and antipathetic to the psyche—and, by extension, the spirit—our society has become. The well-known psychiatrist R. D. Laing recently remarked that we in the West have become "psychophobic," which is to say, terrified of the psyche and things inward. He has more than once castigated his psychiatric colleagues for actually abetting this tendency with their alienating use of clinical labels for mental disturbance and their repressive use of chemotherapy.

Psychophobia, as Laing calls it, is quite endemic in our culture and takes many and surprising forms. One, paradoxically, is the rising interest in "channels" and channeled teachings currently in vogue. Valuable as many of those teachings may be as information, I am led to question the actual form in which channeling popularly is seen.

Very often the practice and the language used by some psychics encourage the idea that all "discarnate entities" inhabit some quite "other" realm that can only be accessed by someone in a state of mediumistic trance, which is to say, a state of fairly deep dissociation, clinically speaking. When a medium is dissociated in such a way sometimes he or she will be consciously present and sometimes he or she knows nothing about the readings until they are over. Either way, ego and "entity" are kept quite apart from each other by the form of the session, a ritualized form of split personality.

Many of the "discarnate entities" that speak through channels sound very much like past life personality fragments. The difference is that the channel seems to *disown* these other selves while past life work attempts to *reown* them. Moreover, therapists believe the realm that depth psychology calls the unconscious is accessible to everyone, while in popular metaphysics only certain people, talented in trance dissociation, are accorded the power to do this.

Many channels rarely mention the unconscious mind, talking instead of "the other side," a term that is once again alienating and dissociative. In this way the popular form of channeling plays right into our prevalent psychophobia. All other selves are fortunately not my business but are left to experts who can contact "the other side" on my behalf. The way these experts treat their own guides as "other" also empowers me to treat mine in that way too.

We have seen how past life recall offers a particularly vivid and emotionally engaging way of encountering our inner figures. First, we engage in dramatic identification —becoming the past life self for the duration of the life story, and then disidentification—dying to that self, detaching from its powerful samskaras, and resolving in dialogue or imagery the unfinished business from a particular story.

As more and more lives accumulate, a second level of the work begins to present itself, namely, a dynamic relationship between the lifetimes themselves. This is where the work, as James Hillman has put it, resembles a symposium, a hearing of all the voices, a seeing of all the interweaving life patterns. The lifetimes remembered are not events to be done with, personality fragments to be exorcised, removed, cast off; instead, they are living energies to be balanced with each other and with the ego, potentially to be integrated in a newer and broader sense of self. Now it is time to face squarely and compassionately the cruel tyrant, the egoistic priestess, the disconsolate beggar woman, the greedy merchant, the cowardly warrior or the terror-stricken child or any of the others who have until this time fueled the most repetitive of our life dramas and drained so much energy where we have most needed it.[3]

The Drama of Psychic Opposites

"Without contraries is no progression" wrote William Blake, an accute commentator on the dynamics of the inner world. Once we begin to explore a whole series of past lives a very prominent feature stands out: there is a constant process of reversal from one kind of personality type to its opposite. There is also a reversal of moral perspective and major themes in the various stories we encounter. So we meet cycles of lives that swing in personality type from concubine to celebate, spendthrift to miser, lord to serf, stay-at-home to adventurer, and so on.

From the moral perspective past life stories may reverse from lives of callous disregard for human life—as warrior, as sacrificing priest, as executioner, to lives of selfless devotion to others—as healer, as contemplative, as surgeon. Themes and settings, too, undergo momentous reversals, from a Roman proconsul ruling all of Spain to a landless Dutch peasant; from an ostracized slave to a Chinese warlord; from a sexually abused child to a battlefield rapist and mutilator. These are the extremes of human nature that we all, it seems, contain within us in a state of uneasy equilibrium.

One of the first to observe the dynamic tendency of the psyche to divide into opposing energies and personalities which are constantly reversing was the little-known Greek mystic and philosopher Heraclitus. He named this dynamic *enantiodromia*—"the movement between the opposites." Jung frequently observed this movement in dream sequences. We now observe it clearly at work when whole series of past lives are remembered.

When the psyche is given permission to flow with these tides of ever-reversing past life stories and personalities and then to contemplate them in all their obtusely contradictory elements a huge psychic tension is set up in the consciousness of the experiencing person. The agonizing challenge now is to find reconciliation and meaning in these polarized personalities with their seemingly irrevocable karmic residues left by past actions. Some examples of the kind of past life reversals that certain of my clients have experienced and which have led them to a deep moral and psychic reevaluation of themselves are as follows:

—A woman first remembers the life of a blue-coat soldier in the American Indian wars. He dies sickened by all the slaughter. The next life she remembers is of a tribal Indian medicine woman whose tribe is being systematically killed off by soldiers. Helpless to change anything, she realizes that her role is to witness and comfort her people as they die one by one, from starvation and bloody attrition. The two lives are seen by her to exactly mirror each other.

—A man remembers a late medieval life where he took great sadistic pleasure in the torture and execution of witches.

After this he finds himself in another life where he is the political victim of the Nazis and is tortured to death for information he does not possess. As he dies he recognizes a version of his previous cruel self in the figure of his torturer and realizes the potential for an endless, hellish, sadomasochistic spiral of vengeful lives. Instead, he is able to forgive his adversary and seems to be released from further karmic violence either to himself or to others.

—A woman finds herself in a past life as a tribal ruler of an island community which is under Roman rule. The Romans force him into all kinds of humiliating sacrifices, including ordering him to execute his own wife. He does all this in order to protect the island community. When she remembers a life seemingly prior to that of the ruler she finds herself as a sea captain who has drowned a whole shipload of peasants who have been captured in a war. On reflection, this woman realizes that the shipload corresponds in number to the size of the island community that the leader felt impelled to protect at such great personal loss.

The Sins of the Fathers—and Mothers: Wendy and Paula

Possibly there is no more tightly bound pair of psychic opposites than that of parent and child. Not for nothing has most of psychotherapy from Freud onward focused very carefully on the drama between the child and its parents. Past life exploration of this powerful diad fully demonstrates the karmic nature of many, if not all, of our past life conflicts, including such things as physical abuse, incest, and abandonment.

When working on a parental complex in past life therapy I will use key themes and phrases that seem to sum up the deadlocked relationship between my client and his or her parent. In this way I allow the unconscious to scan for precise stories of any previous relationship between the parent and the child in question, regardless of the sex or who may have been the parent in a past life. The resulting chains of karmic entanglement are sometimes astonishing. Here are two partial sequences of parent-child "reversals of opposites" that I have encountered in my practice.

Wendy had a history of continual fighting with her father who was a minister and a counselor. She, too, had become a counselor in her profession and she admitted that much of the tension between her and her father was simply plain rivalry. When we explored the intensity of the feelings she had for her father, no less than six past lives emerged in which they seemed to have been together in different ways. Here is the sequence of lives as they came to Wendy:

1. She remembers a life as *a seventeenth-century Scotswoman* whose father is an important diplomat in the Scottish court. Raised to work for him and accompany him on missions, especially secret ones, she finds her whole life given up to his work. She never marries in this life and dies resentful of sacrificing herself for him.

2. Next she remembers a life as *a woman writer* living at the turn of the century. Again, she finds herself working for her father who now owns a newspaper. Her father is very possessive of her and her talents and he effectively sabotages any relationships she might have with other men. Bitterly she turns to drink and dies a spinster.

3. Next she remembers a life as *a man* in a Mediterranean village sometime during the Middle Ages. As this man, she is angry and impatient at her young son for not

being strong. This son grows up to be a healer, but as his father she begrudges him the gift and blocks his development.

4. Wendy now remembers a life when she was *a fisherman* whose ten-year-old son has drowned while out at sea. The fisherman suffers much remorse at the loss of his son.

5. Now she remembers the life of *a man whose father is a village shaman,* but a bad one. The father physically abuses him as a young boy and he runs away eventually to live in the hills. He never again makes contact with people.

6. Finally she remembers the life of *an ancient Chinese village headman* who also has powers as a shaman and healer. In a nearby village there is another reputedly powerful enemy shaman. The headman challenges this other shaman to a contest of powers, but lays a trap for him and instead has him killed. The murder always remains in the headman's conscience, however. Wendy recognizes that he has done this largely out of pride and fear.

From this sequence we can see how Wendy has not only reversed roles with figures like the ones she recognizes as her father, but she has also reversed sexes several times. In half of these lives (1, 2, 5) where she was a daughter or a son to a possessive or abusive father, Wendy would seem to have good cause for residual bitterness at the way all these fathers have treated her. Certainly it was not hard for her to see how she was stuck in rerunning these old tapes about the similarly difficult father today.

But the sequence equally brought out three lives when it was she, as either a father (3, 4) or a powerful leader (6), who had also done things which gave cause for deep regret. It looked as though a whole karmic chain of action and reaction, as it would be called in Eastern philosophy, had been set in motion by her past life murder as Chinese headman of the rival shaman (whom she recognized as her current father). The drowning of a young son (4) and, in addition, jealousy of another son (3) both served, it would seem, to reinforce the residual guilt of the samskara that had been laid down in the Chinese life. In the more recent historical lives (1, 2) we might speculate that Wendy had attempted to serve her father in order to redress the karmic imbalance. But her bitterness had gotten the better of her, with the result that she is once more, in this life, rivals with him.

The challenge, as Wendy was quick to see, was to accept that whatever the negative thoughts she harbored toward her father, they all represented projections of her own inner past life male selves who had abused both societal and parental power. This sequence thus gives us a vivid picture of Wendy's extensive inner struggles with the father aspect of herself that has become bitter, wounded, and jealous. Clearly there was important work to be done dialoguing between these different selves and with an internal representation of her current father.

Paula's conflicts in her current life were with both her mother and her stepdaughter, Tamara. In these relationships she had experienced both sides of a diad. She was, in her current life, as many women are, both a mother and a daughter. Her own mother in this life had been both sexually and physically abusive to her as a child. She still suffered severe lower back pain which she traced to a particular beating she had received from her mother as a baby. As for her stepdaughter, Tamara, they were constantly locked in one kind of fight or another, a pattern that went back to when Tamara was tiny. These were the key past lives that came to Paula when she was working on these issues:

1. Paula remembers herself as *an Egyptian woman who, as a child, is beaten by her mother.* The mother resents her being a girl because she wanted a boy child for reasons of status in the society of that time. Her mother eventually commits suicide when her daughter leaves home at eighteen to be with a man. This Egyptian woman is deeply disturbed after her mother's suicide, and, seemingly possessed by the spirit of her dead mother, she eventually kills herself.

2. Paula now remembers the life of *a European woman who has a daughter but no husband.* The daughter constantly blames her mother for her father's absence and tries to drown herself when she is only four years old. When the daughter is eighteen she leaves home to live with a man, leaving her mother to feel betrayed and despondent.

3. Now Paula remembers a life as *a woman in Spain* in the Middle Ages *with a young daughter.* She is very possessive and tries to control her. When the daughter leaves home at eighteen, the woman cuts her own throat in despair.

4. Paula now sees herself as *a woman in nineteenth-century Europe with a very possessive and controlling mother.* Because of her mother's power, she lives at home, becomes depressed, and, finally, at forty-five kills herself by taking poison.

5. Now Paula slips spontaneously into *a painful childhood memory at two years in this life* when she is being sadistically beaten, twisted, and thrown about and almost choked by her mother.

6. Next Paula remembers a life when she was *a Middle*

Eastern girl of thirteen years. During a desert crossing she is forced by her parents to carry baggage like an animal. Finally her mother demands that she, too, be carried. When she collapses under the burden, her mother beats her savagely. She is left to die in the desert.

7. Paula now remembers a life when she was *an unwanted baby that was brutalized by her mother.* In this short life she is killed because the tribe has no food.

8. Paula now remembers a life when she is *a mother with a tiny child in a primitive tribe.* Because there is no food for this tribe, she takes an ax and kills her baby with a blow on its back. Not long after, the mother herself dies, partly from starvation and partly from being mauled and eaten by a wild animal. After death there is a meeting with her dead child in which there is mutual forgiveness.

9. Finally Paula finds herself as *a woman in Europe at the turn of the century.* She is happy with her parents and has an especially good relationship with her sister. Her sister marries and dies in childbirth. As the woman, Paula feels strongly that the unborn child of her sister may have grown up to be her current stepdaughter, Tamara.

This harrowing sequence of past lives mirrored the intimate and mutually destructive relationships that Paula had with both her mother and her stepdaughter, Tamara. In the first four lives Paula recognizes her present daughter, Tamara, as both the suicidal mother (1) and the controlling mother (4). She also sees Tamara as the daughter she cannot let go of in the second and third lives. This time it is Paula as the mother who is suicidal and possessive. The roles are exactly reversed in each instance. It seems that there is a near-symbiotic/karmic relationship between Paula and Tamara. Their need for nurturance from each other was so great that they could not bear to be parted and had fallen into a guilt-inducing pattern of suicide at each occasion of separation from each other.

In her current life, Paula had struggled desperately to separate from her biological mother and had succeeded only to the extent of joining a religious order when she was eighteen. This compromise solution had, however, still kept her cut off from life. Her guilt at hurting her own mother in past lives was still too great unconsciously for her to be able to leave her fully. Paula's past lives with Tamara reflected her own deep fears of separation from home and mother. Paula realized how she had been projecting her own unresolved fears onto Tamara, and how she had been unconsciously possessive of her and needy. Tamara had, of course, struggled violently against these restraints.

The next four past lives (5–8) reflected the deeply pathological knot that tied Paula to her mother in this life. Both her early childhood experience and the past lives she and her mother seem to have had together reveal Paula's mother to be near-psychotic in her brutality. Nevertheless, Paula also had to face her own shadow in the life (8) when she murders her own child (= mother) with an ax. As she relived this gruesome memory, Paula recognized that the place in the child's back where she had wielded the fatal ax blow corresponded exactly to where her mother had beaten her as a child in this life (5) and where she still had chronic back pain. It is hard to say where this vicious spiral of cruelty and hatred started and with whom, but at some point the vengeful samskaras had become compounded and neither could avoid being drawn to each other karmicly as either mother or daughter.

And yet the bloody denouement to this ghastly se-

quence of past lives where as mother Paula kills her starv-
ing baby with an ax and then dies herself signals a surprising psychic reconciliation with her mother. In the after-
death state there is, in fact, mutual forgiveness between
the two. The reason for this is that Paula, with the help of
the past life vision, has been able to own and vent her own
murderous rage toward her mother. To see one's darkest
shadow—particularly for a woman to see the archetypal
death mother in herself—is a profound and salutary experience.

As a symbolic indication that some considerable degree
of karmic balancing and integration had taken place after
the eighth life, the next past lifetime she remembered
showed Paula with loving parents and being extremely
close to her young sister. Paula became convinced during
this regression that the child which had been lost in childbirth was actually the spirit of Tamara. And although she
felt this spirit's longing for mothering, she said she no
longer felt responsible for her. This was an important
perception, since Paula needed to let go of a huge amount
of both guilt and neediness around both her stepdaughter
and her current mother. A part, at least, of this immensely
tangled karmic skein had been substantially loosened in
our work and Paula had come to accept several forms of
wounded mother and daughter that lived within her.

The Hell of Sadomasochism: The Case of Wayne

Many people will no doubt be disturbed by the number of
past life stories in this book that involve violence and
cruelty. It might strike some as indulgently lurid or even

sensational. But what we find in the psyche is no more than a reflection of our society at large. If violence stalks the streets and subways and is the staple of television and drive-in movies, why should it not be there beneath the surface of the unconscious mind?

When I first met Wayne at a workshop out West, "violent" was the very last adjective I would have used to describe him. A tall, powerfully built man in his thirties, Wayne struck me more as a "gentle giant" type. Indeed, there was a lot of gentleness in him, since, as I discovered, he worked as a teacher for disturbed adolescents at a special education school, where he was very successful at his job.

As our interview proceeded it began to emerge that Wayne was inwardly deeply conflicted. He had little or no interest in women and admitted to having grown up with an extremely poor relationship with his mother. Instead, he was drawn to homosexual relationships with young adolescent boys. Fortunately Wayne knew better than to allow any of this to spill over into his professional life, since, as he knew, this would be devastating. But the fantasies, nevertheless, persisted in him. Mixed in with them were all kinds of sadomasochistic images that he was too shy to talk about much during our first session.

In addition to a poor relationship with his mother, Wayne had never gotten on well with his father, a rather self-destructive man who had turned to drink and gambling before an early death. Somewhat fatherless himself, then, it was not surprising that Wayne was attracted to fatherless young boys.

Wayne, who lifted weights, was powerfully muscled in the upper part of his body, his arms, neck, and shoulders particularly. He manifested a lot of what Wilhelm Reich

termed *armoring*. Beneath this heavily developed musculature I intuitively sensed a great deal of rage that was
held in by Wayne. A further aspect of Wayne's somatic self
was chronic tension that he reported in his upper right
back. He also told me that he had ruptured a disk while
lifting weights not long ago. In addition, he also had a
phobia about drowning and that he could not get enough
air when he was swimming.

Like many "gentle giants" who work out in either gyms
or martial arts studios, I was struck by the contrast between his almost diffident persona and the powerful body
that was kept in the peak of condition, ready for battle.
Was there a warrior story that needed to surface? How did
it connect with the sadomasochistic fantasies and young
boys?

Many people who come into therapy with strongly somatic complaints are often so out of touch with what their
bodies are carrying that the early work is quite gradual;
the more powerful emotions are so split off that it takes
time to get at them. With such clients, I will myself do a
certain amount of body and breath work, or else I will
send them to a competent bodyworker. Past life work that
is just images with no emotion, while a rigid body lies on
my couch hardly breathing, is a waste of time for both me
and my client. All we are doing is compounding the body/
mind split.

Fortunately Wayne was not so split. He had already
done a certain amount of guided imagery in other therapies which had taught him to both value and work with
inner images and to accept that he had active subpersonalities within himself. His ability, then, to own, albeit
with embarrassment, his sadomasochistic fantasies was for
me the symptom that gave the best prognostication for

success. This is because images provide the essential element that is able to bridge that almost impossible chasm of body and mind. A violent image in particular invariably brings with it certain physical sensations: tingling, butterflies in the stomach, dry mouth, palpitating heart, clenched genitals, etc. And such images, once fully owned by the various parts of the body to which they belong, naturally evoke emotions. With the emotions/image/body connection made, the story—past or present—will always emerge spontaneously and, with its own dynamic, lead us directly to some kind of catharsis or intrapsychic resolution.

With Wayne we started with some intense breath work to soften the powerfully held armoring in his chest. I was not too surprised, then, given his openness to darker forms of fantasy, that the first past life he remembered stood in stark contrast to his conscious personality, in a way reminiscent of the famous Dr. Jekyll and Mr. Hyde:

> *I'm seeing this well-dressed woman into a carriage. It seems to be the eighteenth century. I'm dressed as a gentleman— buckled shoes, white hose, long jacket, fancy hat. I'm courteous, but underneath I'm seething. I can't have her and the more I can't have her, the more I hate her. I want to kill her. I want to hurt her the way she's hurt me.*

Seeing that there is already strong and violent affect here I urge Wayne to follow the intensity of this man's feelings and see where they take him:

> *I hate her. I want to kill her. (He repeats, his fists and jaws clenching, his shoulders rising up.) I'll kill you, you slut. Get down. Do it . . . I'm in an upper room at an inn. I'm with this chambermaid or whoever she is. My britches are undone.*

She is servicing me sexually. But there's no relief, all it does is make me angrier about the woman I can't have . . .

Do, do it! You can't! You can't! God I hate you. I hate you all . . . I'm stabbing her, again and again . . . It's with a pair of scissors . . . There's blood . . . Her face, her chest . . . There, she's dead. It's over. I don't care. I urinate on her . . . This is more than you deserve . . . You slut . . . I don't care . . . It feels good now.

Other violent images flood into Wayne's mind now: slapping a stable boy, then somewhere at sea cutting a child's throat. They seem to be a mixture of elements from this eighteenth-century past life and possibly others. Clearly they all belong to the same overall sadistic complex. "See where your rage takes you in the same lifetime," I instruct Wayne.

I'm in the street now. It's cobbled, dark. I'm following this man home. He doesn't suspect because I'm well-dressed. I'm not afraid of anyone, I'm a big man. It's the father of the woman I want so much. He thinks I am uncouth. He won't let me in his house anymore. Now he's got what he deserves.

I've caught up with him. I've got his neck in my hands. I'm very strong. His bones crunch. I drop him, grind his face with my boots. I feel absolute contempt for him. They won't do anything to me because I'm too strong. They're all afraid.

He is referring to the villagers in the country town where all this is taking place. He is indeed known and feared by all as a brutal social menace sometimes out of control. Today he would be labeled a sociopath. But he is wrong about the villagers. A member of the local gentry challenges him to a duel in the woods but, instead, has a whole band of men from the village lie in ambush for the murderer at the appointed place. It is mob justice, but effective. The man is apprehended and killed by a stake being driven through his stomach and his legs pulled off by horses in the manner of medieval quartering. Finally he is stabbed in the chest. His dying thoughts are hateful and vengeful: "I'll get even. I'll hurt more people."

How did such a brutal character evolve? I have Wayne go back to an earlier time in the man's history for any clues. These scenes flash into awareness:

I'm a baby. I'm in a kind of crib, but I'm out in the rain. There's a beautifully dressed woman. She doesn't care. She resents me. I'm very frightened, very alone.

Now I'm thirteen. This older man is coming after me. He's powerfully built. He's the blacksmith on the estate. He says I stole his money. He's whipping me with this many-stranded whip (cat-o'-nine-tails?). I'm so sad inside. I'm worth nothing. They just want to hurt me, but they'll pay for it.

It might seem that this man's callousness is in part a reaction to a rejecting and cold mother which results in his growing up to become a vicious and uncontrollable adolescent. Apparently his father has died when he is very young. Eventually he runs away from the family estate and becomes a violent criminal wanderer: lying, stealing, masquerading—an eighteenth-century confidence man with a huge chip on his shoulder that leads him from one brutal confrontation to another, the final one bloody in the extreme, as we have seen.

In the character whose life Wayne reenacts there is already the dual theme of hurting and being hurt. *"They just want to hurt me, but they'll pay for it"* seems to be his litany of vengeance, a litany directed at both men and women. Can all this violence simply be attributed to a cold and rejecting mother and a blacksmith who beats him? Apparently not, for in our next session an equally brutal figure emerges from another layer of this complex.

This time Wayne finds himself as a professional soldier in one of Western history's most wanton and bloody epochs, the medieval Crusades. Wayne remembers large sections of this life in great detail. More than any of the several violent personalities that surfaced during our work, this one carried both the greatest erotic and the greatest sadistic charge. It was most likely the story that had hovered most balefully in the background of his consciousness, feeding the sadomasochistic fantasies that enticed yet tormented him. Here is the key scene from a past life already replete with violence:

> *I'm a knight in armor, Italian it seems. I'm mounted on a horse with helmet, boots, spear, and I have a tunic with a white cross on it. I'm some kind of leader of this band of soldiers. It's hot, dusty, rocky terrain—Mediterranean or Near Eastern. We're on the edge of this small village. There's a mother with her son of twelve years or so. I spur my horse and run at the woman, impaling her breast upon my spear. I drag her off almost dead, then I kick her off, dismount, stab her, crush her face, run my spear into her genitals. I throw her body off the cliff nearby. The son is watching, horrified, weeping uncontrollably. I wipe the blood off my spear and go up to the boy. I hit him hard, tell him to stop crying and that he's coming with me. Then I order the villagers into their houses and tell my men to occupy the village and take what they need. I ride off with the boy, saying I may or may not return.*

The boy, it turns out, is a homosexual spoil of war for this crusader. But there is an important element to the abduction, revealed in Wayne's soliloquy, as he rides off with the boy:

All of a sudden I feel sad about killing the woman and taking the boy. It reminds me in this life of a younger man I once had as a lover; he was so vulnerable and unprotected.

Evidently early adolescence had been a crucial period in Wayne's psychological development—a time when there is brutality, betrayal, and sadness. The eighteenth-century sadist recalls being whipped at thirteen by the blacksmith and the momentary sadness that arises then, only to be suppressed in favor of vengeance. In his current life, he remembers that his father died at this age. And also that he has chosen a career that has him mostly working with disturbed or displaced young adolescents. This wounded area is, so it seems, multiply determined from these other lives, the pain being reactivated in this life by his father's death.

Wayne's deep ambivalence about giving and receiving love as father to son and vice versa is revealed in the next scene of the crusader's life:

I'm in this castle with the boy. I've terrorized them into giving me room and food. They bring me water for a bath. I wash and oil the boy. He's terrified.

"Do you understand why I killed your mother?" I say to him.

"Yes, sire," he replies.

"I don't think you do. Women are simply for us to get here. They are to be disposed of."

I fondle and suck his genitals. Then I tie him to the table, whipping him but not too hard. It gets me aroused so I have him suck me. Then I penetrate him anally, but it's not satisfactory. I become desperate, sad, enraged. No pleasure seems possible. I take my knife and slice him open, screaming. I cut out his heart. I have the servants dispose of the body.

This shocking episode reveals how painfully this heavily armored warrior self in Wayne longs for love but cannot let go of his encrusted hatred and violence. He swings from tenderness and solicitude to cruelty and contempt. Yet his homosexual desire for the boy is nevertheless an attempt to love and reown a deeply wounded part of himself. But once again hatred, born of his own pains, intervenes. Just such a terrible inner conflict was well expressed by Oscar Wilde as he lay in Reading Gaol on charges of homosexuality, contemplating the imminent execution of a fellow prisoner for the murder of his wife:

> Yet each man kills the thing he loves
> By each let this be heard,
> Some do it with a bitter look,
> Some with a flattering word.
> The coward does it with a kiss,
> The brave man with a sword!
>
> Some kill their love when they are young,
> And some when they are old;
> Some strangle with the hands of Lust,
> Some with the hands of Gold;
> The kindest use a knife because
> The dead so soon grow cold.

The impulse to kill and suppress the image of what we most want but have never had—in Wayne's case the love of both a mother and a father—is deep in us all, as Wilde saw. If we submit to this impulse it seems to create its own repeating circle of karmic hell. In probing for the roots of the crusader's brutality we were taken this time first back to his birth:

"I'm being born . . . There's these big women all around me. My mother, she's weak. Oh, no! She's dying. They don't care. No one cares. They could kill me if they wanted to."

The mother dies in childbirth. The crusader is raised as a loveless orphan, treated almost as a slave by his father. He has a sister who is kind to him, however. Eventually he kills his father at the age of fourteen by setting fire to the house he is sleeping in.

Once again, the same themes as the eighteenth-century life but cruder, bleaker; no mother, a brutalizing father, and a life of embittered cruelty. It starts to become apparent to Wayne how this crusader's killing of the woman and young boy are exact role reversals of what he himself has experienced in this life. By killing this past life mother he renders the boy motherless, just as the crusader had been left motherless at birth. Then, by murdering the boy, the crusader becomes himself an abusing father. It is a chilling example of one of Jung's more thought-provoking dictums, regarding the reversal of psychic opposites: "You always become the thing you fight the most."

The problem of swings of opposites sets up the most vicious of circles when seen karmicly. The more Wayne's past life selves came to hate women, the more they were drawn back to hateful or rejecting mother figures; but the more, as a child, he had come to suffer at the hands of such cruel mothers, the more he grew to hate them in adulthood.

In Wayne's case, we were not able to break out of this circle; perhaps this is precisely why Hell is imaged, in Dante, in the form of circles. Psychologically, circles can represent every kind of self-perpetuating torment, like a snake devouring its own tail. All that can happen in such cases is to find some point of detachment, to take some perspective outside of the karmic deadlock, secure in the knowledge that it is only this particular karmic complex that is struck, not the greater personality as a whole, which has other and broader viewpoints.

In Wayne's next session, he achieved separation from this wretched samskara and experienced a quite remarkable psychic reversal. We had already had a fleeting glimpse of the crusader's death—a suicide by drowning—but it still remained for Wayne to fully experience the ending of this ignominious life and to detach from it. The crusader is not much older than forty when his death occurs as follows:

> *I'm somewhere by the ocean. I've lost my men. I've left my men over in a village. They've got some hostages nearby. I realize that my life has reached the point where all I can do is kill people. I am so full of anger that I don't know how to stop it. I'm ashamed of what I have done, but that only makes me more angry and want to kill again. But a part of me is also sad. I've had enough. I want to die.*
>
> *I take my dagger and walk into the sea. I plunge it into my own belly. My body buckles over. There's blood in the water. I walk farther, stumble and fall, swallowing the salt water. It's cold. I sink down into it. It's noble in a perverted way. I'm sinking now. Water in my lungs . . . I'm lying on the bottom. It's over . . . I'm relieved, very relieved.*
>
> *It's over. It's really over* (tears start to well up in his eyes). *I'm coming out of the body. I'm separating from him.* I can become human again. *I feel so sad for him, for everything. I was so burdened by all the abuse, so terrified of being a victim again, of coming back like my victims again. Now I see that mother and the boy I killed* (he weeps). *And I see the sister that I grew up with; she's smiling.* She *didn't hate me.*

Something about the image of the sister is deeply affecting. It is as though she represents the only available image of tenderness in that life, but one he barely noticed at the time. All of a sudden we find ourselves in a scene from a strikingly different past life:

> *I'm in a dress, a big white dress with sequins. I'm dancing with a partner. He's very dapper. I'm really enjoying this, it's a ball of some kind . . . Seems like France. I'm definitely an aristocratic woman. Young, early twenties. And, oh . . . I've got designs on this man!*
>
> *It's later. The same night. We're in bed, making love. I feel so soft and warm . . . And affectionate. I never knew it could be like this.*

Wayne is shocked but pleasantly surprised to find himself in this woman's body. Here is a personality within Wayne that totally changes how Wayne thinks about himself and the crusader. This is the story, in summary, as it transpires:

> *The Frenchwoman is the total obverse of the crusader: sweet, yielding, sensual, and with never a mean word for anyone. She is a free spirit born into the French nobility in the eighteenth century. She lives a quite licentious life, as is typical of the aristocracy of that period, but she finds a man whom she genuinely loves and marries happily. The Revolution intervenes and she and her husband and two children, a boy and a girl, manage to flee to England, where they live for some years as émigrés in a rather rugged farmhouse. She has no regrets and enjoys raising her children, especially her son, who is particularly handsome as an adolescent. The family moves to London where she takes up some decorative arts that give her great satisfaction. She dies quite young, of a puerperal fever, after a miscarriage.*

The effect that remembering this life has upon Wayne is very marked. He is astonished and relieved to be able to know from the inside, as it were, what female consciousness looks and feels like. He is considerably moved by the warm and very natural quality of givingness of this woman. I remind him that this lovely, sensual, and nurturing woman lives very much in him, an exact counterbalance to the crusader and the sadist.

Wayne has experienced an extreme *enantiodromia,* or reversal of psychic opposites, in this short sequence of lives. From the killer and warrior to the gentlewoman, he has moved archetypally from lives dominated by the god of war, Mars, to the love goddess, Venus. This is an appropriate balancing of the energy of Mars, as both astrology and mythology remind us. In the Greek myths this archetypal pair are called Aphrodite and Ares. Aphrodite, who is born of the waves, is the only one who can quell the fiery, war-like passion of Ares by charming him with her magic girdle into taking off his blood-spattered armor so that he might indulge in the arts of love, not war.

The flow of libido can only reverse, as both Heraclitus and Jung observed, where an extreme has been reached. This seemed to be the case with the crusader; his war-like energy had been exhausted so that, already, glimpses of the sadness in Wayne, so long buried, were evoked by the fleeting image of the sister. She was the first premonition of what Jung would call an *anima* figure, a man's female self.[4] This sister figure and the feelings she personifies are what led him directly to an identification with the fuller and more mature anima self of the Frenchwoman.

Wayne's work is by no means over with the appearance of this female self. What this figure did was set up an enormously powerful exchange of psychic energy between the masculine and feminine sides of Wayne.

Although this was the only female figure to emerge in our sessions, her appearance had a radical effect on

Wayne. He understood his homosexuality much more positively now and could feel less conflicted about it. He was, in fact, recognizing in himself the nurturing mother he never had. The most difficult problem still remained: how to find a strong male in himself that was not brutish and sadistic but who supported rather than wanted to destroy the youthful male self. He was faced with a dilemma well known in archetypal psychology as "the devouring father." In Greek mythology, for example, the god Kronos is jealous of his sons' youthfulness and tries to castrate them all with a sickle.

Several devouring fathers emerged in the subsequent past lives that we worked through in our sessions. In one Wayne saw himself as the son of a peasant father who was forced by that father to commit homosexual acts with him. This father, who was clearly psychotic, had his son blinded and then murdered. In another lifetime, Wayne found himself as a shy young boy who was whipped savagely by his father. In adulthood this man turned to pederasty but found no real happiness in it. Next, he remembered the life of a young Polish adolescent beaten to death by Nazis in a concentration camp. Then, in a predictable reactive swing to this memory, Wayne found himself as a cruel robber in medieval Germany, who, like the crusader, learned brutality as a reaction to being brutalized as a child.

Further light was thrown on his hatred of women and on the sensitivity of his genitals when he saw himself as a little boy being molested sexually by a group of older women. This merged with a painful memory first of circumcision in this life, and then of his genitals being tortured in a Native American life.

All these experiences had to be worked through so that

the residual pain, rage, and humiliation could be released. To help heal these wounded areas we used affirmations that gave Wayne permission to find pleasure and power in his masculine self without the pendulum swinging back toward the aggressive, heavily armored defensive self he had drawn so much security from in his past lives.

The pairs of past life personalities in him became more apparent: brutal father and angry son; homosexually abusive man and submissive boy; sadistic bully and vengeful victim; warrior and lover. Slowly, as Wayne was able to live with, tolerate, and accept the swings of energy and temperament that belong to these inner dueling pairs, two new figures started to emerge: one was a fine Native American man, loved by his mother, proud of his young manhood, a good hunter, warrior, and husband. He lived a good life in harmony with the feminine and the earth. It was a healing vision.

The other healing image of a past life to emerge was of a financial investor earlier in this century in North America. Again, images of a good marriage and healthy children. And now, even a kind of spiritual awakening toward the end of his life. "I am finally learning to trust my tenderness," Wayne said after remembering this life.

Our work, I feel, is finally beginning to pay off. It has been arduous, even grueling, and at times it seemed we would be caught forever in one of Wayne's sadomasochistic circles. There were naturally all kinds of ways these stories resonate with events in his childhood in this life, particularly the harsh treatment he had received at the hands of his parents. But what our work helped him to see was that his outer parents were but a reflection of old, unfinished residues of past life stories in his own unconscious that had hardened into mutually perpetuating complexes: bully and victim, sadist and masochist.

Thanks to the softening influence of the French anima self, Wayne was able to break this miserable deadlock and dare to experience emotional warmth within himself and so rediscover his true capacity for loving relationships. But this had to be achieved through an acceptance rather than through a rejection of the darker parts of himself. Dr. Jekyll *is* Mr. Hyde; Iago *is* Othello *and* Desdemona. We are each of us one, but multiple at the same time. Only when we can welcome this multiplicity of being within us, especially the distasteful parts, can we become truly whole, truly human. This, to my mind, is one of the great challenges and rewards of past life work from a Jungian perspective.

PART IV
THE LARGER PERSPECTIVE

The soul of man is immortal, and at one time comes to an end, which is called dying away, and at another is born again, but never perishes . . . Seeing then, that Soul is immortal and has been born many times, and has beheld all things both in this world and in Hades, she has learnt all things, without exception; so that it is no wonder that she should be able to remember all that she knew before about virtue and other things. And since all nature is congeneric, there is no reason why we should not, by remembering but one single thing—which is what we call learning—discover all the others, if we are brave and faint not in the enquiry; for it seems that to enquire and to learn are wholly a matter of remembering.

Plato, *Meno* 81 B–D,
tr. by Hamilton and Cairns

CHAPTER 10

THE GREAT WHEEL: BIRTH AND BEFORE

I am not yet born; console me,
I fear that the human race may with tall walls wall me,
with strong drugs dope me, with wise lies lure me,
on black racks rack me, in blood-baths roll me.

Louis MacNeice, "Prayer Before Birth"

Thou must be patient; we came crying hither:
Thou know'st, the first time that we smell the air,
We wawl and cry . . .
When we are born, we cry that we are come
To this great stage of fools.

Shakespeare, *King Lear*

At the Hour of Our Birth

One of the most striking psychological facts about the compulsive power of a complex in the unconscious mind is how it can turn the most innocent situation into an occasion for high drama. We saw this in the case of Elizabeth and her cats, for instance. The Freudians early coined the phrase "acting out" in recognition of this huge propensity for drama that our complexes engender. Popular psychology abounds with metaphors of world as stage, of how we identify with role models, follow life scripts, enact family scenarios, etc.

What situation could be more innocent than the birth of a baby? And yet, what more momentous occasion for high drama, as any practicing obstetrician or midwife will tell you with hundreds of stories. Despite the most elaborate prenatal preparations, emergency services, and expert care, babies frequently manage to be born in the most extraordinary circumstances: in elevators, by roadsides, in taxis, plane crashes, football stadiums, and so on. The onset and variable speed of an expectant mother's labor is such a mysterious and unpredictable factor that in millions of cases either the mother doesn't get to the hospital or the midwife cannot make it in time for the home delivery.

And even when the mother has gotten comfortably settled in the hospital or the midwife is there well before the final stages of labor, every kind of complication may and does arise during the process of birth itself: breech births, placenta previa, cranial damage, hemorrhaging, etc, to say nothing of premature births, stillbirths, and the intricacies of delivering twins, triplets, and quadruplets and, of course, cesarean section. Despite every kind of sophisticated fetal monitoring, scanning procedures, and chemical management developed by modern technological medicine, most obstetrics experts seem as helpless to predict accurately what the problems and course of a particular birth will be as the average tribal medicine woman. A woman may have given birth successfully and without complications to four children, for example, then with her fifth a birth with horrendous near-fatal complications occurs.

Critics of modern birthing practices from Frederick

Leboyer onward have charged with some justice that hospital procedures themselves are responsible much more than is realized for the distress and trauma of both mother and child. But these, I believe, are only contributory factors, not the real causes. The real drama takes place between the mother and baby. Mother is the stage, so to speak, and the nascent child is the principal actor or actress struggling with every imaginable piece of karmic stage fright to get out and say his or her first babbling lines. Indeed, as we now know from the investigations of many psychologists working independently of each other in recent years—Arthur Janov, Leonard Orr, Elizabeth Fehr, R. D. Laing, Morris Netherton, and Stanislav Grof[1]—there is a vast and complex array of unconscious factors that are at play in every pregnancy and birth scenario. However much we would like to blame every birth accident or misfortune on clumsy obstetrics, the inescapable evidence is that there are innumerable unconscious forces at work to produce the unique personal drama behind every birth, as befits the individuality of every child who enters the world.

The first psychologist to pay serious attention to the effect of our birthing experience upon the subsequent development of personality was Otto Rank, an early follower of Freud. Rank's classic book *The Trauma of Birth,* written in 1923, remains an indispensable exploration of the symbolic and mythic resonances in the unconscious mind that attend every baby's struggle through the birth canal.[2]

Each dream image of vessel, cave, or dungeon, each scenario of containment or entrapment was convincingly shown by Rank as the way the unconscious of the infant symbolically remembers uterine existence. Literature,

myth, and folklore abounds with stories of perilous jour-
neys through ravines, caves, tunnels, or ocean straits,
which cannot fail to awaken some dim recognition of the
terrors of our own movement throughout the birth canal.
One famous mythological example occurs in Homer's *Odyssey*, where the hero has to make the dangerous passage
between the sea monster Scylla and the deadly whirlpool
Charybdis.

The agonies of delivery itself and all its manifold complications give rise, according to Rank, to images of the
utmost violence in the unconscious of the emergent baby:
drowning, burning, choking, cutting, crushing, dismemberment, decapitation, or even crucifixion. Rank's identification of these extreme images of the archetypal experience of birth was an intuitive generalization from his
casework in the early days of psychoanalysis. The accu-
racy of his insights was vividly confirmed three decades
later by the extensive psychedelic research of Stanislav
Grof. The Czech psychiatrist found that during the course
of ongoing LSD psychotherapy every one of his patients
had visions corresponding in one form or another to precisely the symbolic struggles during birth that Rank had
intuited. Grof was so struck by such imagery that he has
accorded it a whole separate level of the unconscious
mind beneath or prior to the Freudian or childhood unconscious; he calls this level the *Rankian* or *perinatal
unconscious.*[3] (We referred briefly to this level in the Lotus Wheel model in Chapter 5.)

Even though Grof now uses intensive breathing practices rather than LSD, he still finds perinatal imagery fully
accessible to consciousness. Leonard Orr's hyperventilation response, called rebirthing, also elicits this same material, as does Morris Netherton's technique of directed

awareness. The violent birth images such as crushing, strangling, or crucifixion that Rank and Grof report can clearly be attributed to the intense physical stresses and pressures that the infant experiences during the final phases of pregnancy and the constricting and threatening passage through the actual birth canal. In Jungian language, the infant could be said to be replaying archetypal scenarios of deadly peril and gruesome deaths that lie in the repository of the collective unconscious. In this sense, both the physical and the psychic experience of birth must be seen as a universal phenomenon, one in which death and birth coalesce as two aspects of the same all-encompassing archetype.

At both the Jungian and the Rankian level of experience the role of the mother is obviously quite impersonal. It is not as a person that the infant experiences the mother but as the Great Mother, a universal archetypal being whom the greater psyche has known millions of times in similar births. The Mother is for the infant first the archetypal vessel of oceanic bliss, then the crushing or constricting prison or tomb, and finally she is the jaws of death from which the struggling child wins joyous deliverance. The whole process initiates each of us, though we are not fully conscious of it, into the joys and sorrows of being human. It is initiation par excellence and is thus the prototype of all future initiations and transitions in the life that follows.

Every woman when she gives birth participates again in this great transpersonal experience. Many women, particularly when they have been given drugs during labor, find their own birth memories fused with those of giving birth. Some have disturbing visions of death angels or violent happenings. This is all the reactivation of this complex and dual archetype. In giving birth, as in being born, we tap into the universal experience of womankind, which can also include all the losses, sacrifices, and deaths of infants in the Great Memory of the human race. Much despair and guilt can naturally arise spontaneously at such times. It is important to realize that such feelings are not personal, but that they belong to an archetypal or transpersonal experience. Nowhere is the Great Mother in her dual aspect (as life in death and death in life) more present.

Nevertheless, these archetypal experiences at the perinatal level do not constitute the entirety of fetal experience before and during birth. There is indeed a more personal element that has to do with the unborn infant's attunement to the mother's individual consciousness during pregnancy and with the infant's own residual impressions from past lives. With the exception of Morris Netherton's work, little has so far been written about these two other factors of the perinatal unconscious and how they interact. The purpose of the remainder of this chapter will be to sketch this subtle and all-important relationship.

Life Before Birth: Recent Scientific Findings

Recent research by Dr. Gerhard Rottman of the University of Salzburg in Austria has shown how fetal consciousness directly reflects the mother's emotional state during pregnancy. He found that there are four kinds of mothers, distinguished by their different attitudes toward the baby, both conscious and unconscious, during pregnancy. At the two extremes he found what he labeled "Ideal Mothers" and "Catastrophic Mothers."

Ideal Mothers are those who both consciously and unconsciously wanted their unborn babies, according to the psychological tests Rottman administered. These mothers mostly had easy pregnancies and trouble-free births and produced healthy offspring. The group Rottman called *Catastrophic Mothers,* as their name implies, in no way wanted children and, as a consequence, had all kinds of medical problems during pregnancy and bore premature, low weight, and emotionally disturbed children. In between these two extremes were the *Ambivalent Mothers,* who outwardly seemed to want their unborn babies but inwardly were unsure; often this group had behavioral and intestinal problems. Finally there were the *Cool Mothers,* who consciously were very conflicted about having children because of career or financial problems, but unconsciously they really wanted a child. What Rottman found was that the baby, in utero, picked up both messages and was, as an infant, apathetic and lethargic.

These striking findings, and many of a similar nature, are reported in Thomas Verney and John Kelly's book *The Secret Life of the Unborn Child.* This remarkable book is, in many ways, a landmark of psychological research into perinatal consciousness and deserves to be better known. Few people are aware that research of this nature has been going on for two decades. From the perspective of the present book, the authors may seem somewhat cautious in their approach, but considering that their conclusions are based on hard scientific data from up-to-date neurological and physiological research, they are all the more valuable. I will let Verney and Kelly summarize their findings in their own words:

We now know that the unborn child is an aware, reacting human being who from the sixth month on (and perhaps even earlier) leads an active emotional life. Along
with this startling finding we have made these discoveries:

—The fetus can see, hear, experience, taste and, on a
primitive level, even learn in utero (that is, in the uterus—
before birth). Most importantly, he can feel—not with an
adult's sophistication, but feel nonetheless.

—A corollary to this discovery is that what a child feels
and perceives begins shaping his attitudes and expectations about himself. Whether he ultimately sees himself
and, hence, acts as a happy or sad, aggressive or meek,
secure of anxiety-ridden person depends, in part, on the
messages he gets about himself in the womb.

—The chief source of those shaping messages is the
child's mother. *This does not mean every fleeting worry,
doubt or anxiety a woman has rebounds on her child.*
What matters are deep persistent patterns of feeling.
Chronic anxiety or a wrenching ambivalence about moth-
erhood can leave a deep scar on an unborn child's personality. On the other hand, such life-enchancing emotions as
joy, elation, and anticipation can contribute significantly
to the emotional development of a healthy child.

—New research is also beginning to focus much more
on the father's feelings. Until recently his emotions were
disregarded. Our latest studies indicate that this view is
dangerously wrong. They show that how a man feels
about his wife and unborn child is one of the single most
important factors in determining the success of a pregnancy.[4]

Everything that these researchers report, including
Rottman's significant findings, is fully corroborated by my

own less extensive explorations in therapy of intrauterine memories and birth trauma. Yet there is one statement of Verney and Kelly's that I would qualify considerably from my own findings. They see the mother as "the chief source of these shaping messages" in the unborn child's unconscious. I would strongly question this. Instead, I wish to propose that *the mother's consciousness during pregnancy is the occasion for the reactivation of psychic patterns or samskaras previously laid down in the child's psyche in past lifetimes.*

To say this is a major shift of emphasis and may, I hope, relieve many mothers of yet another load of unnecessary guilt regarding premature births, cesareans, brain damage, and more. What needs to be stated very clearly is this: Every infant comes into the world with his or her *own* unfinished karmic dramas. Pregnancy and birth are the first opportunity, as we are beginning to see, to rerun some of them. The incoming child is drawn to certain mothers and fathers not so much out of choice—many of us arrive with distinct reluctance—but because the uncertainties, hopes, fears, and squabbles of certain parents will effectively restimulate old karmic residues within the unborn child's unconscious psyche. In addition, the whole panoply of contemporary birthing technology also provides the unconscious with a wide variety of opportunities to replay a number of unfinished life-death struggles left over from problematic past lives.

What past life research and therapy add to the extremely valuable findings of Rottman and others is this: *The incoming soul or protopersonality is attracted to a mother (and father) who will help mirror his or her unfinished karmic business during pregnancy and birth.* An incoming soul still dominated by catastrophic memories of violent death, deprivation, or abandonment will easily be attracted to Rottman's Catastrophic Mother. When such a mother harbors the unconscious thought "I really don't want this child," it will be mirrored directly by "I really don't want to be here. Nobody wants me" in the fetal unconscious of the unborn child. For the child, these thoughts belong to the remnant of a past life trauma; they are not caused by the mother, but only evoked by her unconscious ruminations. Fortunately the obverse is also true: where a pregnant mother wholeheartedly wants a child (Rottman's Ideal Mother), she will attract to her a child who is relatively free of negative or violent karma.

In between these two extremes, once again, we find Ambivalent and Cool Mothers who attract children whose samskaras reflect thoughts that are deeply divided about being alive or else deeply reluctant. "It's not safe to be here," "I'll never make it," or "I'm just a burden" have been the typical thoughts in the unconscious of such unborn children when remembered during therapy sessions. With the exception of the Ideal Mother, all three of the other categories—Ambivalent, Cool, Catastrophic—will, alas, unconsciously attract candidates for one or more of the many unpredictable dramas that so often surround pregnancy and birthing.

How exactly, then, do the mother's thoughts and feelings feed into the prenatal consciousness of the fetus? And how are the infant's past life samskaras or old karmic dramas reactivated? To begin with, we will look at these highly complex issues separately, then let the overall picture emerge late in this chapter.

There is now a growing consensus among therapists doing deep experiential work involving prenatal and birth memories that even if the fetal infant has no ego consciousness—i.e., an identity—before or at birth, the unconscious mind of the fetus is very much awake. There seems to be no question that the unborn child is absorbing many of the mother's thoughts and feelings as well as images or surrounding events from the moment of conception onward. As Morris Netherton, who possibly has more data on prenatal memory than any other psychotherapist I know of, puts it, "the unconscious of the child in utero is just like a tape recorder; it picks up everything going on around it freed from the filter of ego discrimination."[5]

What this means psychologically is that in the absence of an ego to discriminate, the child cannot distinguish between its own feelings or ideas and those of its mother. So when, for example, the mother thinks "I'm going to have to do this all alone" (when the father is away on business or at war, etc.) the fetus records this thought in the unconscious, where it may activate a potential life script: "I have to do everything alone."

Not just single thoughts, but whole scenes between mother, father, doctor, and others are likewise imprinted in the unconscious of the fetus with the effect of reestablishing patterns that are later often to become debilitating complexes. A woman whose husband drunkenly abuses her during pregnancy may think or say: "He's disgusting. Why doesn't he leave me alone? I hate sex like this." This leaves a residue for later confusion and disgust around sexuality in the unborn child's unconscious. Two short extracts from my casework will also help illustrate the extraordinary complexity and detail of the emotional imprinting that can take place before and around our birth.

1. Miriam was a young woman I saw in therapy. She had difficulty believing her self-worth and in being able to

commit herself fully in a relationship. She also had fears that her boyfriend would leave her. Here is part of how she relived her birthing:

> *I'm all alone, nobody's touching me. I want to go away from it. I don't like the light. It's too bright . . . A white room . . . People in white . . . They put me aside and leave . . . The man hits me on the backside. He makes me cry. I don't want to be here. I don't want to be alone. I'm here but nobody notices me. No one cares. They just push me away. It makes my stomach hurt. They just use you and put you aside.*
>
> *Now mother's voice: "I don't want them to take you. I've got to hold you. It's only natural. Don't take her away. They shouldn't take her away. It has no meaning just to take her away, like she's something bad." They don't even want me to nurse. I feel ugly and dirty. Nobody nurses, they just manipulate you and put things in you.*
>
> *I feel Mother's pain. Her body's in pain. Now it's a glass bottle. It's ugly. The ugliness is between us.*
>
> *Mother again: "She's apart from me. She's ugly because she doesn't want her bottle, so I want to push her away from me."*
>
> *I feel frustrated. I want Mother to nurse and hold me. I want someone to hold me. I feel cold and far away . . . This is the way it's going to be. I'm always going to be alone. They'll manipulate me and leave me alone.*

It is not hard to see how Miriam was prevented from bonding with her mother both emotionally and physically by the sterile impersonality of the hospital routine. The bright lights, the ritual slap, the cold separate bed, and the denial of breast-feeding all created considerable trauma not just for newborn Miriam but for her mother as well. Drugged and exhausted, torn between the authority of the doctors and her natural impulses, Miriam's mother is left feeling bad and ugly and alienated from her child. In her confusion and pain, her feelings and pain become fused with the baby's so that it is the baby who now feels bad and ugly and doubly alone. No wonder that as an adult Miriam finds herself torn by gnawing doubts about herself as a woman and is deeply distrustful of any loving relationship. One form of the pattern is to be found right here at birth. So part of our work in therapy has to be to help her release the old painful feelings and find new ways to trust in relationship.

2. Janice came into therapy with issues not unlike Miriam's. She too had a poor self-image and difficulty in relationships. In addition, she was particularly bitter about men, whom she saw as always letting her down, leaving her feeling perpetually helpless. As a result, she had come to see her life through a cloud of grudging resentment. She had no idea about the circumstances surrounding her conception, which came as quite a surprise when they were revealed in therapy. The scene that surfaced from her perinatal unconscious was of her mother in a doctor's office. The two are clearly discussing an abortion:

> "I'm not ready for this. The time's not right . . . I've got to rid of it. What am I going to do? I feel so helpless . . . What do I do, doctor? Can you help me?"
>
> The doctor's voice now: "There's nothing you can do. It's too late to do anything, Mrs. Wicker. You'll have to go ahead."
>
> "I don't want to do it, but I'll have to do it. Why do I have to get stuck with this?"

From this brief scene we can see how many of Janice's existential issues in her adult life are mirrored in her mother's rejection of her own pregnancy. Janice's poor self-image can be seen as stemming from her mother's not wanting a child to begin with; Janice's feelings of being helpless and stuck seem to have been imprinted right here in the consulting room; her bitterness about men reflects her mother's resentment at both her husband for getting her pregnant and at the doctor for not helping terminate the pregnancy. Once these deeply entrenched attitudes were made conscious Janice was able to begin to find some detachment from her mother's early feelings and no longer be dominated by them.

The Past Life/Perinatal Interface

Those therapies that focus primarily on birth and prenatal memories—Janov's Primal Therapy, for instance—see pregnancy and birth trauma as the ultimate cause of the patterning of all subsequent neurosis. Stories like Miriam and Janice's confirm this picture for them. The infant in utero is portrayed as a purely passive victim, helplessly taking on all of the mother's ambivalence, fear, or negativity, and even her physical addictions.[6] Even Netherton's metaphor of fetal consciousness as like a tape recorder, if taken out of context, can seem to point in this direction.

But such a picture proves rather simplistic, given all that we know about the other aspects of consciousness encompassed by the lotus wheel model that we are proposing. The buck simply does not stop at the mother's door; the overall picture is far more subtle, particularly in terms of the interface between past life deaths and current life perinatal experience. When Susan remembered how the Dutch painter had hanged himself, it took her swiftly into memories of being born and choking on the umbilical cord (Chapter 5).

Frequently the reverse happens. A birth memory of a difficult labor will lead to the remembering of a past life death trapped or crushed, for example. In Chapter 8 we saw how Yvonne went from a choking memory in childhood to a birth memory of the cord around her neck, and thence to a past life memory of being hanged. The symbolic resonances in the birth trauma seem to call up past life dramas, or vice versa. What this seems to imply—at the risk of belaboring Morris Netherton's tape recorder metaphor—is that the psychic tape is by no means blank, either in utero or at birth. There are already preexistent impressions or samskaras laid down in the infant's unconscious at conception. These can be triggered or reactivated and consequently reinforced unconsciously by certain of the mother's thoughts, actions, and interactions throughout pregnancy and childbirth. Later sessions with both Miriam and Janice revealed past life stories whose themes resonated symbolically, not only with their current emotional patterns, but also very clearly as mirrors of their perinatal dramas.

There were several phrases in Miriam's painful memory of her birth that strongly evoked parallels in past life dramas. One was "It makes my stomach hurt. They just use you and put you aside." This triggered imagery of being a young female slave separated from her parents in the days of the transatlantic slave trade. The slave was used sexually by the sailors and flung aside. Another phrase, "Don't take her away," recalled in Miriam's unconscious the life of a young man in a tribe in Central America whose young wife was captured by Spanish soldiers and dragged off for their pleasure. He was left helpless, hid in the jungle, and was eventually killed in a skirmish with the soldiers, never seeing his loved one again. A third theme, that of ugliness and rejection, produced painful memories of a life as a leper driven out by society. The leper lived and died alone in a desert cave.

In Janice's case, there were also a number of past lives that resonated with words she had absorbed from her mother's frustrating visit to the doctor to discuss a possible abortion. For Janice the phrase "I'm not ready for this" took her into a premature past life death on a battlefield as a young recruit. Then "I've got to get rid of this. I feel so helpless" brought up memories of being a mother during a plague and watching helplessly as her family died one by one. The grudging resentment of her mother's that Janice had so strongly identified with—"there's nothing you can do . . . Why do I have to get stuck with this"—brought up the past life memory of a galley slave who was deeply resentful of his captors and overseers.

At this point let me summarize the quite radical position I have arrived at from observing and working with many stories similar to those of Miriam and Janice, a position that is fully in accord with the work of Netherton and Grof.

As infants, we are all conceived with preexistent psychic dispositions or samskaras that are already laid down in the unconscious. These karmic residues latent in the unconscious are reactivated during pregnancy and birth by certain thoughts, feelings, and events in the mother's experience, aided by whatever cast of characters —father, doctors, nurse, etc.—are involved during this period of time. While workers like Verney and Janov see intrauterine patterning as a powerful first cause of neurosis, past life therapy sees it as already karmicly prefigured which is to say, in past lives.

So, for example, the child whose parents engaged in

drunken fighting during pregnancy most likely will have past life issues concerning violence and possibly alcohol or drug addiction. The male child whose mother broods constantly on having a daughter during pregnancy will have past life problems around his sexual identity. Likewise, the female child who in utero overhears her father making plans for his coming son will often have similar past lives concerned with ambivalence around gender.

The period of gestation from conception to birth is therefore one of the most important in the overall scheme of the formation of personality. Not only is the fetal consciousness an uncritical observer and recorder of all the mother does, thinks, and feels, but it is also engaged in a sort of deep rumination over all the still-unfinished business of other lives. The contents of these ruminations will constitute his or her ongoing karma *post natum.* These two streams of consciousness, unmediated by any discriminatory ego, form the matrix of the personality later to emerge.

For most of the infant's gestation it is more the events in the mother's consciousness and in her life that will trigger past life ruminations, and not the physical events of pregnancy itself—unless there are complications, dietary problems, accidents, or violence, of course. In the last stages of pregnancy, however, beginning with the onset of labor, the fetus begins to experience intense physical sensations in addition to the mother's own reaction to labor and the circumstances of the impending birth. The compression of the last month or so and finally the contractions of oncoming labor have the effect of triggering increasingly more violent past life memories as well as archetypal and visionary experiences in the fetus's consciousness—the level Rank observed.

The most thoroughgoing studies of these highly condensed experiences approaching and through birth itself have been made by Stanislav Grof. He has kept copious records of LSD sessions where they have consistently been observed to occur. He has divided the last phase of pregnancy into four stages, which he has termed Basic Perinatal Matrices (BPMs). Grof's pioneering work, which is elaborated in his book *Realms of the Human Unconscious,* should be consulted for the wealth of detail he brings to bear. However, for the simpler purpose of understanding how these matrices relate to past lives, we can summarize them as follows:

Grof's *BPM1* refers to intrauterine life before birth; mostly these are pleasant memories and even experiences of paradisal or cosmic unity. Grof reports disturbances in the mother's emotional life, too, events that we have seen as triggering past life memories.

BPM2 refers to how labor itself brings on physical and psychological suffering in the infant. Grof notes archetypal images of hell as well as apocalyptic visions of war, concentration camps, and the Inquisition. It is here that his subject's reported visions were found to contain a great deal of past life material relating to physical suffering, torture, deprivation, and disease.

BPM3 describes birth itself, that is, the passage through the birth canal. This stage is an intensification and culmination of the suffering encountered in BPM2. The traumatic process of birth itself, fraught with all the complications we described earlier, brings on visions of bloody sacrifice, death, and rebirth in Grof's findings. It is also more likely to stimulate a cosmic octave to the experience of suffering in the form of visionary identifications with Christ, Dionysus, Job, and other archetypal figures.

Clearly there is huge condensed overlap here between the three transpersonal petals of the lotus wheel: birth, archetypal, and past life.

Finally, *BPM4* describes the decompression following birth and with it feelings of rebirth, deliverance, redemption, and universal love. Grof has also observed crisis memories and umbilical pain. In my work I find a great deal of overlap between past life trauma involving separation and difficulties in infant emotional bonding. Frequently, too, there is a correspondence between past life deaths from starvation and neonate feeding difficulties such as colic or allergic reactions to breast milk. Premature birth, as already noted, usually mirrors an untimely death in a past life.

In my own practice I have found that past life stories behind an infant's in utero experiences (BPM1) are often concerned with abandonment, rejection, or lack of support, issues that are usually mirrored by the mother's ambivalent reaction to her pregnancy, as with Janice earlier. Sometimes these take the form of fears of incompetence, of danger or disease: "I'll never survive"; "I can't do this"; "It'll kill me." Whenever there are marital fights, sexually abusing fathers, or absent fathers these two will resonate with past life themes of violence, abuse, or neglect at the hands of men, which then provide the seeds for later distrust in relationships: "All men do is hurt me then leave me," for instance.

It is, however, reserved for the occasion of the birth itself to stimulate the most momentous and dramatic symbolic resonances from past lives and to evoke shattering archetypal visions of death and rebirth. This undoubtably is why Grof devotes two whole stages (BPM 2 and 3) to the relatively short process of birth itself. Certainly it has been my repeated experience that the most effective therapeutic work is often done around the birth trauma, precisely because it interfaces so precisely with unfinished deaths from previous lives. We have already seen from several examples the huge potential for release and the far-reaching insight that comes from working through the death trauma; more examples will be given in the following chapter. The same is true with the birth trauma but doubly so, since it is a precise and highly condensed reminder of the karmic residues of previous deaths.

Deaths and Entrances: The Case of Chris

Whenever there is severe trauma in the struggle to be born, the form of the trauma commonly proves to be an exact and faithful symbolic mirror of accumulated past life death experiences in all their attendant terror and distress. Most often it is the physical circumstances of labor and delivery that activate past life images of violence. For example, forceps delivery will often evoke a memory of being killed by a blow to the head. Here is a selection of other mirror patterns that emerge from this aspect of the work:

—*Choking* on the mucus mirrors death by drowning, strangling, suffocation, or sometimes live entombment.

—*Hemorrhaging* and *blood transfusion* evokes memories of bloody deaths, or of bleeding to death.

—*Cesarean section* triggers violent death memories of being hacked or cut by swords or knives, child sacrifice, too. "Please don't cut me" may be the mother's words which resonate in the infant's unconscious.

—*Breech birth* recalls painful deaths where limbs have

been pulled or stretched, as in racking and other grim tortures.

—*Prolonged labor* inevitably mirrors traumatic deaths of being trapped or dying slowly, as in avalanches, fallen trees, bombings, etc.: "I can't get out," "I'm stuck," "I'll never make it" are common phrases in these instances.

In addition, extreme changes of temperature at birth can trigger memories of death by burning or by freezing, while the bright lights of the hospital room may evoke the bright sunlight of a desert battlefield. The variations are numerous. Ironically, the mechanization and soulless efficiency of many a modern hospital maternity ward can easily conspire to evoke horrendous images of the death machines of modern warfare: the machine guns, tanks, gas chambers, and air raids. The clinical detachment of many contemporary physicians, the routine separation of neonates from their mothers, or else prolonged periods in incubators or with life-support systems so often call forth from the unconscious old stories of brutality by soldiers, incarceration or torture with ropes, wires, or sharp instruments.

The hospitals are, of course, no more to blame from a karmic perspective than are ambivalent mothers. Each individual drama of birth seems to be an occasion for unresolved past life complexes to be revived in the unconscious of the child. Whether or not, as many psychics assert, we "choose" our parents and our incarnation, there is certainly a huge psychic magnetism that seems to draw the raw karmic stuff of a potential new personality to a womb that will remind it of the work that lies ahead.

Few of my clients had been quite so knocked around by life as a young man named Chris who consulted me. The son of a harsh father and an alcoholic mother, Chris grew

up on a farm, accustomed to fights, abuse, and flying fists.
He was born prematurely. At twelve years old his first
attempt to run away landed him in a reform school and
saw the beginning of a pattern of self-destructive behavior and personal violence. He was always in fights, often
coming out the worst. He frequently found himself in
automobile accidents, either as the cause of them or the
victim. He would often hear of the deaths and accidents of
people close to him. Jailed more than once, he wandered
in and out of a dismal spiral of depression, alcohol, and
suicide attempts. Even marriage seemed dogged by the
shadow of death: his infant son had died early of infant
crib death. He had been through all kinds of therapy,
needless to say.

Chris's underlying emotional litany could hardly be
more wretched: "I'm all alone. I'm a piece of shit. I want
to die."

Starting with the phrase "I'm all alone," I encouraged
him to let it take him to any scene in this or another life
where it struck a cord.

*"I'm all alone. It's cold. She never comes. It's a nurse. She
doesn't care. Nobody wants me . . . Bright lights. Things
attached to me. They don't want me. I don't want to be here. I
wanna die. I WANNA DIE."*

Chris is in an incubator. He has been born three months
early. He seems racked with pain and despair. I instruct
him to go back to just prior to being born. What follows is a
confused stream of consciousness in which his mother's
words commingle with his own thoughts.

*"I'm so scared. So scared. I don't want it. I don't want this
kid. It's too much trouble. I don't want to be here. I don't want
to be inside. I deserve to live. Let me live. It's too much trou-*

ble. I'll hurt myself, then I don't have to have a kid. I'll stab myself. Kill me! I'll drink myself to death."

It's Christmas and snowing. She's on the phone. "Ma, help me! I'm gonna have this baby. I don't want it. God help me, I don't want this child. I can't win, Ma! I'm gonna hurt myself."

She's in the bathroom—with a knife. She's going to hurt herself. She's punching her stomach. "Oh, my heart, it hurts." Now she's falling. "Oh, it hurts!" She's at the bottom of the stairs. "Help me!"

We're in a car. She's half-awake. I'm starting to come out. I don't want to be here. There's blood!

A nurse is talking: "She's losing blood. We've got to hurry. It's coming. Oh, it's so small. It's not going to make it. She's weak, too."

I'm so little. She doesn't do anything. She doesn't care. Now I'm all alone. I'm in this box . . . My belly hurts. I don't want to be here. I don't want to be here.

We go back over this scene several times, piecing it together and disentangling Chris's infant thoughts from his mother's drunken, hateful monologue. Things come to a head for his mother, depressed at being pregnant, around the Christmas of Chris's birth. In the bathroom her thoughts are half of killing herself, half of killing the baby inside her. She beats on her own stomach, with Chris inside, and contemplates cutting herself and him with a knife but doesn't use it. Then, after a desperate phone call to her own mother, she falls down the stairs in a drunken stupor. This fall brings on labor and she is rushed to the hospital, beginning to bleed. Chris is born shortly after, three months short of term, and is hooked up to an incubator and intravenous feeding tubes, where he stays for nearly three months.

First I help him detach as far as possible from his mother's negative and violent thoughts about him. He starts to realize he's always seen himself as "too much trouble," a phrase that echoes through his childhood. But most of all he hears how deeply ingrained in his unconscious is his mother's death wish: "I'll hurt myself. I'll stab myself." All kinds of flashbacks to adolescent falls and devil-may-care flirtations with death start to surface in Chris's consciousness. He has unconsciously been trying to fulfill her abortive and suicidal thoughts for most of his life.

Since so much of Chris's misery is encapsulated in his lonely experience of the incubator, I have him explore some of the phrases that reoccur from this unhappy part of his life.

"I'm all alone. I don't want to be here. I want to die. I'll never get out. I'm sick . . . It's a dungeon. I'm chained to a wall. They've left us. Deserted us. The English, the bloody English! The swine! I'll never get out now. I can't last much longer. I'll never make it. It's so cold. They've forgotten, don't care. I'm dying."

It is apparently a wretched death in Scotland as a prisoner. Beaten, sick with dysentery, and left for dead, he hangs in chains, festering with hatred for his brutal captors. The suffering he remembers in the cold, damp dungeon fuses with that of the unwanted and abandoned baby in the incubator. From one past memory of sickness we pass to another. Now, Chris finds himself as a very sickly adolescent in an Indian tribe in the American Northwest. His father has practically disowned him because he is too weak to be trained as a warrior, while the medicine man proclaims his sickness to be evil.

*"I don't want to be here. I'm too much trouble. I've failed."
The tribe is under siege from white soldiers and food has
dwindled during the winter. His father leaves him out to die
in the tribal burial grounds. As he dies, alone and enfeebled,
his thoughts turn again to his father and his mother: "She
didn't want me. You [Father] didn't want me. I'm no good. I
deserve to die."*

The Indian death scene merges briefly with yet another
death, this time another tribal life but in the Old World.
Now Chris is an old man left out to die in a cave. He is
being eaten by a bear while still half-alive. Again the misery of abandonment, violence, and aloneness.

Is there a karmic origin to all the victimization and
violence in Chris's lives, lives that have been so deeply
mirrored in the perinatal dramas attending his birth? I
urge him in a later session to explore further images of
violence, particularly involving knives. Two more past
lives surface that throw considerable light on the complex.

*"I'm a little boy. It seems to be China. Father works on the
dock. He has no time for me. Mother is a prostitute. She's
cruel. She makes me stand guard while she screws them. I
hate that bitch.*

*" 'Stay away from me.' She's always trying to seduce me,
too. I hate her. I hit her with my fists until she leaves me
alone. What a whore!"*

As Chris's anger boils at the memory, his fists clench
and his knuckles whiten. I direct him to see what else
comes of his anger.

*"I'm thirteen or so now. Stronger. God, I hate her—and
women. I'm not at home. I sleep on the docks. I steal. I'm a
criminal now."*

Shortly a terrible image emerges:

"I'm in this house, robbing this woman. She's pregnant. I kill her with my knife—I cut her heart out—and then her baby. All the time I'm thinking of my mother. Oh, God, the blood! What have I done? I didn't want to do it, but I hated her so much."

The intrauterine memories of his mother with the knife weave in and out of this appalling scenario, and a grim sense of justice slowly begins to dawn upon Chris.

The other past life that seems rooted in his hatred of women, and hence a deeply ingrained karmic sense of guilt, is one of an Eskimo man who is something of an uncontrollable psychopath within his tribe. Unhappily married to a shrewish woman he has come to hate, Chris remembers how he takes to forcing himself sexually on as many women in the tribe as will yield to him. He sees it as revenge on his shrewish wife. Eventually he murders her, and the whole tribe turns upon him. He is staked out in the cold and left to die. Again, a bear comes. This time it is a polar bear that is responsible for his bloody end. But he dies unrepentant. His hatred for women carried over in thoughts of violence and thoughts of vengeance, all of which, it would seem, come back to him lifetime after lifetime only to drag him down once more to experience in utero the mirror of all his past brutality.

Our sessions leave Chris considerably sobered and with much to reflect upon. The pattern of violence has been deeply ingrained in him psychically and there is much work of self-acceptance and self-forgiveness to be done. But what he has been through gives him a whole new context for seeing himself. Now he must choose whether to go on blaming his violent parents—who are only a reflection of his own nature—or take full responsibility for that portion of darkness within himself that he was born to work with.

The Cosmic Loop: The Tibetan Picture of Rebirth

Untangling a story as painfully convoluted as Chris's entails no small degree of alertness on the part of the therapist. Slipping in and out of intrauterine events, adolescent brawls, and past life events can be confusing, to say the least. It would be tempting to fall back on psychiatric labels such as "psychotic episode" or "borderline personality" and thus put the lid firmly back on imagery that disturbs our norms of rational and sane experience. Yet, seen another way, these fragmented stories may be a confused cry for help from the depths of a soul seeking understanding and meaning.

The only way I am able to keep my bearings among the stream of words and images that emerge when the unconscious starts to open up is to remember that the psyche is multidimensional. To remind myself of this, I keep the lotus wheel strongly in focus throughout my work. Whichever aspect we find ourself in—biographical, perinatal, past life, etc.—I try to remember that the psyche is following its own chain of resonances to release feelings and images that will take us closer and closer to the core of the complex. What I do is to help my client ride the difficult rapids until they are past, firm in the knowledge that there are still waters ahead.

Nevertheless, it may be evident to the reader from the experience described in this chapter on birth and the following one on death that there are some very subtle symbolic resonances operating in the interface between the three transpersonal aspects of the psyche: the past life, the archetypal, and the perinatal. Regardless of individual experiences, the very process of psychic transition from death *to* states beyond seems to be full of mirror images of the transition *from* the beyond into the body at birth.

We now know that the agonies prior to past life death very much resemble the agonies prior to birth. Equally, we have observed that the blissful or not so blissful states *after* death have strong resemblances to happy or not-so-happy states after birth. Stanislav Grof has charted many of these resemblances and used them in his scheme of the four Basic Perinatal Matrices. This scheme is extremely helpful as a provisional sorting out of the complexity of psychic experience, but it suffers a bit from being overcompressed. There are far too many things crammed into one perinatal drawer in some instances.

We have referred a number of times to *The Tibetan Book of the Dead,* an extraordinary psychospiritual manual of death and dying that has been available to us in the West for half a century now. From a careful study of this and related commentaries, I have arrived at a simplified version of the Tibetan picture of how birth, death, and the beyond are all related to each other. The Tibetan picture has certain advantages over both Grof's perinatal matrices and my own lotus wheel model in that it is both broader, being grounded in an authentic metaphysic, and more dynamic, being focused very precisely on the process of birth and rebirth itself.

Among the Tibetan Buddhist lamas, for whom everything is ultimately a form of mind or consciousness, there is a special term that they use for altered or intensified states of consciousness, namely, bardo states. *Bardo* means something like an intermediary state or realm, by which is naturally meant a psychic state. What is so helpful for our purposes is that the Tibetans have clearly observed not only one but several bardos which correspond very precisely to the states we are constantly trying to disentangle in perinatal and past life work. Thus there is a bardo for the moment of death, a bardo for the after-death visions, a bardo for the process of seeking rebirth, and a bardo for the intrauterine state leading up to birth. In addition there are bardos for the state of dreaming, meditation, and the moment of supreme enlightenment.

The more I meditated on the original texts, on various commentaries, and on my own experiences with clients, the more a simple but—the metaphor is inescapable—pregnant image presented itself: that of a loop. Here, as I finally elaborated it, is how I have come to envision what in the East is called the Great Wheel of Existence.

I will preface a more detailed explanation of the diagram with one or two general comments. First of all, solid lines indicate incarnate or embodied existence, while broken lines indicate discarnate experience. Second, the horizontal lines indicate conscious lives *in time* while the circular loop indicates a *timeless* state in the unconscious mind which is nevertheless accessible in meditation, therapy, etc. This said, we can now follow the dynamic flow of the diagram according to the numbered sequence.

1. *Death Experience:* The Tibetan lamas lay great emphasis on the last moments of embodied consciousness. As we noted in the previous chapter, consciousness is at the highest degree of intensity at death, with the result that thoughts and feelings that occur in this transition are deeply imprinted on the transmigrating consciousness. In

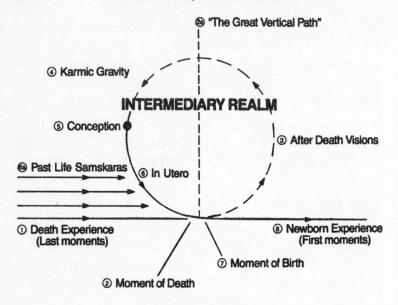

The Loop of Rebirth

Indian terms the samskaras can be strongest at death and the karma created correspondingly great. Attention to the moment of death is thus regarded by the Tibetans as of supreme importance. Naturally a peaceful death is greatly to be desired so that one can consciously let go of all attachments and in so doing incur little or no karma. But as we have seen with the past life work, the opposite frequently occurs. We often die alone or in pain, nursing bitter, despairing, or vengeful thoughts that create the seed kernels of complexes in other lives.

2. *The Moment of Death* is therefore not only one of heightened psychic intensity, but one where heightened consciousness can lead to the release from karmic attachments. When a person dies violently but accepts the justice of his or her life or else bears no grudges or rancor,

then no karma is incurred, no samskara is laid down for future lifetimes. Part of the value of remembering past lives is that the negative thought patterns and feelings that accumulate at death can be brought to consciousness and detached from the samskaric complex, depotentiating it. We saw, for example, how when Edith relived the shocking loss of her limbs as a Russian anarchist she could detach from the dying thought "I'll never use my arms and legs again."

Although I have no examples of it in this book, I will briefly mention that the Tibetans also distinguish an exceptional form of the bardo for the moment of death. This rarely attained level of consciousness is what is called the moment of supreme illumination when not just certain karmas are released, but *all* karma. In a state of enlightenment the dying person not only sees the Clear Light of the Void—which many glimpse only briefly—but is fully absorbed into it. This is called *"The Great Vertical Path"* (2a) and manifestly symbolizes total transcendence of the Wheel of Rebirth for all Buddhists. The Hindu scripture *Svetasvatara Upanishad* describes this conception beautifully:

> This vast universe is a wheel. Upon it are all creatures that are subject to death and rebirth. Round and round it turns, and never stops. It is the Wheel of Brahman. As long as the individual self thinks it is separate from Brahman it revolves upon the wheel. But when through grace of Brahman it realizes its identity with him it revolves upon the wheel no longer. It achieves immortality.[7]

3. *After Death Visions:* This bardo state describes consciousness after it has left the body. There may be brief visions of the Clear Light of the Void but they fade. Other

images then appear, connected in one way or another with the life that has just been lived on earth. In the next chapter I will describe in detail many of the post-mortem experiences that my clients have reported, some painful but mostly pleasant. Figures in white are quite common and would correspond to what the Tibetans call the peaceful deities. These figures review and help explain the karmic lessons of a particular life. Visions of demonic or maleficent figures—for the Tibetans, wrathful deities— are much less common in my experience, but they occasionally appear. One client experienced a vision of Kali, the death goddess, lopping off limbs and drinking blood after a particularly violent life she had just remembered as a soldier.

4. *Karmic Gravity* is my term for what the Tibetans call "the bardo of seeking rebirth." It refers to the psychic magnetism within the karmic complex, that is to say, all the unresolved thoughts and feelings now lodged as a samskara that once more provide the dynamic for seeking expression in human form. The opportunity to work them through on a purely visionary level with spirit guides and/ or the demonic images of one's karma has now passed; now it is time for consciousness to "seek out a womb" as *The Tibetan Book of the Dead* so matter-of-factly puts it.

I have observed that karmic gravity usually operates through the symbolic resonance in the samskaric residues in one way or another. Either the sword wound will lead directly to other lives of physical disability or down into a womb that is about to undergo a cesarean section, for instance. Or else the image of a child that has died painfully in a violent situation will be imprinted on the psyche and lead the rememberer directly into a lifetime where he or she is a child suffering in a similar way.

When we do not follow the symbolic resonances directly into a specific scene in another lifetime but follow the whole process of death and rebirth, it is possible to observe the moment of *Conception* (5) in exactly the way that *The Tibetan Book of the Dead* describes it. One sees one's future parents copulating and there is a sexual attraction to the opposite sex parent—exactly as Freud described it in the Oedipus complex but seen from a slightly different angle.

6. *In Utero* consciousness is wisely accorded a separate bardo state by the Tibetans. From the diagram of the cosmic loop and from what I have described earlier in this chapter we can see why. The timeless intrauterine state is here symbolized as a slow descent into incarnated being. During this state of deep rumination, as the fetus overhears the various thoughts, words, and dramas that belong to the mother's consciousness, *Past Life Samskaras* (6a) begin to be triggered and reactivated.

7. *The Moment of Birth* is the most intense transition from these timeless ruminations of the intrauterine bardo to fully embodied existence. The loop shows how all the unresolved samskaras deriving from unhappy or painful deaths accumulate around the experience of this perilous passage through the birth canal. It is the most psychically concentrated and pivotal experience of the whole cycle—as Grof's studies so brilliantly demonstrate. Here, as in the crisis moments of death, huge karmic residues can be reexperienced and, with help, released.

8. *Newborn Experience:* The life-death struggle is over. The ghastly memories of death reactivated in the birth passage have passed and there is the release and decompression of birth. For many this is a time of heightened consciousness, comparable to the moment of death. Often

there are transcendent moments of loving recognition of mother and father, a deep knowing of why one has returned once more, or simply a god-like state of rapturous being. For others, alas, paradise is soon lost with the obstetrician's whack on the rump, bright lights and silver nitrate in the eyes. The system goes into convulsive shock. Once more an old karmic pattern is reactivated and replayed in the unconscious. It is played out on the fully mechanized stage that modern medicine has generously provided.

But worst of all, there is for many the deep shock of separation. Premature or not, many a crying infant is left for (subjectively) long periods of time in a separate bed far from the mother beneath merciless fluorescent lights. Frequently, these infants will fall into reiterated memories of aloneness, separation, or abandonment. Or, if there are medical complications where surgery or other procedures are urgently indicated, past life memories of infanticide, child sacrifice, or abortion will often be stimulated in all their agonizing intensity in the unconscious of the terrified and disoriented infant.

Much as parents and birth attendants struggle to create ideal conditions for birth, the karmic compulsion of old patterns and traumas seems ever to powerfully reassert itself. A perfectly orchestrated home birth will end up in a desperate race to the hospital, just as a well-planned hospital birth will be scotched by a precipitous labor that happens somewhere well out of reach of the hospital.

These, then, are the various dramas that may, like the good and wicked godmothers of fairy tales, attend any birth. The Tibetan image of the loop of rebirth shows very precisely how we come trailing clouds of misery every bit as much as clouds of glory. For it is thus that we are initiated into the inescapable duality of human existence. No one knew this duality better than William Blake with his poems of innocence and experience. Among them he wrote:

> Man was made for Joy & Woe
> And when this we rightly know
> Thro the World we safely go
> Joy & Woe are woven fine
> A Clothing for the soul divine . . .[8]

CHAPTER 11

THE GREAT WHEEL:
DEATH AND BEYOND

Did he live his life again in every detail of desire,
temptation, and surrender during that supreme moment
of complete knowledge? He cried in a whisper at some
image, at some vision,—he cried out twice, a cry that was
no more than a breath—
  "The horror! The horror!"

                              Joseph Conrad, *The Heart of Darkness*

Thine own consciousness, shining, void and inseparable
from the great body of radiance hath no birth, nor death,
and is the immutable light—Buddha Amitabha.

                              "The *Bardo* of the Moments of Death,"
                              The Tibetan Book of the Dead

Dramas of Death: The Cases of Michael and Burton

"Men fear death as children fear to go into the dark"
wrote Francis Bacon four centuries ago. For all our modern medical advances, assurances by the spiritualists of
"another side" and now even a science of dying,
Thanatology, we are just as afraid of death as Bacon's
sixteenth-century contemporaries. If anything, the abject

failure of materialist science and medicine to conquer this "last enemy" has left modern men and women even more terrified of this awesome power. The "American way of death" as Nancy Mitford called it, is one of sheer denial: corpses are cosmeticized to look as if they are sleeping in the bloom of health; talking of terminal illnesses is more taboo than sex; the act of dying is a secret kept from children and adults alike. Except for the Hospice movement, it is almost impossible to die in a hospital with quiet dignity without being subjected to the intrusive frenzy of medical heroics. Saving life seems much more important than simply giving death its due.

I believe that past life work has enormously important insights to contribute to our understanding of death, especially when seen as a psychological process. Although I have personally sat with only a handful of people through their physical deaths, I feel like a fully fledged Thanatologist from the thousands of past life deaths I have taken my many clients through.

In foregoing chapters we have already observed a number of death scenarios, many of them dramatic, violent, and often tragic. Most past life work in therapy tends to be focused on the more painful memories because they are images or reflections of present suffering—in clinical terms, the pathology—in the life of the person who has sought out therapy. Since the majority of traumatic samskaras are imprinted from scenes of violence or unhappy deaths—battlefields, disease, famine, separation, execution, etc.—a great deal of our work has to do initially with the cleaning or catharsis of these old psychic wounds. The only other category of past life trauma that is nearly as frequent as death is that of abandonment and separation, as we have seen from examples in Chapter 5.

But regardless of whether the death is violent or not, there is always much that can be gained from the experience of transition. During a past life session I will almost without exception take my client to the point of death and beyond, since it brings a sense of completion, detachment, and, often, though by no means always, resolution.

Two examples may give an idea of the variety of transition scenarios that may occur quite spontaneously and how they can be guided toward resolution.

Michael, a man in his thirties who tended to keep his feelings well hidden, remembers a life as a woman in New York City in the early part of this century. Unable to find work in the 1920s, the woman ends up as a high-class prostitute, selling her favors to rich businessmen out of better-class bars. Quite singlemindedly, she hooks a man who falls in love with her, makes her his mistress, and, after he has become divorced, marries her. Being out only for herself, she finally finds that all her material gains count for very little. Here is how Michael reenacts her deathbed scene:

> "I'm quite sick and old now. It is pneumonia. I know I am going to die soon. So do they [the family]. They're all there. My husband, grown children, Fred, Angela, and Minny . . . They don't give a damn. They're just going through the motions. Making nice noises. They can't wait for me to go . . . Oh, my chest, I can't breathe . . . It hurts . . . I'm very weak. I'm going now." Convulsions, coughing, then he goes quite limp on the couch.
>
> "What happened?" I ask.
>
> "I'm not there anymore. I seem to have floated above my body. I'm not in it now, no more breathing. Thank God that's over! My, how they hated me. And I gave them good cause. I manipulated all of them, especially Henry [her husband].

There, Minny's crying, but she was always sentimental. She didn't care about me any more than the rest. Well, I'm leaving now. It's beginning to seem very far away. I'm floating off somewhere else. Oh, my chest hurts."

"Take some deep breaths and just say what seems to be in your chest," I instruct him.

Michael breathes deeply for a while and tears start to well up in his eyes. "Oh, I was so selfish. I did everything just so as I could control them." Begins to sob bitterly. "I thought love could be bought, but it can't. They never loved me because I never loved them. Oh, what a waste, what a waste! All that money, it meant nothing once I had it. Oh, my chest, it hurts!"

"Look back over your whole life"—I am still talking directly to the woman—"and see how your selfishness arose."

"Oh, I see myself as a little girl in a tenement in Brooklyn, playing. Mother was bitter. She never had much after father left. I learned to grab, that you didn't get anything unless you grabbed."

"Do you blame that little girl?" I asked.

"No, I don't blame her. She closed up, like Mother."

"Is there anything you might say to her now, looking back?"

"Yes, don't close up. Life is hard, but you don't have to become hard-hearted." He touches his chest, quite unaware of the body symbol, and a new burst of sobbing starts.

"I want to tell them I'm sorry," he says.

"Good. See your husband and family now. Tell them you are sorry."

"Please forgive me, Fred, Angela, Minny . . . And you, Henry, how I used and bullied you. You were really a dear, simple man. I never thanked you for anything. How can you forgive?"

"Ask them."

"Can you forgive me? . . . They're smiling. They just couldn't get through to me. Yes, they forgive me. They do."

"What happens now?"

"I'm in some kind of simple room. It's not on the earth. I've been sent here. I just have to sit and think about my selfishness. How it's still in me . . . I'm here for a long time before I come back again."

The process reported here is what many past life therapists call the review stage of the past life story. The separation from his past life body that Michael has just experienced is a typical death transition in past life work. Obviously there is no way to verify whether this is a true account of how death is really experienced, but it is so common that I never question it. Instead, I use the state of detachment to help the departing past life personality evaluate him/herself within the context of that life. I take the woman back to her childhood "defeat in life" and have her express the thoughts and feelings unsaid in that life as a whole.

These after death dialogues are a kind of psychodrama created by deliberate intervention on my part. Sometimes an exchange of recriminations will occur and lead to further conflict in yet other past lives. But when, as with this woman, there is genuine remorse, there can also be genuine forgiveness and repentance. Frequently, when karma releases in this way, there is a remission of physical symptoms associated with blocked emotions. Certainly this man's chest had carried a "frozen heart" memory that was here opening and unburdening.

Another poignant example of a physical unburdening that came from reliving a past life death was the case of Winifred. Winifred was a middle-aged woman who had had chronic sinusitis since her early life. During the workshop she relived the lonely death on a battlefield during World War I of a young man who had grown up in London as an orphan. The young man had made friends for the first time in the trenches during the campaign. When he suddenly found himself choking on mustard gas, in the middle of a surprise attack, he realized momentarily, as he lay dying, how much he was about to lose in terms of his newly found friendships. But the gas blocked all the possibility to weep and grieve. When Winifred relived this experience she was able to realize how much grief the young man had never expressed and was at last able to let it go. Almost miraculously, her sinuses unblocked. And when she came back to a later session in the workshop she reported that she had woken up that particular morning for the first time in over twenty years able to breathe through her sinuses.

When the life remembered has been relatively happy and fulfilled, there will be little need for such after death psychodramas. The departing consciousness will usually say things like "It was a good life. I did what I had to do. Maybe I failed here and there, but it was good on the whole." Leonard's life as the Chinese ruler in Chapter 6 is an example of this kind.

Quite different and more difficult to bring to any satisfactory resolution were the past life memories of Burton. Burton was an architect in his thirties struggling to hold a small business together. He came to therapy with a very specific fear of dying. Various somatic symptoms had been troubling him, but the predominant and gnawing anxiety at the back of his mind was: "Life is passing me by. I'm going to die soon." I invited him to explore the anxiety by simply repeating the phrase "I'm going to die soon," with his eyes closed, lying on my couch. Almost immediately the nature of his unconscious conflict emerged with great vividness and anguish. Here he is as a young soldier of sixteen or so, lying mortally wounded on a battlefield during what seemed to be the Napoleonic Wars:

> *"I'm going to die soon. No, I won't let it happen. I've got to keep moving. I have to. I can't stand it. I can't get out of it. I'm gaining control . . . No, I'm not going to die. I can't die. I'm going to hold on. I won't die, I won't! They're trying to move me . . . 'Don't move me! I'm going to fight. Leave me alone! Don't throw me on a heap. Leave me alone!' They're not listening. But I'm staying here. I'm a soldier. I'm terrified. I'm not going to die."*

Burton continues this agonizing half-delirious, half-conscious monologue for some time. The young soldier now is in a state of total denial that he is in fact dying. He apparently lies, left for dead, for many hours before death finally ensues.

> *"I can't move my lower body. It's numb. It's gone. I might be more hurt than I think. That's why they left me. There's no help. I can't die. I mustn't die. I don't know how to die. I don't know how to let go. I know how to fight. It's a good quality. That's why people liked me. I don't want to die. It's harder and harder without a body. There's no pain now. Just numbness in the lower body. I'm angry. I'm much too young to die. There's no angels, no people, nothing . . . I'm leaving now. It's so sad. Such a waste . . . I was so naive, so young."*
>
> *"What's happening now?"* I ask.
>
> *"I'm not in his body. I'm seeing him from the side. He has a white coat. Blond hair. His hip, belly, and guts are all blown away."*
>
> *"What kind of person are you?"*
>
> *"I'm a romantic. A good-natured fellow. I was all for Napo-*

leon, freedom and all that. I had a sister I cared about a lot. It's so sad." He weeps for a while.

"Does any part of your body still hurt?" I ask.

"Yes, my lower back."

"I want you to go back into your body as the young soldier and say what your back is feeling," I instruct him.

"I'm trying to hold my body together. I am angry. It isn't working. I can't hold it together."

"Do you recognize those words in your current life as Burton?" I ask.

"Oh, yes. That's my struggle. I'm always afraid it's all going to fall apart. That I'll fail."

"Be aware that these words belong to the soldier's life. Not yours, now. You can let them go when you are ready," I say to him. Then I give him some affirmations to help release the old negativity he has been carrying symptomatically in his lower body. He repeats as follows:

"I am letting go of that soldier's pain and bitterness. I am letting go of his fear of dying. I am letting go of the need to control. My whole life is ahead of me. I have all the time I need."

The pain lessens and Burton feels greatly relieved, but there is still a lot of work to do. I have him let the unhappy frustrated soldier in him speak out some more so that his full script is clear:

"I'm dead, but I'm sad. It was so unfair. Back there is my sister and mother and friends. They don't know where I am. I could fight forever. I feel cheated. I hate you [to God]. You should have put me together."

All that could be done for the moment was to live with this past life figure now that his pain had been made conscious. It would take Burton some time. I encouraged him to start a journal and write dialogues with this inner figure. This would keep the soldier's bitterness and anxiety that had been dogging Burton in the foreground of consciousness now. Slowly it would start to lessen. As for Burton's deep fear of death, this was completely alleviated by this one session. It was absolutely clear to Burton how he had unconsciously been carrying the young soldier's anxieties from the life of being prematurely cut off into his daily life today. Whole new stores of energy were now available to him after our work.

Dying to Self: The Practice of Non-attachment

Working through the death experiences like those of Michael, Winifred, and Burton, as well as the others cited in this book, has two main therapeutic aims. In the first place, the death experience, traumatic or peaceful, is frequently the locus or the point of accumulation of all the negative thoughts, feelings, and sensations of a particular past life. We work to express, release, and probably reverse these psychic residues in several ways: psychodramatically, or with dialogue, affirmations, or meditation.

Second, when properly handled, the death experience can provide a valuable ritual for psychodramatic healing by virtue of its very archetypal structure. Undergoing a visionary death in all its terror and sublimity creates a psychic event of such intensity that it allows an individual to *consciously* detach from the highly charged impressions or samskaras that have accumulated in that or many lifetimes. We are, in fact, doing something comparable to Patanjali's Yoga. Yogic meditation teaches the practioner to become *non-attached* to the samskaras of the mind, a version of what St. Thomas à Kempis called "dying to self" in his manual of spiritual practice, *The Imitation of Christ.* In more modern psychological jargon, we undergo a kind of cathartic ego death by virtue of our intense identification with the secondary personality or other self that has been dominating our thoughts and behavior unconsciously.

The practice of figurative or symbolic dying to self has an even richer source in the series of manuals for the dying called the *Bardo Thodol* or *The Tibetan Book of the Dead,* which I have mentioned before. These texts, which have reached us from an ancient Tibetan Buddhist tradition, actually concern themselves with the possibility of dying consciously. Although a superficial knowledge of their use might suggest that they are simply ritual texts to be read at a funeral wake, closer examination of the tradition reveals that they are also meditations to be made prior to and in preparation for death. A student learns that by meditating on all aspects of death, both before and after, even though he or she is not actually dying, he or she will be fully prepared to undergo eventual death fully conscious—and possibly he or she will be able to avoid being sucked down by precisely the kind of negative thoughts we have been describing. Stanislav Grof is fond of quoting the saying "He who dies before he dies, does not die when he dies."

All this may sound rather exotic to Western readers unless we take into account a fundamental tenet of Buddhism that might be called *the principle of determining power of thought.* In the seminal text called the *Dhammapada* (loosely translated, *The Way of Truth*) we read in the opening lines:

All that we are is the result of what we have thought: it is founded on our thoughts, it is made up of our thoughts.

If a man speaks or acts with an evil thought, pain follows him as the wheel follows the foot of the ox that draws the carriage . . .

If a man speaks or acts with a pure thought, happiness follows him, like a shadow that never leaves him.[1]

Here in a nutshell is the Buddhist doctrine of karma in its purest psychological form. What the Tibetan masters do in the *Bardo Thodol* texts is to emphasize the supreme importance of this principle at the two major transition points in human existence: birth and death. At these junctures it has been observed, from time immemorial, that there is a heightened intensity of consciousness as the soul of the individual moves from the nontemporal to the temporal and vice versa.

Everyone knows, in popular folklore, the legend of the drowning man whose life supposedly flashes before him in an instant. William Golding's novel *Pincher Martin* exploits this theme. As we saw in the previous chapter, a brief period of heightened consciousness also occurs for the newborn child at the time of birth. When clients relive their births, as did Susan (Chapter 5), they will often become very conscious of a particular thought or realization that comes to mind as they emerge into the physical world. It may be a loving recognition of the mother as an old, good friend, or else—such is karma—a fearful recognition of an old, old enemy. Or else, as in my own case, the depressing thought "I don't want to be here."

The heightened consciousness that occurs at death imprints with exaggerated intensity the dying thoughts, feelings, or sensations on whatever we call the vehicle—soul, spirit, subtle body, or *akasha*—that is transmitted to a future life. Frequently it will be reactivated during the birth trauma. Susan's birth with the umbilical cord around her neck recalled her guilty death from hanging, for instance. But whether this happens or not, the dying state of awareness in a past life will inevitably "fix" the samskara or karmic complex in some form of the transmigrating psyche.

We saw how Helen (Chapter 2) died angry and bitter at the man who jilted her, only to ruminate continually on this theme in her novels today. Gregory (Chapter 4) bore his dying guilt in his genitals. Edith (Chapter 7) carried over into her body the idea that "my limbs will never work again." Michael (above) was tormented by a fear of premature death derived from his battlefield memory. In the last chapter we also saw how complex and devastating the dying thoughts of a rape or torture victim can be when their karmic ramifications are followed into other lives.

Here, in summary, are some examples of karmic imprinting at death that I have encountered from taking my clients through this psychological rite of passage:

—A woman counselor remembers being a little girl who accidentally sets her parents' house on fire in a past life and dies thinking, "It's all my fault. I didn't do enough to save them." This thought makes her overly solicitous in her work today and guilty about all her friends' problems without knowing why.

—A man remembers a World War II life as a pilot bombing Dresden. He is deeply conflicted about dropping the bombs, thinking, "Is this the right thing to do?" He is shot down shortly after. In his current life and career he is plagued with indecision.

—A woman remembers being a particularly cruel male

ruler in the ancient world who delights in having his slaves whipped. He dies thinking, "I don't deserve power." In her current life the woman experienced huge resistance to taking positions of responsibility, despite obvious ability to do so.

—A woman remembers being raised as the honored human sacrificial victim of a South American tribe. "I will become one of the Gods" she thinks as her heart is torn out. In her current difficult life she takes a secret glory in her suffering (similar stories derive from early Christian martyrdom).

—A man is tortured to death as a female (witch) in a medieval life thinking, "It doesn't matter what you say." He is seriously blocked and cynical about expressing himself in this life (many women remember similar stories, too).

—A woman who is chronically depressed remembers a life as a man whose dearly loved wife dies in childbirth. He never recovers from the loss and hangs himself with the thoughts "Nothing seems worth anything. I don't want to be in this life." The depressing thought lodges in the neck and shoulders of this woman and depletes her vitality in this life.

Other very common past life death scenarios that take their karmic toll are: losing parents as a young child ("I've got to do it all alone"), dying from a sudden accident or surprise attack ("It's not safe to go out/be in the world/be alone, etc."), being betrayed by a lover of either sex ("I'll never trust or show my feelings to a man/woman again"), physical accidents or torture ("I don't ever want to be in the body again").

There are, of course, numerous variations on these themes as well as hundreds of other themes to be found in the growing literature of past life therapy. They all confirm abundantly the ancient insights of the Tibetan Yogic masters that the most powerful karma may be either created or relinquished at the very moment of death. As one of the Tibetan sayings puts it:

> In a moment of time, a marked differentiation is created; in a moment of time, Perfect Enlightenment is obtained.[2]

For most people who have not been initiated into meditation or learned to remember their past lives, such moments of enlightened clarity are extremely rare. Because of our ignorance and the reactive fears to which the mind is most prone, the moment of death is much more likely to be one of confusion or panic where "a marked differentiation is created"—which is to say, desiring or choosing some human composition or refuge. Rather than take what *The Tibetan Book of the Dead* calls "the great vertical path" to enlightenment in which individual consciousness is released from the endless cycle of rebirth and is reabsorbed into the divine unity, most of us are drawn once more down to a womb by the compulsive power of karma and particularly the power of thoughts that have again and again crystallized at the final hour. Nevertheless, even if Perfect Enlightenment is rarely within the grasp of those who do remember this transition, there can still be all kinds of freeing from particular karmic complexes using the methods I have described.

Spontaneous After Death Visions

Much of the time when I work with memories of past life transitions through and beyond death I will make active interventions and suggestions to facilitate the process of detachment from karmicly laden thoughts. I have cited the dialogues and meditations used with Michael and Burton. But there are also occasions when clients have had such profound releases during the death transition that a state of lucidity is reached after death where visions of great luminosity and great spiritual beauty spontaneously manifest. It is important to record some of these extraordinary "shewings"—to borrow a word from the medieval mystics—to balance the rather grim picture already painted. But before I do that, there follows a brief survey of what my clients have reported of the after death state both in therapy and from explorations during workshops my wife and I have led.

For the majority of the rememberers the actual moment of death, regardless of their thoughts, is experienced as a great release, a peaceful separation from all the usual as well as the exceptional sufferings and conditions—old age, loneliness, and illness. In about 95 percent of my selected sample the dying personality reports floating above the body and eventually on up, way beyond the earth to some barely definable realm of peace and rest. A small portion of these subjects remember seeing brief visions of light. Of the remaining 5 percent of my cases, about half of them report being reabsorbed peacefully back into the earth and the remainder fall into strange vortices or barely describable dark places. Compared to "hellish" states on earth, classical after death images of hell have been quite rare in my practice, but they do occur. An example of them is given in the following section. It seems likely—and here I am in agreement with Stanislav Grof—that most of the hellish experiences do not occur after death so much as in the perinatal state prior to birth when all the negative samskaras accumulate, as we saw in the previous chapter.

Out of the 95 percent who float upward and the 2.5 percent who are reabsorbed into the earth, the majority—

very roughly 80 percent—quickly find themselves back in another past life or in this incarnation. They either report being immediately inside a womb or in the body of a fairly young child. Often a particular last thought will catapult them directly into an adult drama in this or another life, bypassing childhood altogether. One woman dying with the thought "I was too selfish. I need to care about others" went directly from dying as a fat old Semitic patriarch to finding herself as a nun in a leper colony. I could cite hundreds of such examples.

Of the smaller proportion who are not thus thrust back on earth, there are those who "spontaneously" (as opposed to being directed by me) see non-embodied or "spirit" figures in the intermediary realm above or beyond the earth. These will frequently be the departed companions or family from the life just remembered, often a spouse or lover who died earlier, or an especially beloved child or parent who died when the rememberer was on earth. Encounter with an enemy or enemies that have been killed does happen spontaneously, but not that often. More often some person or persons resembling the old adversaries will be encountered in the next life to be remembered rather than between lives. Many of the smaller proportion will meet old teachers or gurus from the life just lived or known from another one. Some report returning to the same teacher, each of them as different personalities, over a number of lifetimes.

A quite common experience of this nature is one where, after death, the discarnate personality meets some robed figure in white who radiates love and wisdom. Frequently several of these figures come in small groups, a kind of "karmic committee," as I have come to call them affectionately. This group helps review and advise the departed personality about the lessons of the life lived.

One woman reported being taken by such a luminous being to a celestial temple, where she was shown a huge book in which the life she had just remembered and "many more" were clearly written. Another woman was similarly guided by a spirit figure and shown part of a huge tapestry that represented her many interwoven lives. Celestial gardens, mountains, and islands are sometimes glimpsed. I also have several reports on record of clients who remembered lives as tribal Native Americans and who, after death, went to celestial forests strongly recalling the "happy hunting grounds" of legend.

Visions of Jesus will often occur for those who remember devout Christian lives or lives of innocent martyrdom, but they seem as much contingent upon those particular lives as the celestial forests belonging to lives lived in a tribal hunting culture. A special category of after death vision, which has resonances with shamanism, is meeting a sacred animal or bird—bears, wolves, deer, eagles, and hawks have all been reported—and in some cases there is a transformation into these animals in spirit form.

Such visions usually come only after many of the more painful lifetimes have been worked through. They seem to belong to a stage of integration when a large proportion of karma is about to reach resolution. It is for this reason that I am reluctant to direct my clients to find spirit guides or former teachers, or to go to celestial watering holes. It seems to me that such experiences are graces that are freely bestowed by the wisdom of the Greater Self only when and if a person is ready. To go seeking them prematurely reminds me of those eighteenth-century dramatists who rewrote the endings of Shakespeare's bleaker tragedies because they offended their Enlightenment vision of what a perfect world should be like.

A lot of these past life after death experiences resemble the well-known reports of near death experiences collected by Dr. Raymond Moody and by Dr. Kenneth Ring and others.[3] From the testimony of hundreds who have been declared clinically dead and who have afterward been revived we now have similar stories of floating out of the body and above the earth, of celestial lights, of dead relatives and spirit figures in white. About the only major experience reported in such studies that I cannot corroborate is that of feeling propelled through a tunnel, but my private sample of cases cannot be compared to the rigorous research work of these investigators. Even so, the apparent resemblances are striking enough for me to be persuaded personally that these are archetypal or universal experiences of death and transition that are recorded in the collective unconscious of the individual.

Learning from Dying

To conclude this survey of my gleanings from past life experiences of death and transition I want to cite three short examples from transcripts of actual cases in which the rememberer experienced some marked new level of awareness at death. Whether these are what would technically be called religious experiences or more simply moments of expanded understanding of the Self in all its multiple and conflicting forms, I cannot say with certainty. But they are striking as archetypal visions that in one way or another integrate the sublime heights and barbaric depths that go to make up the human comedy—a comedy in which it would seem that we have all played many parts.

1. Madeleine, a young teacher in her thirties, was in a state of near suicidal depression when she sought out past life work. She had been in primal and other therapies for some years and felt stuck to the point of despair in her life and in her therapy. Over the course of several sessions both I and my wife, Jennifer, worked with her and found a series of past lives in which violent deaths, torture, and rape came up one after another. It seemed that she was caught in a circle of karmic hell in which the dominant thought that kept repeating life after life was, "It's all my fault. I am a wicked person and deserve to suffer."

What had occasioned this crippling negative thought? There turned out to be two crucial past life stories, one recent and one very ancient, that lay behind the cycle of despair and punishment. The first one very much resembled the life that Yvonne remembered (Chapter 8), a life as a pirate. Madeleine described in gory detail numerous executions, rapes, and mutilations; here is a sample:

> "We're at sea. We've captured a ship. The first victim is a young officer in uniform. We behead him. His eyes are staring, the body crumbles . . . Now another man. We shoot him in the face. Half his face is gone: there's an eye hanging down . . ."

This bloody life drags on and on with more killing, but unlike Yvonne's pirate life there is no retribution. Too old to go back to sea, the pirate hangs around in bars at port and eventually dies of a fever, alone and destitute in the upper room of a tavern:

> "I am dying slowly. I'm cold. Now I'm hot, sweating . . . I'm no longer there . . . I don't understand where I am . . .

It seems to be a dark mist . . . Oh, help, I'm seeing the faces of the people we killed. They're coming back to haunt me. I see their protruding eyes, the blood; there are so many of them, young and old, it's a kind of hell. I'm a ghost, too. It seems like I have to walk the earth as a ghost for a long, long time. There's no place for me. I am totally alone. No one is aware of me. This is my punishment. It's not on this earth but on some other desolate planet, dark and full of cold mists. I remain here for a long, long time. It seems like an eternity.

"I'm punishing myself. In this dimension a part of me knows that this is what I have to do to atone for what I have done to others and in order to be human again I have to feel what my victims must have felt before they died, desolate, alone, and without hope."

Madeleine continues to traverse this awful psychic wilderness for a long time in this and other sessions and it seems that she recognizes the faces of every man, woman, and child she had brutalized in the pirate's life. It is an extraordinary act of contrition that she seems driven to perform. Eventually an amazing reversal occurs:

"I'm walking from right to left. There's a light ahead of me; it's starting to get warm. I'm stepping onto the grass. There are people and voices ahead of me and I hear an authoritative voice which says: 'Enough, enough. You have done enough.' I know now that my punishment is over."

Very shortly the scene changes again and Madeleine finds herself briefly inside a mother's womb, and she is born as a baby boy. The scenes that follow reveal a simple but fulfilled life in which the boy comes to maturity, works as a carpenter, marries the woman he loves, and experiences great happiness.

"How could I deserve such a good life?" Madeleine asks herself when it is over. To which the voice of wisdom inside her replies, "You must learn through love, not just from suffering."

Madeleine has traversed a state not unlike that known to Buddhist teachings as the after death realm of the *pretas* or hungry ghosts, only for her these ghosts were images of the happy life she had denied in others and in herself. Once she had reowned her capacity for happiness there was no need to endlessly repeat the cycle of self-punishment reflected in both the lives of violence she had remembered previously and this hellish state. She had descended into her own karmic hell and returned ready to embrace life fully and joyfully now. There was other important work to be done to be sure, but this vision was for her the crucial turning point in her past life experiences.

2. Milton was a middle-aged man who had recently separated from his wife not long before he consulted me. At first we worked extensively on lives that mirrored his patterns in relationships. It emerged that in several of these lives he had been betrayed or abandoned by women he loved, leaving him with the thought that "passion needs to be controlled." In searching for the origins of the cycle of abandonment, the opposite picture began to emerge, as it often does with extended work: lives of robbers, soldiers, slave owners, etc., which mirrored a cruel, callous, and abandoning side of Milton, the side that Jung calls the shadow self or selves. Not unlike Madeleine, Milton needed to look at the very darkest impulses in his nature to become reconciled with himself at a deeper level.

The culmination of the series of lives of power and cruelty was one where Milton found himself as a Moroccan bandit leader. His life as this leader consisted almost entirely of raiding, looting, and killing. Here is how he relived a typical scene:

"We're riding on horses, we're starting to cut them down. They're poorly armed. My men behead some of them. I cut down some women. They're herding others into houses and setting them on fire. Now I'm with this woman. I'm raping her. It's wonderful. Now I cut her throat. It makes me feel strong and masterful to have another's life and pleasure at my command." (Such an image of omnipotence is the very obverse of the vulnerability that Milton had felt in earlier lives; the victim has now reversed into persecutor.)

Having lived by the sword, this bandit dies by the sword; he gets a pike in his belly and his throat cut in one misjudged raid. He floats out of his bleeding body, still stirred up by the fury of the battle. But as he goes higher a certain calm takes its place and a spirit figure, some kind of guide, appears to him quite spontaneously (he has not encountered any such figure previously in our past life work). The figure begins to speak:

"You must meditate long on this life, to look at what you have done. You must see the people you have killed, examine the deeds you have done, see if what you have done is good. You will have much time to examine these things—things you have not thought of much in that life, thoughts you had put aside. This task will take as long as you need to perform it."

Milton then described his meditation in the following words:

"I find myself in a great aloneness, alone but not alone. Nothing there, not even a sense of time. It seems to take forever, but somehow no time at all. No new thoughts come, all thoughts are known to me. I become aware of the souls of those I slayed, their presences; all equally strong because all equally important. I feel sorrow for these souls, that I robbed them of their chance to grow further in that life—sorrow for myself that I did not grow close to the spiritual nature I feel about me. But at the same time I feel gladness that I removed these souls from the material realm at the appointed time and that I was thus removed. I feel happiness in the knowledge that those who lived, lived and those who died, died.

"I feel wonder at the glory of it all, at everything. I feel an awareness, almost of the whole universe and still the awareness of myself here. Such peace, such glory! And all creation, material, immaterial, animal, vegetable, and mineral—all this is a manifestation of Truth, Truth as it is. There is nothing else. I am aware that that life was a life of action, a life when I did things without concern for good or evil, but only of pleasure and pain. In that life I had power and used it without regard for right or wrong, or even awareness of right or wrong. I took no more than casual concern for Allah. I was a force in the world as I knew it, but not a thinking force. Yet it was a life I had to go through. In that life I killed, raped, looted, without thought or concern for what I was doing, being an instrument only of the passion of the moment . . ."

In this deeply reflective state, images of other lives come to Milton—a Spanish nobleman who kills for jealousy, a runaway who attained power among the Indians, a woman victimized during the Civil War, a loner cowboy who rejected power—and several more. He is shown a panorama of the entire spectrum of responses to power and passion in these various lives ranging from utter powerlessness to the thoughtless abuse by the bandit. All the

extremes of the karmic complex have been faced in some
sense, and in some sense known only to Milton reowned,
accepted, reconciled. We are both deeply moved and
sobered by this moment. The session ends practically in
silence; further comment by me seems redundant. As I
went home that day in the back of my mind the closing
words of Coleridge's Ancient Mariner returned to me:

> He went like one that hath been stunned,
> And is of sense forlorn:
> A sadder and a wiser man,
> He rose the morrow morn.

3. Sherry was an attractive young woman suffering
from depression and a general sense of poor self-worth. "I
don't want to be here," she said. "It all feels hopeless."
Relationships always seemed to fail for her. She felt
doomed to do it alone. Yet she yearned for some kind of
religious experience that had not been fulfilled either.

Most of the lives that came to her to begin with had
themes of victimization, abandonment, desolation. But
among them there were lives as a monk and then of a nun
that reflected her religious seekings. It was in this context
that the following story of religious awakening emerged
in one of our sessions. Sherry saw herself as a Roman
soldier in Rome at the time when the early Christians
were being persecuted by the official decree of the Emperor Decius:

*"It's the army. You obey orders. If not, you are killed. I'm in
charge of part of the prisons under the Colosseum. Those who
don't worship Caesar are sent here to be killed by the animals
and gladiators. It's very bloody, they kill them all: women,
children, everyone. But they are amazing people. I can't help
being struck by their courage and patience . . .*

"I'm walking through a corridor in a prison. There is a woman singing. I hear a lion roaring in the background. This woman has been set apart for some reason. She is quite beautiful. I ask if she wants to change her mind. She looks at me directly and intently. "Do you want to change your mind?" she says. I ignore this and say that I could help her get out if she wanted to.

"Over the next few days I keep returning to her. Her beauty, her self-possession, her light and calm are affecting more than I realize. Am I falling in love with her? I want to save her, but it's too late. Her calm faith makes me feel that I'm not good enough, that I must be close to damnation. After all I've done, I could never be a Christian.

"I think of moving her to the room of women where the soldiers take their pleasure, but it would only prolong her agony. She says I'm missing the point if I only want to save her for my own peace of mind. One day I'm watching her and it seems she is surrounded by a kind of golden light. It grows and envelops me. Suddenly I am expanded and out of my body. I'm above the Colosseum. For a brief moment I experience the other side of death. I see choirs of departed martyrs like a dome over the arena. It's all over suddenly. I feel I must do something for her so I stay with her until the soldiers come to take her. In those last moments she talks to me about Christ and his love. I don't know what I'm going to do now. I've never felt my heart open before. She talks about forgiving, of the need to forgive myself. I'm awed by her. She's not afraid to die. It's part of her faith in life. I realize I set the scene for her fulfillment.

"They take her away. I stay in her cell and the light around me is there even when she has left. I feel her physical agony in me somehow. I feel enraptured but at the same time a big hole within me. It's as though she's still trying to help me. I hear her voice like a whisper: 'Be at peace.' "

This experience shatters the soldier's life. He manages to relinquish his post in the army and retires to live in a small village by the sea as a farmer. Secretly he is baptized and attends secret meetings with other Christians where they sing, heal, and pray. He lives to old age and dies one night out on the beach under the immensity of the stars. As he leaves the body he reflects:

"I am deeply grateful that my life turned around. I no longer have any issue around power, but now I know I have something to learn about love. The vision of the Colosseum I had earlier returns to me and once more I am above the arena. I see all the martyrs. Not all of them are pure, some of them are caught up in their own bitterness. I feel tangled up among these, since I feel in part responsible. I see a vision of the woman. She tells me to go still higher, into the realm of Christ, where it is clearer, more full of being. She tells me I can't help those from down there. I can only call them up.

"I realize as I reflect that much of that life and of this one has been motivated by self-interest. I must want others to advance for their own sakes, not for mine. It's time to let go of my self-interest. I still feel the grief for this woman: she was a kind of soul mate. She will always be with me."

The figure of this inspiring teacher from Sherry's past life is most certainly a historical image of someone who had a profound influence on her past life self. But such a figure is also impossible to separate from archetypal teacher who dwells within each of us. The beauty of such an experience is that, once conscious, such teachers do stay with us in our dreams, fantasies, and meditations and can be cultivated for their continuing wisdom and love. Sherry now had a resource and an inspiration which was uniquely hers and could always be called upon. And of course she also had within her the powerful soldier who was capable of change. Whoever the woman was in the gory history of the Decian persecutions, her luminous image is now an enduring part of Sherry's psyche. And from the extraordinary after death vision of the souls above the Colosseum, Sherry was left with a symbolic choice of sinking down lower into a bitter form of martyrdom or allowing herself to be drawn further upward into the spiritual power that Christ represents. All this is mediated by the beautiful inner teacher who is an image of her own potential evolution.

Such moments are rare in past life work, yet when they occur they add a humbling sense of the infinite variations and the particularity of how the soul comes to know itself. For every one of the countless ways in which human beings have died there exist countless potential moments for such openings of grace and enlightenment.

CHAPTER 12

BEYOND THERAPY: SOME CONCLUSIONS

The cure for pain is in the pain. Good and bad are mixed. If you don't have both, you don't belong with us.

Jalal Al-Din Rumi, Sufi mystic

That happiness endures which comes from the grinding together of anguish and ecstasy and from the intensity of the grinding.

That knowledge is true which comes from the searching into doubts and beliefs and from the depth of the searching.

Discourse on Vegetable Roots
Anonymous Chinese sage,
Ming Dynasty

The Limitations of Past Life Therapy

It would be easy to make extravagant claims for past life work as the therapy of therapies. I could say that past life therapy rarely fails where other therapies fail, that it brings new insight to physical complaints of all kinds, that it integrates many therapeutic disciplines and offers a humanistic as well as a transpersonal perspective on the psyche.

Such claims would be both exaggerated and false. Past life therapy does not work for everyone. In some cases it simply does not work. I get stuck with some of my clients, as every therapist does. Stuckness—failure—is sometimes a major metaphor in a client's life, and therapy may be just another place to say, "There, I told you so." In some cases past life therapy fails because a person is so deeply identified with a complex that neither in this life nor in any other one do they seem willing to relinquish it. A man who had brutally killed in other lives and who had left his wife in this one when she was dying of cancer was so deeply entrenched in the samskaras of guilt—"I deserve to suffer"—that I could bring him nowhere near the point of forgiveness. He had assumed what Jung called a negative inflation, seeing himself as "the greatest of all evil-doers," and, like the archetypal Wandering Jew, Ahasuerus, felt he deserved to suffer to the end of time.[1]

While it is true that past life work can bring striking relief from certain physical symptoms and illnesses in ways I have described, it would be rash to generalize from the successes of only my own private practice and the self-selected participants at my workshops to some universal claim about psychosomatics. True, I have witnessed some remarkable remissions of chronic physical complaints, but so have many bodyworkers with other orientations. Past life work, with its emphasis on the power of body imagery and the embodied story, can often move symptoms to another level, where resolution occurs, but it is only one avenue of our growing understanding of the psyche-soma continuum.

As for the eclecticism of the past life technique and the broad range of its philosophy, it could be argued that it tries to encompass too much and complicates the picture where other therapies have the elegance of simplicity and one-pointedness. For some, the introduction of Yoga terminology and the metaphysics of reincarnation is off-putting and distasteful. For many, the very idea of past lives is either intellectually bothersome or simply too alien, culturally speaking.

For some of my clients, past life work is too intensive, too overwhelming. They do not need the raw areas of their psyche to be exposed yet again. Instead, for them it is the personal factor in the therapeutic relationship that helps them rebuild their trust and confidence in life. Others find imaging and working inwardly either too difficult or too dissociating. Even if they can remember past lives with ease, some clients do better to reinforce their connections with this life rather than wander further off into another world. Other clients who are able to image other lives comfortably enough often do so rather flatly and with a certain rigidity in their bodies. In their case, I will usually prescribe a course of bodywork or some other kind of experiential work. If the body is not alive and sensitive, the past lives that are reproduced will merely mirror back the emotional and somatic deadness of that client with stories of characters like monks, hermits, outcasts, or others whose lives symbolize detachment, emptiness, and a reluctance to be embodied.

There are two other categories of clients I am wary about working with at the past life level. The first is those with schizophrenic tendencies in whom there is already a tendency for the psyche to become enamored if not totally seduced by the many subpersonalities within. Such clients attempt to turn readily available theories of reincarnation and metaphysics into grists for their own personal philosophical mills. Their wonderfully appealing theories often end up being nothing more than a huge and elaborate defense against the simple fact of being alive and present on this earth.

It does, however, seem highly possible that many of the visions and voices that flood into the psyche of many a schizophrenic are indeed past life fragments. But such a sufferer will always be tempted to *over-identify* with such fragments. A sense of self that in normal individuals we call a strong ego is essential in order to integrate and balance the other selves that people the unconscious. Otherwise there can be no successful *Auseinandersetzung,* or "having it out with" the unconscious. Appealing as past life personalities may be for the schizophrenic, it is the ego that must rule in this life and be the arbiter of present reality.

Since one of the chief symptoms of many schizophrenics has to do with a profound denial of being fully present in this life, i.e., what is often called a poor reality sense, there is often important work to be done around their birth traumas. Their deficient ego sense is often, in my experience, bound up with not having ever been fully born into this world. With the few schizophrenics I have worked with I have encountered enormous resistance to doing birth work. My hunch in this connection is that these clients were still stuck in utero, caught up in a disembodied or partially embodied bardo state or one of Stanislav Grof's Basic Perinatal Matrices. Rudolf Steiner apparently had a similar insight. He thought that schizophrenics—suffering from what was called in his day dementia praecox—were improperly incarnated souls.

The other category of client I have limited success with includes those who are psychologically healthy but who come to me with all kinds of theories about their past lives, possibly derived from Cayce, Seth, Theosophy, or a psychic they have been to. It is not the origin of the client's beliefs that I find myself suspicious of but of a certain obsessiveness in their attachment to these beliefs. The theories or doctrines they subscribe to already have a certain "saving" quality to them and I begin to suspect that I am somehow required to put a nice rubber stamp of approval on what they seem already to know quite clearly.

Unfortunately, any philosophy, theology, or metaphysics can all too easily become an ego defense against the shadow sides of the personality. A little like the schizophrenic, this kind of client is already a little intoxicated by some secret and glamorous fantasies about his or her past lives. It is the ego that seeks to benefit from the process, not the personality as a whole. As we have seen again and again in this book, the past life stories and personalities that emerge from this process are often far from flattering to the ego of the experiencer and produce characters that are rarely illustrious or famous. For such seekers of selective enlightenment I can only reiterate Jung's sobering remark that "we do not become enlightened by imagining figures of light but by making the darkness conscious."

The Uniqueness of Past Life Therapy

As I took some pains to explain earlier, past life therapy, as a rule, does not set out to prove anything. Proof or disproof of reincarnation is strictly the province of parapsychology and research. Nor does past life therapy necessarily subscribe to any religious, spiritualist, or "metaphysical" doctrine about reincarnation. Where I do use terms like karma and samskara from these disciplines

OTHER LIVES, OTHER SELVES

it is simply because, to my mind, they offer better explanations for the psychological phenomena that emerge during a session. I prefer them to existing psychoanalytic terms like "projection," "fantasy," and "suggestion" or the overworked explanatory concept of cryptoamnesia.

Preference for one explanatory hypothesis over another often boils down to *how many* of the phenomena can be explained by it and *how satisfactorily*. I prefer Hindu and Buddhist psychological and metaphysical explanations precisely because of their broader application as concepts, but why I find them more satisfactory than conventional psychological theories could certainly be seen as a matter of personal prejudice. When it comes to metaphysics, one man's cosmic revelation is another man's gobbledygook.

Be this as it may, any concern with explanation must remain secondary to the immediate task of the therapist, which is to help his or her clients to obtain relief from and to understand troublesome symptoms and behavior patterns over which they have no control. The form of past life therapy described in these pages must be judged by its effectiveness in relieving psychological distress. In this sense the way I work with past life stories and personalities and the framework in which I see them are, as I stated earlier, a means to an end, not an end in themselves.

As a means to relieving symptoms, the ability to access past life memories and secondary personalities has a number of advantages over established therapies. One great benefit of working through phobias, separation anxiety, guilt, etc., as past life stories is that the process displaces the conflicts from the stuck places in the rememberer's current life to an entirely new context. By becoming "another person" through the suggestion of the therapist, the ego is relieved of the burden of confronting "real" parents, "real" losses, "real" disabilities, and so on. The psyche is freed by the magical *as if* to produce stories that do not threaten the living ego, which is invited to sit back and watch the drama, as it were.

We have seen, for instance, how child abuse scenarios that resist conventional treatment open up when displaced onto past life traumas. The worst possible catastrophic fears or phobias can be entertained in this process without "real" threat to the ego or the body. Deeply guarded sadistic or masochistic fantasies can also be given far greater freedom for both expression and resolution when experienced as part of past life war, persecution, or torture scenarios. A part of the psyche seems to understand and be comforted by the realization that these terrible or fearful happenings *are both me and not me.* The psyche, then, is able to accept both its own duality and its own multiplicity through this process. It is a less threatening and indirect way of coming to accept the most difficult parts of ourselves.

The obverse of the displacement of our psychological problems onto a past life is the process of reintegrating the past life story back into *this* life. As we have seen, this is done partly by the therapeutic ritual of taking the client through a death experience and then various encounters with and between ego and past life selves. Having totally identified with the imagined "other self," I encourage my client to partially disidentify with this character through the visionary experience of dying. I say "partially" because a major concern is to consciously reown this secondary or past life personality as a part of oneself so as not to be dominated or possessed by it. It is thus a process of discrimination: differentiating various aspects of ourselves and thereby releasing the ego from its thralldom to their unfinished stories and obsessions—the samskaras. The various after death psychodramas I have described provide all kinds of opportunities for release, detachment, reconciliation, or self-forgiveness. In this respect, past life work adds a quite new dimension to more conventional Gestalt therapy or psychodrama.

Another advantage of the past life work within the broader context of the lotus wheel image of the multilevel complex is its high degree of condensation. Stanislav Grof's pioneering work acknowledges, by the very term COEX, a system of *condensed* experience. Not just one but several issues—contemporary, childhood, somatic, past life—may successfully be worked on in only a single two-hour session. Past life work, therefore, tends to be swifter and more concentrated than many therapies, with the one possible exception of psychedelic therapy.

Another reason for the accelerated pace of past life therapy as described in this book is that it is primarily experiential and only secondarily interpretive. Insights into the meaning and interrelationships of several past lives and present problems often come spontaneously from the client's realization and interpretation. This is not to say, however, that I will not direct the person's awareness to obvious parallels or symbolic resonances or make direct interpretations where it seems appropriate. Usually, though, that comes near the end of the reenactment of the life.

One distinctive feature of past life work as proposed in this book is that in practice it is thoroughly holistic. Despite its spiritual-sounding name, past life therapy actually works on all three of the levels—body, mind, and spirit—that constitute the defining feature of a holistic therapy. We have shown in this regard how past life residues of violence, sickness, and deprivation lodge in the tissues of the body, how behind every psychological complex there lies a past life theme and how in the after death state subtle spiritual realizations may occur.

Possibly one of the most striking proposals of past life therapy is the notion of inherited complexes or samskaras. Our rejection of the tabula rasa dogma sets past life therapy radically apart from almost all other therapies except the Jungian. By relocating the traumatic roots of psychological disturbance in previous lifetimes we turn the whole of Freudianism and child psychology on its head. When children's problems are seen to originate from previous lives, these problems can no longer be solely the result of parental abuse, neglect, or absence. Of course this means re-visioning all childhood trauma, especially the actual or imagined sexual abuse of children by adults in a totally new light; that is, as triggering events evoking residual karmic memories rather than as first instances of such happenings. What this amounts to is that every psychological quirk from ticks to colic, from incest to sadism need no longer be blamed simplistically on feeding schedules, hospital incubators, or those universal scapegoats, the parents.

The Three Levels of Past Life Therapy: An Overview

Past life therapy as I practice it is not a "nice" therapy. It is not full of warm fuzzies, cozy sharing, or spiritually uplifting messages from "the other side." It is work, hard work, in which I challenge my clients to face the most difficult parts of themselves, not the easiest. As we saw when we looked at the concept of the self as multiple, the psyche, and especially its past life components, consists essentially of disparate opposites that have to be held together in a difficult tension of coexistence; Dr. Jekyll must somehow live with Mr. Hyde, Othello with Iago. F. Scott Fitzgerald once remarked that the hallmark of genius is to hold two totally opposite ideas in one's mind at the same time and work with them. We could say that the road to self-realization—what Jung called the individuation process—entails holding pairs of radically opposite past lives or subpersonalities in consciousness and reconciling them. This, I believe, is what the anonymous Chinese sage meant when he talked of the enduring happiness which comes only from "the grinding together of anguish and ecstasy and from the intensity of the grinding."

No one has described this process of living with the tension of opposites as well as the great German psychologist and Zen teacher Karlfried Graf von Dürckheim. I had the privilege of meeting him briefly on two occasions when I visited the Black Forest in Germany many years ago at a time when I was learning to meditate. He had known Jung personally and had developed his own extraordinary synthesis of Zen and Western depth psychology. He had also created a unique retreat community which fully honored the psychological, the bodily, and the spiritual levels of being as a living unity. That meeting and his writings have been a constant inspiration to me.

I often recommend Dürckheim's remarkable book *The Way of Transformation*, subtitled "Daily Life as Spiritual Exercise," to my clients in therapy who are starting to meditate. The following passage speaks eloquently about not only meditation practice in the Buddhist tradition but also Jung's psychology of the opposites, which is for me a *sine qua non* of past life therapy.

Only to the extent that man exposes himself over and over again to annihilation can that which is indestructible arise within him. In this lies the dignity of daring. Thus, the aim of practice is not to develop an attitude which allows a man to acquire a state of harmony and peace wherein nothing can ever trouble him. On the contrary, practice should teach him to let himself be assaulted, perturbed, moved, insulted, broken and battered—that is to say, it should enable him to dare to let go his futile hankering after harmony, surcease from pain, and a comfortable life in order that he may discover, in doing battle with the forces that oppose him, that which awaits him beyond the world of opposites. The first necessity is that we should have the courage to face life, and to encounter all that is more perilous in the world. When this is possible, meditation itself becomes the means by which we accept and welcome the demons which arise from the unconscious—a process very different from the practice of concentration on some object as a protection against such forces. Only if we venture repeatedly through zones of annihilation can our contact with Divine Being, which is beyond annihilation, become firm and stable. The more a man learns wholeheartedly to confront the world that threatens him with isolation, the more are the depths of the Ground of Being revealed and the possibilities of new life and Becoming opened.[2]

It has been beyond the scope of this book to describe the much longer process of the integration of many past life personalities and their unfinished business into consciousness. Most of the cases described here have focused on specific problems and issues, which is to say, one or two major complexes but not necessarily the whole personality. In clinical terms, what I have presented is best called short-term, intensive therapy. Long-term work with past lives would resemble much more the traditional Jungian path of individuation, which is a more gradual, reflective, if painful, assimilation of whole series of polarized or split-off or secondary personalities and complexes.

It would require a separate book to describe what such a process would look like, and such books are already beginning to appear.[3] We have mostly seen only excerpts from that process in the cases I have described. Nevertheless, it may be of great value to give a kind of bird's-eye view of the overall development that can occur during a therapy spread over a longer period of time where the contents are mostly drawn from past life recall. For more classical versions of the Jungian individuation process, which relies more upon dream symbolism, the reader is referred to standard accounts by Jung and his followers given in the notes.[4]

What has become increasingly clear as I have studied the broader movement of individuation both in my clients and in my own process is that there are three distinct stages or levels that we may all need to go through. The first level I call *the realistic-cathartic stage;* here we treat the stories and past life personalities *as if* absolutely real. The second level I refer to as *the symbolic-archetypal stage,* when a certain overall detachment begins to occur with specific insights into the metaphorical and often the spiritual meanings of the lives. The third level, rarely attained, I have named *the integral-mystical stage* when a kind of transcendent realization of the meaning of the entire process may begin to occur.

Searching for an image to encapsulate the subtle move-ment between these three levels, I came across a celebrated Zen Buddhist koan, or teaching saying. It reads as follows:

> Before a man studies Zen, to him mountains are mountains and waters are waters. After he gets an insight into the truth of Zen, through the instruction of a good master, mountains are *not* mountains and waters are *not* waters. After this, when he really attains to the abode of rest, mountains are once more mountains and waters are waters.[5]

1. *The Realistic-Cathartic Stage:* "Mountains are mountains and waters are waters."

This is the level at which we may legitimately take all stories literally, as if there were a linear cause-and-effect sequence that operates within and across lives. We treat the complex as absolutely real, the product of a living trauma that is in need of healing and often catharsis. First, the trauma must be brought to consciousness and then, if necessary, allowed to express and release all blocked pain and emotion associated with it. We noted that Jung's maxim "A complex arises where we experience a defeat in life" can easily be extended to encompass a defeat in *any* life. Throughout this book we have seen how a past life complex or samskara arose where there was an area of hurt, of loss, of grief, anger, or bitterness: a parent dies when we are very young; we see our whole family brutally killed; we become crippled; a community, nation, or empire collapses; poverty overtakes us; a spouse or ally betrays us; sickness prevents us from ever working or being productive; we are exiled, imprisoned, or unjustly oppressed; we are disgraced or humiliated publicly; we find we are sterile or impotent; an accident alters our mental capacities; we are persecuted and hounded for our beliefs.

In every case such as these the ego or the past life self

has suffered a deep hurt and more often than not all kinds of emotions have been buried. We build huge defensive walls, rationalizations, whole lifestyles to avoid ever repeating such a situation and, it seems, lifetime after lifetime the same defensive pattern persists in structuring egoic reality.

We saw how in guiding individual sessions it is necessary to take these experiences as completely real—*as if they were literal experiences.* Absolute respect for the psychic reality of the experience is necessary so that this "other life" can be reconstituted and relived in all its fullness. The stance of the therapeutic *as if* provides an attitude of unconditional concern and is the basis for the successful release and expression of the story in all its confusion, pain, or fragmentation. And whatever embroidering, distortion, or unconscious reworking may have occurred, each client's story needs nevertheless to be heard totally without judgment or without interpretation, fully encouraged to be told *as real.*

The young woman who reported severe nightmares remembered monsters peering at her from the darkened room when she was a three-year-old. Her mother had pooh-poohed it all, telling her that she was "imagining things," but the fear and insecurity persisted into adulthood and interfered with her relationships. In our regression we went back to childhood and allowed her to see the monsters again. When she was asked to look more closely, the monsters became fierce dogs, and she found herself in the medieval past life as the child who became the hunting victim of men and hounds. *Once relived as if all the horror and pain were absolutely real,* the phobia and the other related symptoms disappeared.

We also saw how a part of taking the story literally to

begin with also concerns the body: the persistent ache in the neck that emerges as a buried image of a beheading; the sexual blockage that carries a memory of rape or torture; the blocked breathing or asthma that stems from a suffocation memory; the ulcer that derives from the terror of a concentration camp deportation. All such stories speak of the karmic residue of a complex that has become embodied psychosomatically.

Yet powerful as the cathartic release of the emotions buried in the complex's story may be, there are some that resist such treatment. Certain clients do not let go of the trauma. Instead, they seem to relive it over and over again and remain stuck in the circle of their own emotional hell. The opposite pole of the complex, reversal of victim into attacker or slave into master, does not appear in these cases. To dig further into the birth trauma or intrauterine experiences or into even more dramatic or violent past lives sometimes has the opposite effect than that intended and gets the client more and not less entrenched. The realistic-cathartic model now gets us unaccountably stuck. Something is being missed, or else there is a subtle attachment to the old dramas. T. S. Eliot's words may apply here: "We had the experience but missed the meaning."[6]

It is at this point that I start to encourage a more reflective and detached stance in therapy. We may simply practice imaginal dialogues with the past life personalities, rework their stories fictionally, paint, draw, or sculpt or make masks of them; dramatize them or treat them as dream stories. Now the perspective reverses to the second level.

2. *The Symbolic-Archetypal Stage:* "Mountains are *not* mountains and waters are *not* waters."

In the realistic stage we encouraged full identification with the past life self, a complete role reversal for the purpose of inner psychodrama, a relativization of ego identity to favor the shadow selves or disowned parts of ourselves. But now that we fully recognize their power to oppress, depress, possess, and obsess us we must start to free ourselves from their subtle and not-so-subtle thralldom. Instead of saying "I *was* that slavemaster, temple prostitute, tribesman, etc.," we begin to say instead, "I have a slavemaster, temple prostitute, tribesman *within me.*" We move from identification to disidentification—a sorting out of the influencing other selves, an observation of their inner dance so as to spot their moods and tempi. We may now begin to recognize quite clearly certain thoughts and their provenance. "There's never enough time," the old fleeing refugee in us may grumble, or, "I don't want to let him in," a sexually abused child may murmur in the middle of lovemaking. But now that we know each of them better, and their old repeating tapes, we can mentally pull them aside, talk to them, cajole, comfort them, remind them that circumstances have changed now, and even press them into service as Prospero did with the monster Caliban in Shakespeare's *The Tempest.*[7]

This is the stage that Yoga meditation calls the detachment from the samskara and which James Hillman's archetypal psychology calls de-literalizing the complex.[8] We now ask for *meaning* rather than catharsis, for *metaphor* rather than realism. Why are we always stabbed in the *back?* Why have we so often lost our *head?* Why the reiterated theme of losing land, earth, territory? How are we still dominated by thoughts, such as "There's never enough," "No one will ever stop me," "It's always too late"?

As an example of the movement from the first to the second level I cite the case of a middle-aged woman who worked as a psychiatric nurse. She relived the gruesome death of a medieval peasant who had been dispossessed of his land and who had tried to take revenge upon his feudal lord. Having lived for a long while in the woods, he had plotted a nighttime assault on the castle. The attack was foiled by the guards, who captured him and thereupon brutally disemboweled him and flung him to die at the bottom of a disused stairwell. Not surprisingly there was important work to be done cathartically and much emotion held in the lower body was actually released. But then, in the after death state, looking back on the life, we asked the meaning of this brutal death. "I lost my guts when it came to standing up to the tyrant," said the client. Immediately a flood of associations came to her from her life in the hospital where she worked. She had been extremely disgruntled with her medical superiors and was full of complaints that she had not had the "guts" to make directly to them. No doubt the blocked anger she felt toward them and other authority figures had accumulated in her belly area and remembering this trauma released it. But the more important release was at the level of understanding the symbolic nature of the complex: the drama of power and powerlessness, courage and cowardice played out in her guts.

Help in understanding the symbolic meaning of the physical aspects of a complex can sometimes come from surprising sources. In Chapter 4 I briefly described how "the body tells its story too." In it I mentioned the case of Jane, who remembered a pioneer woman's death from a broken back when a horse and trap overturned. She connected the back pain which the memory revived with a mysterious near-fatal kidney disease she had had at twenty-seven in her current life. Most important, she recognized that common to both the past life injury and the contemporary disease was an unresolved conflict between love and independence. At the time I did not understand exactly why her *kidneys* and not just her back should be hurt in the rerun. But later, in discussing the case with my friend Charles Poncé, a psychologist who is an authority on esoteric symbolism of all kinds—astrology, alchemy, Kabbalah, for instance—I learned the answer. Poncé pointed out that in the Chinese medical system (which includes acupuncture) there are subtle energy meridians that connect and replenish the various organs with *T'chi* or life force energy. Furthermore, he said, this system has symbolic names for each organ which point to specific emotional, i.e., psychosomatic, correspondences. The kidneys are known as "the seat of passion"! Clearly Jane's kidneys were carrying and protesting the deeply felt disappointments in love she had incurred, but which she was inclined to bury.

In another case a young man, who was a teacher, had been experiencing an almost paralyzing stage fright whenever he lectured to audiences larger than a small class. A seemingly unrelated body problem was that he had poor circulation in the hands and feet and constant stiff necks. In a past life session he relived a life as an influential wandering teacher in the Middle East who had attracted such large crowds that he and his following had threatened to disrupt the stability of a small caliphate. The caliph had him arrested and then brutally martyred. First his hands and feet were cut off and then he was left crucified overnight on a gibbet, to be beheaded, barely alive, the next morning.

There was an agonizing catharsis that continued for many months during massage sessions whenever his hands, feet, or neck were touched. But sometime later, in processing the death experience more fully, the following remarkable experience occurred: he went above the earth and was met by a loving group of figures in white who, when asked why he had died so horribly, answered like cannon shots:

You lost your hands because you were out of touch with the people.

You lost your feet because you were off the earth.

You lost your head because it was too puffed up with knowledge.

These words struck him so deeply that he spent nearly a year meditating on them. Almost as a sign that his penitence was over, he was offered a job lecturing to large audiences and found that his stage fright had now disappeared. He was also to find, as the circulation in his hands and feet returned, that he had some talent as a healer.

In both cases the breakthrough came in the after death state when the two clients were able to stand outside, detach from the subpersonality or the complex they had each been dramatically reliving, and see it more as a story, a dream reality pregnant with meaning. This is similar to a technique developed by J. L. Moreno in classic psychodrama in which the protagonist appoints substitutes to play himself and all his alter-egos, as well as familiar figures in his life. By standing outside our whole story we can see exactly how we are caught up in the drama of our complex. Psychologically speaking, we are now encouraging, by this use of detached or disincarnate perspective, the development of what certain meditation disciplines call the witness point. Also, in the case of the guides, we allow a "higher" subpersonality to offer wisdom and insight.

Jung's term for the witness point was "the transcendent function" and it is interesting to note that this phenomenon occurs, in his view, at a point where the two polarities of a complex or else a pair of archetypal opposites become reconciled.[9]

In these two cases the past life stories of each person each expressed ways in which their different complexes had become polarized. For the psychiatric nurse the vengeful would-be murderer in her became a mutilated victim; both extremes were present in one life. For the teacher with stage fright the issue of spiritual pride swung to its opposite in an utterly humiliating death, again within the same life.

We have seen how, when a client is encouraged to run a number of lives with instructions simply to "go to another life" after one is completed, the psyche will also spontaneously produce a life that is the seeming mirror image of the one just completed.

Once the client views such pairs for their symbolic meaning (and sometimes there may be more than two polarized), either in the after life review stage or at the end of the session, a major piece of work is done. A shadow figure becomes integrated, a split is healed, a lost part of the soul, like a prodigal son, is redeemed through love and acceptance.

If we are unable to take this witness point outside the diad, there is often a continuing spiral of lives of reaction and counterreaction; more and more brutal soldier lives and more and more victim lives, or else, chains of increasingly spiritual lives (monks, shamans, priests) contrasted with purely material lives (peasants, merchants, beggars) that elude any resolution because the question of their psychic opposites is not confronted. We stay stuck at realistic-cathartic level.

To confront the shadow and sit with the warring opposites in us is not an easy task, in whatever form it comes to us. It is sobering, humiliating, and inevitably requires a kind of death in us, and, as D. H. Lawrence came to see, "long, difficult repentance." Such work is indeed long, hard, and often takes us to the verge of despair and disillusion. Not for nothing did the great Catholic mystic St. John of the Cross coin the term "the dark night of the soul" to describe the slow death and detachment from all our lesser selves. But St. John of the Cross reminds us, too, that "he who knows how to die in all things will have life in all things."

Jung once remarked that work with the darker, disowned parts of the self, which he called the shadow, "is a moral problem that challenges the whole personality."[10] To see that all those people out there whom we particularly dislike, hate, or disapprove of—from our slovenly next-door neighbor all the way to some nationalistic despot—are reflections of our own inner shadow and past life selves takes considerable courage and self-detachment. For many clients who have had the "dignity of daring" to go deeply into past life work, there is often a renewed sense of respect and tolerance for even the harshest of parents, the cruelest of circumstances. We come to see that our samskaras and the unrelenting effect of karmic gravity before birth have drawn us both to these parents and to these wretched beginnings. We need to face and be finished with some old, old story within us that they mirror precisely.

We come to have compassion not just for cruel or neglectful parents or guardians. We must also face the implications of other characters in our unconscious that are quite remote historically speaking, quite removed from our cultured and immensely privileged modern Western ego selves. As well as facing primitive cannibals, torturers, or near-brutes in themselves, some clients have also had to look at memories of lives as cripples, dwarfs, cretins, and more—the freakish side of human nature which is nevertheless full of symbolic reflections of the embodied ugliness or self-loathing that can afflict the soul. Yet even in the cruelest, simplest, and most materially primitive of lives we still stumble upon the same human lessons of forbearance, tolerance, and fidelity that are to be learned in every society from cave dwelling to modern suburb.

For those prepared to sit and meditate on these challenging images of their other selves, there often arises a distinct feeling of solidarity, of empathic identity with other cultures and peoples that suffer in our own day in far-off parts of the world. Knowing that one has within one an African herdsman or a Russian peasant of previous eras, or memories of victimization and massacre by conquistadores, Romans, or earlier, warlike Israelites, leaves one listening to the media reports of the killing of Guatemalan peasants, Palestinians, or South African blacks with more than a pang of echoed sadness. In the famous words of John Donne's great sermon:

> Any man's death diminishes me, because I am involved in Mankind; And therefore never send to know for whom the bell tolls; It tolls for thee.[11]

When deep chords like this begin to reverberate we may be approaching the third stage, that of integral awareness.

3. *The Integral-Mystical Stage:* "Mountains are once again mountains and waters are waters."

In any thoroughgoing meditation on the symbolic meaning of one's present life, one's dreams, or the fragments of past life stories residing within us, glimpses of a greater pattern may often come to us quite unbidden. Such all-encompassing flashes of insight often defy verbal description and logic, which is why mysticism is usually couched in strange, evocative imagery, full of pregnant paradoxes.

At the first level events were literal: real pain, real cancer, real executions. Then they became symbolic: pains in the neck, being cut off from life, feeling crippled, being starved for love, needing to come down to earth, life a perpetual sacrifice, etc. But finally things and events become accepted purely and simply for what they are and we are left to utter words that only we can fully comprehend. "All this is a manifestation of Truth" as my client Milton put it.

This stage can only be hinted at and we are obliged to turn to images and metaphors from the great artists and mystics to understand it. In Mahayana Buddhism, for instance, there is the image of the one who no longer meditates on the manifold contents of his or her own mind because distinctions no longer matter. This is the *bodhisattva,* the enlightened meditator who has gone beyond all the opposites in his/her own nature, and, being indifferent to the play of opposites in the outer world as well, finally returns to the marketplace. The famous ox-herding pictures of Zen tradition show a man potbellied and beaming, "entering the city with bliss-bestowing hands," where he lives in the marketplace among wine-bibbers and butchers.[12]

Visionary artists who attain the unitive level of the mystical vision, like Dante and Shakespeare, return again and again to the metaphor of the drama, the divine comedy, the world as stage, as dream play. The reason why Shakespeare often inserts a play within a play is a visual koan. If we, the audience, are watching actors on the stage who are in turn watching a play (as in *Hamlet*), then perhaps we are ourselves only actors in a play that is being watched by some other consciousness.[13] Seemingly a regress, but not necessarily an infinite one—a regress or return to the I or Eye who in seeing truly sees, the knower who (behind all) truly knows, as the Hindu Upanishads put it over and over again.

Jung once had a profound dream that reflected for him the paradox of the knower and the known. In his dream he was on a hiking trip and came across a little chapel by the wayside. On entering he expected to see the customary image of the Virgin or a crucifix on the altar, but to his astonishment he saw a yogi, in lotus posture, deep in meditation. Jung continues: "When I looked at him more clearly I realized that he had my face. I started in profound fright, and awoke with the thought: 'Aha, so he is the one who is meditating me. He has a dream, and I am it.' I knew that when he awakened I would no longer be."

At the integral level of consciousness all past lives are present to the Self and all roles are known as aspects of the Self. Good and evil roles exist but merely as parts of the greater drama, not as absolutes in themselves. We can no more have a universe without good and evil than without height or depth, as Ananda K. Coomaraswamy once put it. Such are the axes of spiritual and phenomenal reality. They create that dynamic tension of opposites necessary for created reality to become conscious of itself.

To mystical consciousness, all is both one and many, and everything is in its place in the ever-transforming play of creation. We are called upon simply to know and embrace our part of this whole, to know that this part is perfect in and of itself.

A Zen master, Sengstan, put it in these sublime words:

> The Great Way is not difficult for those who have no preferences. When love and hate are both absent everything becomes clear and undisguised. Make the slightest distinction, however, and heaven and earth are set infinitely apart. If you wish to see the truth, then hold no opinions for or against anything. To set up what you like against what you dislike is the disease of the mind.[14]

From such a perspective *there is no reincarnation* because the individual soul that is said to be reborn has no separate reality except as one of the billions of sparks of the Greater Mind. At the hub of the Great Wheel of Existence we would see that the spokes all emanate from the Center. Only at the rim are the spokes seen as separate and in a sequential relation to each other. "Verily," said the great Indian sage Sankara, "there is no transmigrant but the Lord," by which he meant the *atman*, the Self at the heart of all beings and of all Being.

If our moral being and our sense of self as part of the greater whole is challenged by past life work, it is inevitable, too, that we will be left to reflect on such great philosophical and religious issues. After all, this is a practice that produces in almost everyone who undergoes it distinct visions of death and birth and the realms between and beyond.

When the Tibetans wrote down their "books of the dead" they intended them to be used as manuals for meditating on the imagery of dying well before actual physical death occurs. This suggests that it is the images that are the actual key to the process. "He who dies before he dies does not die when he dies" would seem to express the Tibetan belief very precisely. Death must be understood symbolically. Few such traditional practices of the *ars moriendi*, "the art of dying," remain in the West today, though possibly the technique of past life remembering in many ways offers a modern equivalent.

Certainly many clients and even onetime workshop participants have been left with a quite new feeling about death and dying. Whether this "proves" anything about actual death in any scientific sense is impossible to say, but these experiences do touch a profound archetypal sense of "yes, this is how it is" in many people.

Naturally such experiences provoke the great religious questions: What is permanent? Who am I? Does this "I" continue? From the viewpoint of the multiple psyche it would seem to me that only traces of the "I" or ego survive, to become constituents within the unconscious minds of some future personality. It is a very moot point as to whether an *individual* soul survives as a complex personality, as popular metaphysics teaches, or simply *soul*, an unindividuated agglomeration of psychic experiences and samskaras. This "soul mass" may simply break apart after death and be reabsorbed piecemeal into new soul formations as they accumulate around or are drawn toward a newly conceived child.

In trying to picture how the multiple self reincarnates I
often imagine the individual psyche as like a car that has
been built from spare parts at a huge Cosmic Junk Heap.
It may have a Chrysler engine, a Buick chassis, VW
wheels, Saab upholstery, etc., but the overall composition
is a hybrid. Of course the Buick chassis may know what it
was like to have been a complete Buick before it was
broken up and sent to the great Cosmic Junk Heap—and
so may the VW wheels, the Saab upholstery, etc., remember their originals. But in what sense is this new car a
remake of any of the previous individual cars? By analogy,
in what sense am I, as a multiple being, a reincarnation of
all the other lives I remember?

Both Buddhism and Hinduism sidestep this issue
slightly.[15] The Hindu master Sankara maintained that the
Self (or the divine essence) is the only transmigrant, not
the ego self. The Buddha refused to make a definitive
statement on this matter, although asked more than once.
In fact, Buddhism later developed a doctrine of "no-soul"
possibly in reaction to even the idea of the transmigrating
atman. Buddhism, however, does allow for the transmission of karma, as part of the self-reproducing wheel of life,
though not of individual souls carrying it. In the West, by
contrast, occultism, Theosophy, and "metaphysics" have
developed an elaborate picture of the developmental
evolution of the individual soul. In the light of these conflicting views, the reader will have to decide for him- or
herself, but hopefully he or she will do so based upon
personal experiences rather than hearsay or dogma.

Envoi: No Man Is an Island

> These are only hints and guesses,
> Hints followed by guesses; and the rest
> Is prayer, observance, discipline, thought and action.
>   T. S. Eliot, "The Dry Salvages"

When I look back over the many case notes that have been accumulating in the files of my wife and partner, Jennifer, and I, from workshops or private therapy sessions for nearly a decade, I am staggered by the sheer range of human experience and pathos that those we have been privileged to witness have worked through. From the harrowing tragic last moments of a child going to a Nazi gas chamber or a prostitute's remorse at murdering her unwanted baby to the passionate oratory of a Roman senator trying to dissuade the Senate from war, or the quiet mysticism of a shaman's initiatory communion with the animal spirits around him, we have found ourselves challenged at all levels of our being to find a compassionate human response to each of them. Some of the stories are too shameful and grueling even for print, some are visions too intimate in their spiritual nuance to make public; for those it is enough that they have been told.

Increasingly I am left with a humbling respect for the inexhaustible dignity of the human spirit in its capacity to become ennobled by harsh circumstances and suffering. In most cases the soul, or whatever it is that is passed on, really does seem to mature over many lifetimes. I find Shakespeare's famous lines in one of his greatest plays, *King Lear*, take on an even more profound meaning:

Men must endure
Their going hence, even as their coming hither:
Ripeness is all.

In the light of this richly varied array of human experience, the question of whether reincarnation is proved by all or any of this seems to me somehow irrelevant. At best, the question strikes me as an intellectual defence against daring to search more deeply into one's own soul for what we have in common with all humanity. A Roman moralist, Terence, tried to say it in the aphorism, "Homo sum; humani nihil a me alienum puto": "I am a man; nothing human do I regard alien to me."

In a world where we are constantly being taught by our leaders to think of the Russians as epitomes of evil, where we fear to walk the streets or share our clubs with those of other creeds and different-colored skins, simply to know that we are connected with the whole of humanity by the memories we carry in our own unconscious minds is immensely sobering—and surely challenging. If we are indeed to work for one world, one planet, we must first accept that we are one people and let go of the absurd prejudices and superior attitudes that have divided us for so long. A change is needed if, in the theologian Dietrich Bonhoeffer's words, "mankind is to come of age." Perhaps, in its small, yet quite radical way, the practice of remembering our past lives may help us make that much needed transition. If what has gone before brings us closer to each other and the commonality of our shared struggles, this book will have more than succeeded.

EPILOGUE

Follow poet, follow right
To the bottom of the night.
With your unconstraining voice
Still persuade us to rejoice:

With the farming of a verse
Make a vineyard of the curse,
Sing of human unsuccess
In a rapture of distress;

In the deserts of the heart
Let the healing fountain start,
In the prison of his days
Teach the free man how to praise.

W. H. Auden, "In Memory of W. B. Yeats"

. . . Now I want
Spirits to enforce, art to enchant;
And my ending is despair,
Unless I be relieved by prayer,
Which pierces so that it assaults
Mercy itself and frees all faults.
As you from crimes would pardon'd be,
Let your indulgence set me free.

Prospero's farewell,
Shakespeare, *The Tempest*

APPENDIX 1

The Legacy of Depth Psychology

"The dwarf sees farther than the giant when he has the giant's shoulders to mount on" wrote the poet Coleridge. What Coleridge says about poets applies equally to psychotherapists. Any therapist practicing today draws upon an extraordinarily rich tradition of exploration and research into the human psyche and the soul. We are all indebted more than we realize to the giants of the past: William James, Freud, Jung, Adler, Reich, Moreno—to name only the best known. Obviously it is beyond the scope of this book to summarize their various contributions, but it will be valuable to mention briefly how some of their major insights inform past life therapy.

Depth psychology is usually defined as the study of unconscious processes in the psyche. Contrary to a popular story that Freud "discovered" the unconscious somewhat around 1900, there had already been a huge amount of clinical investigation into the unconscious mind using hypnosis throughout the nineteenth century. During that time major research into multiple personality, somnambulism, personality dissociation (or splitting), and hysteria took place. Furthermore, it is not generally realized that the acutal term *unconscious mind* was already in common use among European philosophers by the 1850s.[1]

Arguably, the true founder of modern psychotherapy was Franz Anton Mesmer (1734–1815), whom we met

briefly in Chapter 3. As well as discovering, with the help
of his close associate, the Marquis de Puységur, the therapeutic use of trance states or hypnotic sleep in healing,
Mesmer also proposed the existence of a universal magnetic fluid which, when blocked, leads to sickness or the
loss of psychic vitality. This idea was further elaborated a
century later by Freud in his theory of the libido or
psychic energy, which when repressed or unconsciously
held back leads to neurosis and depression. Mesmer and
his associates also observed that as part of his "magnetic
cure" the patient may need to go through some kind of
healing crisis, by bringing to a head dammed-up emotions
and thoughts. By the late nineteenth century this was
widely accepted in hypnotic treatment and known as the
cathartic method (in Greek *katharsis* means purgation or
purification). Freud later talked of the abreaction or emotional release that occurs when buried affects come to the
surface.

A more recent and highly effective form of cathartic
method was practiced after World War II by psychiatrists
seeking to alleviate shell shock. With the help of sodium
pentothal (the "truth drug") and hypnosis, severely shell-
shocked soldiers were regressed to the particular battlefield horror that had left them so emotionally scarred.
Once it was fully relived in all its pain and terror, the
symptoms would usually disappear. Today, shell-shocked
veterans of Korea and Vietnam are still treated in this
fashion with comparable success.

Provoking catharsis by bringing inner psychic conflicts
to a head was also practiced in a somewhat different way
by J. L. Moreno earlier this century. He had his patients
reenact unresolved emotionally laden situations by
shared role playing or by what he called psychodrama,

still a powerful tool in any therapist's repertoire and a crucial metaphor for past life work.[2]

Even if Freud did not discover the unconscious mind, it was his observations about the dynamic interaction between conscious and unconscious processes that made him such a key figure in the development of psychotherapy. By seeing neurosis as the outcome of the denial or the repression of huge underground currents in an individual's emotional and instinctual life, Freud turned the focus away from a tendency to idealize the rational mind and instead initiated the first intensive study of the energetic principles of the unconscious itself.

First of all, Freud developed free association as a precise method for capturing the ways in which the contents of the unconscious are perpetually seeping into conscious awareness. Eventually he came to realize that when "primitive" instincts and emotional impulses—desire, rage, lust, revenge, etc.—are denied access to the "civilized" conscious mind, they do not disappear but continue to live out an entirely independent psychic existence in the unconscious. There they drain away energy from the conscious system, causing depression, anxiety neurosis, phobias, etc., or else they erupt as physical symptoms, irrational moods, or slips of the tongue.

Freud first observed the residues of these unfinished emotional patterns in dreams, where they expressed themselves in fantastic but meaningful dramas. Jung arrived independently at very similar conclusions from his clinical study of the association experiment. (Most people are now familiar with this test in which any unusual lapse of time in responding to certain commonplace words from a long list was found to indicate an emotional association to the word in question.) Jung was the first to call the kernels of these emotional situations, which are full of disruptive and unresolved emotional energy, feeling-toned complexes, stressing, too, that they lead a powerful, autonomous life in the unconscious mind.[3] Both Freud and Jung concurred on this fundamental picture of the human psyche: *that each of us carries within us a whole other world, shadowy and fantastic, to be sure, but teemingly alive with inner figures, melodramas, grievances and fears, that are constantly exerting their influence over our every word and deed.*[4]

Freud and Jung later parted company on two major issues of Freud's theory: the predominance of sexuality and of childhood in the origin of neurosis. It is the Freudian perspective, the emotional triangle between the child and his or her parents (the Oedipus complex), that has become a cornerstone of our psychological thinking. Nowadays, it is almost a cliché to search for the cause of a present psychological disturbance in early childhood. Not just Freud but psychotherapists who specialize in the use of hypnosis have also tended in this direction, using the technique of age regression to return to an earlier traumatic event in the past, whether imagined or real. Of course, regression to traumatic events was also commonly practiced by nineteenth-century clinicians who pioneered the use of hypnosis—Liébeault, Charcot, Janet, for instance—but it was Freud who claimed to have uncovered the highly complex inner life of the child.

Skeptical of Freud's picture of childhood, Jung raised the still highly controversial question of whether the complex did not also have an innate core to it in the form of an inherited disposition. Jung came to see the Oedipal drama of jealousy, possessiveness, and lust as not about the real parents, but instead as an inner drama that all mankind carries, not a personal but a universal or archetypal story. As he put it:

> In reality the whole drama takes place in the individual's own psyche, where the "parents" are not the parents at all but only their imagos: they are representations which have arisen from the conjunction of parental peculiarities with the individual disposition of the child.[5]

Freud himself, contrary to attempts by later followers to drive a wedge between the two schools, also arrived at strikingly similar conclusions:

> It seems to me quite possible that all things told us today in analysis as fantasy were once real occurrences in the primeval times of the human family.[6]

If anything, the major differences between the two schools is not so much about the literal origins of complexes but which complexes are primary. Freud and his successors wanted to boil everything down to parental complexes, while Jung argued for a far wider range of complexes at the root of psychic disturbances. When the unconscious is examined, Jung discovered, we find not just the images of parent and child, but also heroes, tyrants, slaves, queens, merchants, charlatans, seductresses, scapegoats, priests, generals, lords, peasants, and so on. Each of the figures is a personified complex that inhabits the inner melodramas of our dreams and fantasies and invests them with every bit as much energy as memories of our personal mother or father.

What Jung observed was that the dramatic scenarios that our complexes stage in the unconscious mind strongly resemble not just Oedipus but many of the universal stories known to mankind in myths, legends, folktales, and literature. One man may feel inwardly pursued by devastating guilt, as Orestes, the Greek hero, was pursued by the Furies. T. S. Eliot's play *The Family Reunion* uses this archetype. Another may have to go on an archetypal hero quest to prove his manhood. Reluctant heroes from Hamlet to Dustin Hoffman's *Marathon Man* have enacted this mythic theme often enough. A woman whose daughter leaves home for an unknown man may experience the rage and grief of the Greek goddess Demeter when Hades abducted her daughter Persephone. Another woman's life may be entirely given to amorous adventures with powerful men, thus enacting stories of the love goddess, Aphrodite/Venus.

Ultimately, then, Jung was to regard the neurosis of modern men and women as a kind of punishment for failing to honor these greater powers that dominate our lives from the unconscious. "The gods," he once said, "have become diseases." Only by uncovering the archetypal patterns behind our personal stories can we, to some extent, be freed from the fateful compulsion of "the gods." The poet Keats wrote that "the life of man, if properly understood, is a continual allegory." It is this understanding that is sought by Jungian psychology today and by its highly creative offspring, the archetypal psychology of James Hillman. Hillman believes that only a psychology which is founded upon an understanding of how archetypal images inform *all* cultural and creative activity— arts, science, religion, politics, philosophy—can do justice to the multiple realities we call "soul." For Hillman the true aim of psychology is, with Keats, one of "soul-making."[7]

APPENDIX 2

Did Jung Believe in Reincarnation?

In the years between 1920 and 1940 Jung immersed himself in many classic Indian, Chinese, and Buddhist texts on
Yoga and meditation. Tentatively he began to introduce
some of the concepts from these writings into his matur-
ing vision of a psychology that would eventually encompass both the personal and the transpersonal levels of the
psyche. Most notable is his proposal of the archetype of
the Self, the transcendent image of the divine that lives
within everyone. The introduction of this term was inspired by the Hindu concept of the *atman*, translated
variously as the "eternal Self," the "Higher Self," or the
"Oversoul" by other writers. The concept of the Self is
first elaborated in Jung's work *Psychological Types* (1921).

From 1932 to 1940 Jung gave regular seminars at the
Zürich Federal Polytechnic (Eidgenössische Technische
Hochschule). In 1933, as well as elaborating on his own
psychological ideas, Jung lectured on Kundalini Yoga and
later, in 1938–39, he discussed a number of Eastern texts,
including the *Yoga Sutras of Patanjali*, generally considered the written foundation of all Yogic teaching. These
lectures contain many of his reflections on karma, the
klesas, and the samskaras, as well as the difficulties of
translating these alien terms into Western equivalents. In
the first of the Kundalini lectures Jung is reported to have
said:

The mind in a child . . . is by no means a *tabula rasa*. There is a rich world of archetypal images in the unconscious mind and the archetypes are conditions, laws or categories of creative fantasy, and therefore might be called the psychological equivalent of the samskara.[1]

He added that he thought the Eastern mind would perceive this doctrine quite differently and left it at that. His caution was repeated in his commentary on *The Tibetan Book of the Dead*, referred to several times in this book:

We may cautiously accept the idea of *karma* only if we understand it as *psychic heredity* in the very widest sense of the word. Psychic heredity does exist—that is to say, there is inheritance of psychic characteristics such as predisposition to disease, traits of character, special gifts, and so on.[2]

Despite these extremely close rapprochements between Jung's theory of archetypes and Yoga's conception of samskaras, the bridge between an Eastern and a Western psychology was never quite built. Jung continued to insist that the archetypes had no content, that they were formative principles only, dry riverbeds with no river. His was a theory of samskaras without the vasanas and klesas, which is to say, without specific memory traces. As he put it in the same commentary;

So far as I know, there is no inheritance of individual prenatal or pre-uterine memories, but there are undoubtedly inherited archetypes which are, however, devoid of content, because, to begin with, they contain no personal experiences.[3]

By 1942 Jung had modified his position somewhat, recognizing what he called "a karmic factor" within an archetype and stating that it expresses itself in mythological images:

We mentioned earlier that the unconscious contains, as it were, two layers: the personal and the collective. The personal layer ends at the earliest memories of infancy, but the collective layer comprises the pre-infantile period, that is, the residues of ancestral life. Whereas the memory-images of the personal unconscious are, as it were, filled out, because they are images personally experienced by the individual, the archetypes of the collective unconscious are not filled out because they are forms not personally experienced. When, on the other hand, psychic energy regresses, going beyond even the period of early infancy, and breaks into the legacy of ancestral life, the mythological images are awakened: these are the archetypes. An interior spiritual world whose existence we never suspected opens out and displays contents which seem to stand in sharpest contrast to all our former ideas.[4]

In what seems to have been an afterthought, Jung writes in a footnote to this passage:

The reader will note the admixture here of a new element in the idea of the archetypes, not previously mentioned. This admixture is not a piece of unintentional obscurantism, but a deliberate extension of the archetype by means of the *karmic* factor, which is so very important in Indian philosophy. The *karma* aspect is essential to a deeper understanding of the nature of an archetype.

Nevertheless, there still remains a big difference between past life memories and archetypal or mythological images. Nor does Jung ever explain how this "karmic factor" in an archetype operates.

Jung does not seem to have accepted actual past life memories until the last decade of his life. Even then his statements were extremely cautious. A colleague whom he had trained, Erlo van Waveren, brought him a series of dreams interwoven with clear past life memories. During their sessions, Jung apparently opened up a lot to Van Waveren about his own experience. As Van Waveren reports it:

> In our conversation, he was as open, frank, and revelatory as he would ever be with me. Our discussion then was at such an intimate level that the next day he requested Mrs. Jung to speak to me at the Jung Institute and tell me not to talk to anyone about our conversation. In our Western world, Eastern concepts are often sooner accepted when presented in a more or less scientific light. Professor Jung was a past master at that. Whenever he spoke to me about an incarnation, it was referred to as an ancestor; "ancestral components," "psychic ancestors," "ancestral souls" are all expressions which Professor Jung used to express the idea of metamorphosis . . .[5]

Jung's scientific reserve is also to be found in his posthumously published autobiography, *Memories, Dreams, Reflections,* dictated shortly before his death in 1961. In it he writes that he personally had come across no empirical evidence of personal rebirth, but then he adds:

> Recently, however, I observed in myself a series of dreams which would seem to describe the process of reincarnation in a deceased person of my acquaintance. But I have never come across any such dreams in other persons, and therefore have no basis for comparison. Since this observation is subjective and unique, I prefer only to mention its existence and not to go into it any further. I must confess, however, that after this experience I view the problem of reincarnation with somewhat different eyes, though without being in a position to assert a definite opinion.[6]

This, then, is the final evidence of Jung's memoirs. But is it? It is well known in Jungian circles that large segments of *Memories, Dreams, Reflections* were excised by members of his family as being embarrassing to the family name; every single reference to his close collaborator Toni Wolff was removed before publication, for example.

Was Jung's growing belief in reincarnation also embarrassing in some way? Apparently it was, according to a colleague of mine. This colleague visited Zürich recently and called upon one of Jung's daughters in order to interview her specifically about Jung's past life beliefs. She told him that her father had written quite a lot about the subject in his autobiography, but that it had all been changed by his Zürich editors.

"How do you know?" my colleague asked.

In answer to his question she led him into another room and showed him a glass case containing the manuscript of *Memories, Dreams, Reflections*. She then proceeded to show him where certain words and passages had been altered by the editors to tone down the specific reincarnational content. Apparently Jung's family and editors had put pressure on Jung to make these changes out of some fear that he might appear senile to the public.

What of Jung's own past life experiences? Again, there is no clear published evidence, but I am led to wonder if the famous Personality No. 2 he writes of in his memoirs is not a past life fragment. Here is how Jung described his authoritative second self, which emerged when he was twelve years old:

> . . . to my intense confusion, it occurred to me that I was actually two different persons. One of them was the school-boy who could not grasp algebra and was far from sure of himself; the other was important, a high authority, a man not to be trifled with . . . an old man who lived in the eigh-

teenth century, wore buckled shoes and a white wig and went driving in a fly with high, concave rear wheels between which the box was suspended on springs and leather straps.[7]

The boy Jung had actually seen such an antique carriage from the Black Forest once and the sight of it had aroused in him the thought "That's it! Sure enough, that comes from *my* times." It sounds as though seeing the carriage triggered an eighteenth-century memory fragment in Jung. Interestingly, in a crucial dream of a multistoried house that Jung had in adulthood (which also contains the seed of the idea of the historical layers of the collective unconscious)[8] the upper story was "a kind of salon furnished with fine old pieces in rococco style." This could easily describe an eighteenth-century house. The lower story dates from the fifteenth/sixteenth century in the dream.

If there is a single eighteenth-century personality who came close to obsessing Jung it was Goethe. The parallels between Jung's and Goethe's interests are not hard to see. Both were scientists and visionaries, both immersed themselves in alchemy, the problem of evil, and the eternal feminine; the contents of parts I and II of *Faust* parallel exactly Jung's personal and archetypal levels of the unconscious.

Naturally Jung was absorbed in reading Goethe as a child. But could Jung also have had a past life personality fragment of the deceased Goethe in him? There is no way of knowing, of course, but there was a family story that Jung's grandfather may have been one of Goethe's "natural," i.e. illegitimate, offspring.[9]

And if Jung had part of Goethe in him from the eighteenth century, what did he have from the fifteenth/sixteenth-century layer of his psyche referred to in his dream? I would suspect a fragment of the great Swiss alchemist and healer Paracelsus.

I had always kept such highly speculative thoughts to myself, but several years ago I was fortunate to meet with Erlo van Waveren himself and learned that he too had arrived independently at similar conclusions regarding Goethe and Paracelsus.

Could it be that larger personalities like Jung whom we honor with the term "genius" are able to reabsorb and pass on the psychically inherited remnants of certain creative spirits from previous ages? This would explain not only the extraordinary breadth of vision that belongs to a genius such as Jung's but also the inner torment that he and others like him have suffered in order to remain whole and not go the way of "the divided self"[10] that succumbs to madness. It is not a path that we should necessarily envy, but one whose fruits put us infinitely in the debt of those who have trodden it.

PAST LIFE THERAPY ORGANIZATIONS

The following may be contacted:

1. Association for Past Life Research and Therapy
   (APRT)
   P.O. Box 20151
   Riverside, CA   92516

Offers public conferences, professional training workshops, and publishes a newsletter and the journal *Regression Techniques*.

2. Association for the Alignment of Past Life
   Experience (AAPLE)
   1147 Hacienda Blvd.
   Hacienda Heights, CA   91745

Offers professional training in the Netherton method.

3. Laughing Bear Productions
   5 River Road
   New Paltz, NY   12561

Limited professional training seminars offered by Roger Woolger; also seminars on Jungian psychology and related fields.

GLOSSARY

Active Imagination: the practice devised by C. G. Jung of sitting with a dream image while awake and participating in its further unfolding or development as a waking dream.

Age Regression: see Hypnotic Regression.

Archetypal Psychology: a derivative of Jungian psychology developed by James Hillman which seeks to reveal the archetypes or root metaphors which underlie human culture and to restore the imagination to a central place in psychological theorizing.

Archetype: loosely, a typical image or motif that recurs in fairy tales, myths, and world literature and which is also to be found in the dreams, fantasies, and delusions of individuals (e.g., the hero, the trickster, the witch); more strictly, the formative and structural principle behind any image, idea, event, symptom, etc. (see Jung, *CW*, Vol. 9, Part I).

Catharsis: (Greek: *katharsis* = purgation) the emotional release and unburdening that can occur during psychotherapy (q.v.) of various kinds.

COEX: "a system of condensed experience" (Grof); see Chapter 5 for a full definition.

Collective or Transpersonal Unconscious: "the collective unconscious contains the whole spiritual heritage of mankind's evolution born anew in the brain structure of every individual" (Jung, *CW*, Vol. 8, p. 158); in Jung the contents of the collective unconscious are the archetypes (q.v.).

Complex: "Complexes are psychic fragments which have split off owing to traumatic influences or certain incompatible tendencies" (Jung, *CW*, Vol. 8, p. 121). A complex may take the form of a neurotic complaint or behavior pattern, a physical symptom, or a dream or secondary personality (q.v.).

Depth Psychology: broadly, the psychological movement from Mesmer to Freud and onward that attempts to understand and to work with the unconscious mind; includes psychoanalysis, Jungian analysis, and hypnosis (q.v.).

Gestalt Therapy: a method of psychotherapy (q.v.) developed by Fritz Perls which utilizes one's immediate awareness of emotional, mental, and physical states.

Holistic, Holism: a philosophy commonly associated with alternative healing practices that treats body, mind, and spirit as inseparable parts of the whole person.

Hypnosis, Hypnotism: an artificially induced state of trance, superficially resembling sleep (Greek: *hypnos* = sleep), in which the unconscious mind is open to various kinds of suggestion, including the vivid recall of lost memories. (Different degrees of trance are possible during hypnosis; susceptibility to hypnosis is highly individual.)

Hypnotherapy: a form of psychotherapy (q.v.) that directly or indirectly induces hypnosis (q.v.) in order to gain access to and to alleviate unconscious conflicts and buried traumas.

Hypnotic Regression: the use of hypnosis to enable a person to relive a recent or distant past experience. **Age regression** is the form of hypnosis that induces the reliving of long-past events, usually from childhood or even back to intrauterine states. **Past life regression** resembles age regression in that a "past life" is imagined to be prior to both present and early childhood experience; compare Past Life Recall (q.v.).

Jungian Analysis: a method derived from Freud's psychoanalysis (q.v.) which also uncovers unconscious processes and complexes (q.v.) but which also posits a collective or transpersonal unconscious (q.v.) through which the transformative power of the archetypes (q.v.) may manifest.

Karma: (Sanskrit = deed, action, work) 1. the spiritual law of moral cause and effect by which good or evil acts or thoughts are eventually meted out to the originator in a later incarnation; 2. the actual psychic inheritance, good or bad, accruing from previous deeds in this or another life; 3. destiny or fate.

Klesas: Sanskrit term for wounds or afflictions from a current or past life that give rise to persisting negative thoughts or feelings; part of the samskaras (q.v.).

Mesmerism: the practice and school of psychic healing developed by Franz Anton Mesmer and others, which used trance-inducing passes to obtain states of trance later to be called hypnosis (q.v.).

Parapsychology: a division of research psychology (occasionally repudiated by them) that investigates paranormal phenomena and various psychic claims using empirical, statistical, and experimental methods.

Past Life Complex: see Samskara.

Past Life Recall: the ability to recall past lives either 1. spontaneously; 2. through hypnotic regression (q.v.); or 3. through other forms of induction such as guided imagery or focusing on images, feelings, words, or sensations.

Past Life Regression: see Hypnotic Regression.

Primal Therapy: a method of psychotherapy (q.v.) developed by Arthur Janov, that encourages the strong emotional release of early childhood and birth trauma.

Psychiatry: the branch of medicine concerned with psychological illness, especially psychosis, which regards many such abnormalities as organic in origin and which commonly prefers drug treatment over other forms of psychotherapy.

Psychoanalysis: the method and school of depth psychology (q.v.) established by Sigmund Freud. As a *method* it is a verbal psychotherapy (q.v.) that uncovers unconscious processes, complexes (q.v.), and conflicts. As a *theory* it postulates elaborate structural interelationships between the conscious and the unconscious mind.

Psychodrama: a group psychotherapy (q.v.) devised by J. L. Moreno in which a person's psychological and social problems are dramatized through role-playing, role-reversal, and other devices.

Psychology: traditionally defined as "the science of the mind," but academically more narrowly defined as "the science of behavior"; depth psychology (q.v.) would include the unconscious as well as the conscious mind.

Psychosomatic medicine: an approach that believes certain organic and systemic physical illnesses may be due to psychological stresses or other unconscious conflicts.

Psychotherapy: a very general term covering many kinds of treatment for psychological disturbances; it may refer to verbal therapies (e.g., psychoanalysis, Jungian analysis), experiential and expressive therapies (e.g., psychodrama, Primal, LSD therapy), or body-oriented therapies (e.g., Reichian therapy), as well as behavior therapy and psychiatric drug treatment.

Rebirthing: an intensive breathing therapy devised by Leonard Orr which utilizes hyperventilation to achieve deep catharsis (q.v.) of emotional and somatic blocks, particularly the birth trauma.

Samskara: Sanskrit term for the dispositions, propensities, or "tendencies to act according to certain patterns established by reactions in the past" (Zimmer). In Yoga theory a samskara can carry over from lifetime to lifetime; it may therefore be regarded as a past life complex (see Chapter 6).

Secondary Personality, Subpersonality (also Personality Fragment, Split-Off Personality): all synonyms for the personality formations other than the ego-self, which live an autonomous existence in the unconscious mind and which are accessible in our dreams, fantasy, active imagination (q.v.), guided imagery, or hypnosis (q.v.).

Shamanism: a form of spiritualistic healing involving trance communication with spirits and with other realities; more commonly practiced in tribal and non-Western cultures; the term can equally refer to witch doctors, medicine men and women, and other tribal healers.

Symbolic Resonance: the symbolic or metaphorical associations made by the unconscious mind that link together the different thoughts, images, feelings, and sensations that make up a complex (q.v.; see also Chapter 5).

Theosophy: the spiritual and metaphysical teachings that derive from the mediumistic writings of Madame H. P. Blavatsky, co-founder of the Theosophical Society (see Chapter 3).

Transpersonal Psychology: a general term for a number of psychological theories and practices that have in common the recognition of a spiritual component to the psyche; includes studies of meditation, mysticism, spiritual awakening and development, psychedelic experiences, shamanism, healing, and traditional spiritual disciplines.

Vasanas: Sanskrit term meaning memory traces from a current or past life, which form part of a samskara (q.v.; see also Chapter 6).

FURTHER READING

The following list, by no means exhaustive, is a representative selection of writings on past lives, reincarnation, and psychology from a variety of different perspectives. A number of standard or classic works not mentioned in the text are also added. Further titles are to be found in the Notes.

1. ON PAST LIFE THERAPY

Fiore, Edith, *You Have Been Here Before*, Ballantine Books, New York, 1979.

Kelsey, Denys, and Joan Grant, *Many Lifetimes*, Doubleday & Company, Garden City, N.Y., 1967.

Lucas, Winafred, ed., *Past Life Therapy: A Handbook for Professionals*, forthcoming.

Moore, Marcia, *Hypersentience*, Crown Publishers, New York, 1976.

Moss, Peter, and Joe Keeton, *Encounters with the Past*, Doubleday & Company, Garden City, N.Y., 1981

Netherton, Morris, and Nancy Shiffrin, *Past Lives Therapy*, William Morrow & Co., New York, 1978.

Schlotterbeck, Karl, *Living Your Past Lives*, Ballantine Books, New York, 1987.

Sutphen, Dick, *Past Lives, Future Loves*, Pocket Books, New York, 1978.

Williston, Glenn, and Judith Johnstone, *Soul Search*, Turnstone Press, Wellingborough, England, 1983.

2. REINCARNATION AND KARMA IN RELIGIOUS TRADITION

Evans-Wentz, W. Y., *The Tibetan Book of the Dead*, Oxford University Press, New York, 1960; with Commentary by Jung and Forewords by Woodroffe and Govinda.

John, Da Free, *Easy Death*, Dawn Horse Press, Clearlake Highlands, Calif. 1983

Kapleau, Philip, and Paterson Simons, eds., *The Wheel of Death*, Harper & Row, New York, 1971.

Lauf, Ingo Detlef, *Secret Doctrines of the Tibetan Books of the Dead*, Shambhala Publications, Boston and London, 1977.

McGregor, Geddes, *Reincarnation in Christianity*, Quest Books, Wheaton, Ill. 1978.

Meher Baba, *Discourses*, Volume III, Sufism Reoriented Inc., San Francisco, 1967.

Neufeldt, Ronald W., ed., *Karma and Rebirth: Post Classical Developments*, State University of New York Press, Albany, N.Y., 1986.

O'Flaherty, Wendy Doniger, ed., *Karma and Rebirth in Classical Indian Traditions*, University of California Press, Berkeley, Calif. 1980.

3. ON PARAPSYCHOLOGY AND REINCARNATION RESEARCH

Bernstein, Morey, *The Search for Bridey Murphy*, Doubleday & Company, Garden City, N.Y., 1965.

Currie, Ian, *You Cannot Die*, Methuen, New York, 1978.

Haynes, Renée, *The Seeing Eye, the Seeing I*, St. Martin's Press, New York, 1976.

Iverson, Jeffrey, *More Lives than One?* Warner Books, New York, 1977.

Lenz, Frederick, *Lifetimes, True Accounts of Reincarnation*, Fawcett Books, New York, 1971.

Mishlove, Jeffrey, *Roots of Consciousness,* Random House, New York, 1975.

Rogo, D. Scott, *The Search for Yesterday,* Prentice-Hall, Englewood Cliffs, N.J., 1985.

Stevenson, Ian, *Twenty Cases Suggestive of Reincarnation,* University Press of Virginia, Charlottesville, 1974.

4. GENERAL AND CRITICAL WORKS ON REINCARNATION

Collin, Rodney, *The Theory of Eternal Life,* Samuel Weiser, New York, 1974.

Cranston, Sylvia, and Carey Williams, *Reincarnation, A New Horizon,* Julian Press, New York, 1983.

Ducasse, C. J. *A Critical Examination of the Belief in a Life After Death,* C. C. Thomas, Springfield, Ill. 1961.

Fisher, Joe, *The Case for Reincarnation,* Bantam Books, New York, 1985.

Head, Joseph, and Sylvia L. Cranston, eds., *Reincarnation: the Phoenix Fire Mystery,* Warner Books, New York, 1979.

Hick, John, *Death and Eternal Life,* Harper & Row, New York, 1976.

Moore, Marcia, and Mark Douglas, *Reincarnation, the Key to Immortality,* Arcane Publications, York Cliffs, Maine, 1968.

Walker, Benjamin, *Masks of the Soul,* Aquarian Press, Wellingborough, England, 1981.

Wilson, Ian, *All in the Mind,* Doubleday & Company, Garden City, N.Y., 1982.

5. ON REINCARNATION AND POPULAR METAPHYSICS

Cerminara, Gina, *Many Lives, Many Loves,* William Sloane Associates, New York, 1963.

Hall, Manly P., *Death to Rebirth: Five Essays,* Philosophical Research Society, Los Angeles, 1979.

Kardec, Allan, *The Spirits' Book,* Starlite Distributors,

Reno, Nevada, no date. (Originally published as *Le Livre des Esprits*, Paris, 1857.)

Langley, Noel, *Edgar Cayce on Reincarnation*, Warner Books, New York, 1967.

Montgomery, Ruth, *Here and Hereafter*, Fawcett Books, New York, 1968.

Roberts, Jane, *Adventures in Consciousness*, Bantam Books, New York, 1979.

Roberts, Jane, *Seth Speaks*, Bantam Books, New York, 1974.

Steiger, Brad, *You Will Live Again*, Dell Books, New York, 1978.

Yarbro, Chelsea Quinn, *Messages from Michael on the Nature of the Evolution of the Human Soul*, Playboy Press, New York, 1979.

6. ON JUNGIAN, DEPTH AND ARCHETYPAL PSYCHOLOGY

Avens, Roberts, *Imaginal Body: Para-Jungian Reflections on Soul, Imagination and Death*, University Press of America, Washington, D.C. 1982.

Brown, Norman O., *Life Against Death*, Wesleyan University Press, Middletown, Conn., 1959.

Coward, Harold, *Jung and Eastern Thought*, State University of New York Press, Albany, N.Y., 1985.

Ellenberger, Henri, *The Discovery of the Unconscious*, Basic Books, New York, 1970.

Frey-Rohn, Liliane, *From Freud to Jung*, G. P. Putnam's Sons, New York, 1974.

Hillman, James, *The Myth of Analysis*, Harper & Row, New York, 1978.

———, *Re-Visioning Psychology*, Harper & Row, New York, 1977.

Jung, C. G. *Memories, Dreams, Reflections*, Random House, New York, 1973.

———, *Psychology East and West*, Princeton/Bollingen, Princeton, N.J., 1978.

————, *Psychology and the Occult,* Princeton/Bollingen, Princeton, N.J., 1977.

Storr, Anthony, ed., *The Essential Jung,* Princeton/Bollingen, Princeton, N.J., 1983.

Von Franz, Marie-Louise, *C. G. Jung: His Myth in Our Time,* Little, Brown & Co., Boston, 1975.

Watkins, Mary, *Waking Dreams,* Harper & Row, New York, 1976.

7. ON TRANSPERSONAL PSYCHOLOGY

Assagioli, Roberto, *Psychosynthesis,* Viking Press, New York, 1965.

Grof, Stanislav, *Realms of the Human Unconscious,* E. P. Dutton, New York, 1976.

————, *Beyond the Brain,* State University of New York Press, Albany, N.Y., 1985.

————, ed., *Ancient Wisdom and Modern Science,* State University of New York Press, Albany, N.Y., 1984.

Grof, Stanislav, and Christina Grof, *Beyond Death,* Thames & Hudson, London and New York, 1980.

Huxley, Aldous, *The Perennial Philosophy,* Harper & Brothers, New York, 1945.

James, William, *The Varieties of Religious Experience,* Longmans, Green & Co., New York, 1902.

Ring, Kenneth, *Life at Death,* Quill, New York, 1980.

————, *Heading Toward Omega,* Quill, New York, 1984.

Sannella, Lee, *Kundalini: Psychosis or Transcendence?,* H. S. Dakin, San Francisco, 1976.

Smith, Huston, *Forgotten Truth,* Harper & Row, New York, 1977.

Stone, Hal, and Sidra Winkelman, *Embracing Our Selves,* De Vorss, Marina del Rey, Calif., 1985.

Verney, Thomas, and John Kelly, *The Secret Life of the Unborn Child,* Delta Books, New York, 1981.

8.   On Holistic and Psychic Healing

Achterberg, Jeanne, *Imagery in Healing: Shamanism and Modern Medicine*, Shambhala Publications, Boston and London, 1985.

Bailey, Alice, *Esoteric Healing*, Lucis Publishing Co., New York, 1953.

Krippner, Stanley, and Alberto Villoldo, *The Realms of Healing*, Celestial Arts, Berkeley, Calif., 1976.

Locke, Steven, and Douglas Colligen, *The Healer Within: The New Medicine of Mind and Body*, E. P. Dutton, New York, 1986.

Markides, Kyriacos C., *The Magus of Strovolus*, Routledge & Kegan Paul, Boston and London, 1985.

Tansley, David, *Subtle Body*, Thames & Hudson, London and New York, 1977.

9.   On Meditation

Dhiravamsa, *The Way of Non-Attachment*, Schocken Books, New York, 1975

Dürckheim, Karlfried, Graf von, *The Way of Transformation*, Allen & Unwin, London, 1971.

Suzuki, Shunryu, *Zen Mind, Beginner's Mind*, Weatherhill, New York, 1970.

Tarthang Tulku, *Gesture of Balance*, Dharma Publishing, Berkeley, Calif., 1977.

NOTES

Abbreviations:
CW = Collected Words (Jung),
SE = Standard Edition (Freud).

CHAPTER 1: A SCEPTIC ENCOUNTERS PAST LIVES

1. The classic Oxfordian demolition of metaphysics is A. J. Ayer's *Language, Truth and Logic,* London, 1936. Metaphysics is not part of the standard philosophy curriculum at Oxford University.
2. See the Glossary for short definitions of technical terms used in the book.
3. Author's translation.
4. Jung, "Psychological Commentary on *The Tibetan Book of the Dead,*" 3rd edition, 1957, p. xiv.
5. With John Kelly, New York, 1981.
6. My review appears in the *Journal of the Society for Psychical Research,* December 1970, pp. 422–42.
7. See C. G. Jung, *Synchronicity,* Princeton, N.J., 1973.
8. C. G. Jung, *Psychological Reflections,* Princeton, N.J., 1970, p. 220.
9. See Leonard Orr and Sondra Ray, *Rebirthing in the New Age,* San Francisco, 1977.
10. Stanislav Grof, *Realms of the Human Unconscious,* New York, 1976.
11. Morris Netherton and Nancy Shiffrin, *Past Lives Therapy,* New York, 1978.
12. Stanislav Grof, *Beyond the Brain,* Albany, N.Y., 1985, pp. 28ff. and passim.

CHAPTER 2: PAST LIFE THERAPY: HOW IT WORKS

1. All cases described are disguised for reasons of confidentiality.
2. From the perspective I am taking, a strong case could be made that many historical novels and plays are in fact fictional reworking of past life memories. Certain novels, like Virginia Woolf's *Orlando* and Marguerite Yourcenar's *The Abyss* seem to be memories that are hardly touched up at all. It is also striking how Shakespeare in his cycle of plays keeps returning to three historical periods: Ancient Rome, Ancient Britain, and fourteenth-century England.
3. *Leviathan,* i, 13.
4. *Mythologies,* New York, 1959, p. 345, cited in Gerhard Adler, *Dynamics of the Self,* London, 1979; Adler's essay "Remembering and Forgetting" is highly recommended.
5. See Joseph Head and Sylvia L. Cranston, eds. *Reincarnation, the Phoenix Fire Mystery,* New York, 1979, for numerous others.
6. See René Guénon's *Theosophy, History of a Pseudo-Religion,* a devastating critique of the movement and its branches. Guénon had himself been absorbed in occult studies for many years before becoming a scholar of Vedanta and then a convert to Sufism. His personal involvement and profound knowledge of traditional religion make him a unique commentator of Theosophy. Unfortunately *Théosophisme, histoire d'une pseudo-religion,* Paris, 1921, has never been translated.
7. *Théosophisme,* p. 103.
8. *Introduction générale à l'étude des doctrines hindous,* Paris, 1921, p. 287.
9. My description derives from Rudolf Otto's classic work *The Idea of the Holy (Das Heilige),* 1917 (Oxford University Press, New York, 2nd ed., 1958).

CHAPTER 3:   TERRA INCOGNITA: EXPLORING UNKNOWN PSYCHIC REALMS

1. C. G. Jung, *Memories, Dreams, Reflections,* New York, 1973, p. 150.
2. See James Hillman, "Psychology: Monotheistic or Polytheistic?" in *Spring,* 1971.
3. Jung, *Psychological Reflections,* p. 25.
4. James Hillman has perceptively observed that the Jungian movement is caught in a split that derives in part from Jung himself, a conflict between the mediumistic side of his family (his mother) and the rational-scientific side (his father). Many Jungians today heavily favor Jung's "clinical" writings and play down his religious and spiritual investigations. See Hillman, "Some Early Background to Jung's Ideas," *Spring,* 1976.
5. A serious scholarly account of one such revival is: Frances Yates, *Giordano Bruno and the Hermetic Tradition,* University of Chicago Press, Chicago, 1964.
6. For a good general account of these various movements, see Colin Wilson, *The Occult,* Vintage Books, New York, 1973.
7. Mircea Eliade, *Occultism, Witchcraft and Cultural Fashions,* Chicago, 1976, p. 49. Eliade's essay "The Occult and the Modern World" is probably the best short account of the subject available.
8. See René Guénon, *The Spiritist Error (L'Erreur Spirite,* Paris, 1921, not translated) and *Théosophisme.*
9. During the 1890s the oriental scholar William Emmette Coleman documented two thousand plagiarized passages in *Isis Unveiled* and charged that *The Secret Doctrine* was largely compiled from standard nineteenth-century reference materials. For details see Bruce F. Campbell, *Ancient Wisdom Revived,* Berkeley, Calif., 1980, p. 33ff.
10. Wickland, p. 421.
11. Mircea Eliade, *Shamanism,* Princeton, N.J., 1964; Michael Harner, *The Way of the Shaman,* New York, 1980; Stephen Larsen, *The Shaman's Doorway,* New York, 1976.
12. See Sylvia Cranston and Carey Williams, *Reincarnation: A*

New Horizon in Science, Religion and Society, New York 1984, for Chapter 12, "Judaic Teachers and Prophets."

13. See Henri Ellenberger, *The Discovery of the Unconscious* New York, 1970, p. 313.

14. *The Search for Yesterday,* Englewood Cliffs, N.J., 1985, p 88.

15. In C. G. Jung, *Psychology and the Occult,* Princeton, N.J. 1977, and *CW,* Vol. 1.

16. Ian Stevenson, *Twenty Cases Suggestive of Reincarnation,* Charlottesville, Va., 1974.

17. Lawrence, *Apocalypse,* 1931.

18. John Hick, *Death and Eternal Life,* New York, 1976, p. 392 Hick takes Weatherhead and others to task for their igno rance of Early Church doctrine. Hick's scholarship would also cast doubt on the widely held view that Early Chris tianity was reincarnationalist, as found in Langley, *Edgar Cayce on Reincarnation,* New York, 1967, and Head and Cranston's *Reincarnation, the Phoenix Fire Mystery.*

19. From *Shiva and Dionysus,* London, 1982, p. 8.

20. As quoted in Joe Fisher, *The Case for Reincarnation,* Toronto, 1984, p. 50.

21. Quoted in Philip Kapleau and Paterson Simons, eds., *The Wheel of Death,* New York, 1971, pp. 46–47.

22. Two representative anthologies from this movement are Charles H. Tart, ed., *Transpersonal Psychologies,* New York, 1975, and Roger Walsh and Frances Vaughanm, eds., *Beyond Ego: Transpersonal Dimensions in Psychology,* Los Angeles, 1980.

CHAPTER 4: THE FOURTH WAY: A PSYCHOTHERAPIST'S APPROACH TO PAST LIVES.

1. Jeffrey Iverson, *More Lives Than One?* London, 1976.

2. Helen Wambach, *Reliving Past Lives: the Evidence Under Hypnosis,* New York, 1978, and *Life Before Life,* New York, 1979.

3. For an account of de Rochas's work see D. Scott Rogo, *The Search for Yesterday,* pp. 16–17.

4. Denys Kelsey and Joan Grant, *Many Lifetimes,* New York, 1967.
5. See Peter Moss and Joe Keeton, *Encounters with the Past,* New York, 1981, Netherton and Shiffren, op. cit., and Edith Fiore, *You Have Been Here Before,* New York, 1978.
6. Jung describes active imagination in "The Transcendent Function," *CW,* Vol. 8, also in Joseph Campbell, ed., *The Portable Jung,* New York, 1976.
7. On Milton H. Erickson, see Jay Haley, *Uncommon Therapy,* New York, 1973.
8. *The Tibetan Book of the Dead,* Evans-Wentz, tr., p. liii.
9. See, for example, Ron Kurtz, *The Body Reveals,* New York, 1976, and Ken Dychtwald, *Bodymind,* New York, 1977.

CHAPTER 5: THE MULTIDIMENSIONAL PSYCHE

1. *Spring,* 1971, p. 157.
2. Borges, *A Personal Anthology,* New York, 1968.
3. Kant, *Critique of Pure Reason,* A 33 B 50, p. 77.
4. Grof, *Beyond the Brain,* p. 76.
5. Ibid., p. 97.
6. Ibid., p. 97.
7. See Fritz Perls, *Gestalt Therapy Verbatim,* New York, 1976.
8. For a good account of the religious aspects of the Self, see Edward Edinger, *Ego and Archetype,* New York, 1972.
9. St. John of the Cross, *Ascent of Mount Carmel,* various editions.

CHAPTER 6: UNFINISHED SOUL BUSINESS: THE PSYCHOLOGY OF KARMA

1. In Wendy Doniger O'Flaherty, ed., *Karma and Rebirth in Classical Indian Traditions,* Berkeley, Calif., 1980, p. 243.
2. Heinrich Zimmer, *The Philosophies of India,* Princeton, N.J., 1951, p. 324.
3. Jung, *Psychological Reflections,* pp. 38–39.
4. Zimmer, *The Philosophies of India,* p. 325.

CHAPTER 7: SUBTLE BODY, DENSE MIND: PAST LIVES AND PHYSICAL ILLS

1. For a refreshing reappraisal of the whole body-mind-spirit issue see: Huston Smith, *Forgotten Truth, the Primordial Tradition,* New York, 1977.
2. See O. C. Simonton, S. Simonton, and J. Creighton, *Getting Well Again,* Los Angeles, 1978, and Steven Locke and Douglas Colligan, *The Healer Within,* New York, 1986.
3. Sydney, 1968. For an introduction to Reichian therapy see David Boadella, *Wilhelm Reich, the Man and His Work,* London, 1973, and Boston, 1985.
4. London, 1954.
5. From "Lupus erythematosus" in *The New Columbia Encyclopedia,* New York, 1975.
6. Heinrich, Zimmer, *The Philosophies of India,* Princeton, N.J., 1951, p. 324.

CHAPTER 8: EROS ABUSED: THE PAST LIFE ROOTS OF SEXUAL AND REPRODUCTIVE PROBLEMS

1. *Realms of the Human Unconscious,* p. 176.
2. Boston, 1958, and *CW,* Vol. 10.
3. See Anthony Storr, ed., *The Essential Jung,* Part 4.

CHAPTER 9: THE MANY LIVES OF THE SOUL

1. From *Views from the Real World,* E. P. Dutton, New York, 1975, p. 75.
2. From *Loose Ends: Primary Papers in Archetypal Psychology,* Spring Publications, Dallas, 1978, p. 182.
3. For an excellent account of how therapists work with sub personalities see: Hal Stone and Sidra Winkelman, *Embracing Our Selves,* Marina del Rey, Calif. 1985.
4. See Anthony Storr, ed., *The Essential Jung,* Part 4.

CHAPTER 10:   THE GREAT WHEEL: BIRTH
AND BEFORE

1. For example: Arthur Janov, *Imprints: The Lifelong Effects of the Birth Experience*, New York, 1983; Leslie Feher, *The Psychology of Birth* (on Elizabeth Fehr); R. D. Laing, *The Facts of Life*, New York, 1976. For Orr, Grof, and Netherton see notes to Chapter 1.
2. *The Trauma of Birth*, English translation, London, 1929.
3. *Realms of the Human Unconscious*, Chapter 4, "Perinatal Experiences in LSD Sessions."
4. *The Secret Life of the Unborn Child*, pp. 12–13.
5. *Past Lives Therapy*, p. 125.
6. Verney's data does not show the fetus as entirely passive. According to Dr. Albert Liley of Auckland, New Zealand, "it is the fetus who guarantees the endocrine success of pregnancy and who triggers physical changes in the mother's body." These findings "raise the possibility that the unusually high rates of physical and emotional damage in the offspring of rejecting or unhappy mothers may not be solely due to harmful maternal hormones. It seems at least a possibility that if a fetus does have partial control over a pregnancy and senses himself in a hostile environment he may withdraw his physiological support, thereby harming himself" (*Secret Life*, pp. 90–91).
7. From *The Upanishads* (tr. by Prabhavananda and Manchester), New York, 1957.
8. From "Auguries of Innocence" in *The Complete Poetry and Prose of William Blake*, revised edition, ed. by David V. Erdman, Anchor Books, Anchor Press/Doubleday, Garden City, N.Y., 1982, p. 491.

CHAPTER 11: THE GREAT WHEEL: DEATH
AND BEFORE

1. Translated by Müller in E. A. Burtt, *The Teachings of the Compassionate Buddha*, New York, 1955, p. 52.
2. *The Tibetan Book of the Dead*, p. 168.

3. See Raymond A. Moody, Jr., *Life After Death*, Atlanta, 1975; Kenneth Ring, *Life at Death: A Scientific Investigation of the Near Death Experience*, New York, 1980.

CHAPTER 12: BEYOND THERAPY: SOME CONCLUSIONS

1. Of the universal or archetypal nature of guilt, the philosopher Vincent Vycinas has written: "Karmic guilt is a kind of illness of man's inner self. It can be compared to neurosis. This illness befalls man not totally by his own disconcern for the godly laws of the world. To be sure, man *is* guilty and his is the cause of his karma; nevertheless, the event of reality, Nature's play, is the prime source of man's karmic guilt" *(Search for Gods,* The Hague, 1972, p. 271). This issue takes us unavoidably into thorny theological problems such as original sin in Christian terms and the origins of evil. Do we all share in "Adam's sin" or must God Himself/Herself take some of the responsibility for the evil in creation? Jung wrestled with this conundrum in *Answer to Job,* Princeton, N.J., 1969.
2. *The Way of Transformation,* London, 1971, pp. 79–80.
3. For example, Erlo van Waveren, *Pilgrimage to the Rebirth,* New York, 1978.
4. Recommended are: Anthony Storr, ed., *The Essential Jung;* Joseph Campbell, ed., *The Portable Jung;* Jung's autobiography, *Memories, Dreams, Reflections;* Edward C. Whitmont, *The Symbolic Quest,* New York, 1969; June Singer, *Boundaries of the Soul,* Garden City, N.Y., 1972; Marie-Louise von Franz, *C. G. Jung, His Myth in Our Time,* New York, 1975.
5. From D. T. Suzuki, *Essays in Zen Buddhism I,* London, 1949, pp. 22ff.
6. "The Dry Salvages" in *Four Quartets,* Harcourt, Brace & Company, New York, 1943.
7. Shakespeare's final play, *The Tempest,* can be read for its mystical and symbolic allusions to the process of individuation. Prospero has gained full access to Ariel, the spirit, because he also accepts his own darkest shadow, the monster Caliban: "This thing of darkness, I acknowledge mine," he says. In this extraordinary summation of all Shake-

speare's work on his own inner opposite selves, a pair of
warring brothers (Prospero and Antonio) are reconciled
and the prince and princess (Ferdinand and Miranda) are
married. At the center of this stands Prospero, the magi-
cian, image of the Higher Self, like the Superior Man of
Chinese philosophy.

8. Hillman, *Re-Visioning Psychology*, Part 3, "Psychologizing
   or Seeing Through," pp. 149–54.

9. Jung, *CW*, Vol. 8, pp. 67–91.

10. Jung, *CW*, Vol. 9, Part II, p. 8.

11. *Devotions*, XVII.

12. For the Ox-herding Series of Images, see D. T. Suzuki, *Man-
    ual of Zen Buddhism*, New York, 1980, pp. 148ff.

13. Jorge Luis Borges certainly understood Shakespeare in this
    way; his biographical parable about him concludes: "His-
    tory adds that before or after his death he found himself
    facing God and said: *I, who have been so many men in vain,
    want to be one man, myself alone.* From out of a whirlwind
    the voice of God replied: *I am not, either. I dreamed the
    world the way you dreamed your work, my Shakespeare:
    one of the forms of my dreams was you, who, like me, are
    many and no one"* ("Everything and Nothing" in *A Per-
    sonal Anthology*, New York, 1967).

14. Translated by The Zen Center, Rochester, N.Y., published
    Boulder, Colo., 1974.

15. For one of the very finest discussions of Hindu, Buddhist,
    and Platonic doctrines of reincarnation and the Self see
    Ananda K. Coomaraswamy's essays "Recollection, Indian
    and Platonic" and "On the One and Only Transmigrant" in
    Roger Lipsey, ed., *Coomaraswamy: Selected Papers II*,
    Princeton, N.J., 1977.

APPENDIX 1: THE LEGACY OF DEPTH PSYCHOLOGY

1. A good concise history of the concept of the "unconscious"
   is L. L. Whyte's *The Unconscious Before Freud*, New York,
   1960. For an encyclopedic history of depth psychology
   from Mesmer onward see Henri Ellenberger, *The Discovery of the Unconscious*, New York, 1970. Ellenberger's in-

dispensable work places psychology within its broader social, philosophical, and cultural context as no other history does.

2. For a good introduction to J. L. Moreno's work see Jonathan Fox, *The Essential Moreno: Writings on Psychodrama, Group Method and Spontaneity,* New York, 1987.

3. For Jung on complexes see Anthony Storr, ed., *The Essential Jung,* Princeton, N.J., 1983, Part 1. Jung had originally wanted to call his psychology "complex psychology."

4. For a comparative study of Freud and Jung's psychology of the unconscious see Liliane Frey-Rohn, *From Freud to Jung,* New York, 1974.

5. Jung, *Symbols of Transformation, CW,* Vol. 5, Princeton, N.J., 1952, p. 328.

6. Freud, *Introductory Lectures in Psycho-Analysis III, SE* XVI, p. 371.

7. See Hillman, *Archetypal Psychology, a Brief Account,* Dallas, 1983.

APPENDIX 2: DID JUNG BELIEVE IN REINCARNATION?

1. Jung, "Commentary on Kundalini Yoga," *Spring,* 1975, p. 8.

2. "Psychological Commentary on *The Tibetan Book of the Dead,*" p. xliii.

3. Ibid., p. xlv.

4. *Two Essays on Analytical Psychology, CW,* Vol. 7. p. 77.

5. Van Waveren, *Pilgrimage to the Rebirth,* p. 23.

6. *Memories, Dreams, Reflections,* p. 319.

7. Ibid., pp. 33–34.

8. Ibid., pp. 158–59.

9. Ibid., pp. 35 and 234n.

10. On the spiritual torments suffered by creative geniuses, see especially "The Sick Soul" (Lectures VI and VII) and "The Divided Self and the Process of Its Unification" (Lecture VIII) in William James's masterpiece *The Varieties of Religious Experience,* New York, 1902.

INDEX

Faculty X, 61, 62
Family struggles, 18
Fantasies, past lives as, 30-34, 88-89
"Far memory," 41
Fathers
  "devouring," 240
  success of pregnancy and, 252
  See also Parents
Fa Tsang, 108-9
Faust, 46, 348
Fear
  of abandonment, 17
  irrational, 17
Fehr, Elizabeth, 247
Feminist therapists, 211-12
Fiore, Edith, 88
Fitzgerald, F.Scott, 316
Flournoy, Theodore, 64-65, 67
Fox family, 55
Franklin, Benjamin, 42
Free association, 339
Freud, Sigmund, 41, 45, 87, 121, 142, 337
  catharsis in therapy of, 338
  Jung's disagreements with, 5, 47-48, 340-41
  study of the unconscious by, 339-40
  trance states in couch therapy of, 92
From India to the Planet Mars, 65

Gallup poll, xviii
Gestalt therapy, 16, 28, 107, 122, 352
Gnostics, 61, 71, 72
Goethe, Johann Wolfgang von, 42, 46
  Jung's absorption with, 348
Golding, William, 290
Grant, Joan, 41, 61, 88
Great Memory, 41-42, 250
Great Mind, 41
Great Mother, 250

"Great Vertical Path, The," 274, 275, 293
Great Wheel of Experience, 273
Griffin, Susan, 191
Grof, Stanislav, 21-22, 77, 107-9, 127, 185, 202
  on birth, 247-48, 262-63, 272
Group therapy. *See* Past life therapy—group
Guardians of the threshold, 12
Guénon, René, 43-44, 56, 58, 63
Guilt complex, 17-18
Guirdham, Arthur, 8-9
Gurdjieff, G.I., 213
Gynecological problems, 190-212

Halprin, Anna, 104, 161, 169
Hardy, Sir Alistair, 64
Harner, Michael, 60
Haynes, Renée, 8, 9
Head, Joseph, 54, 72
Headaches, 22
Heraclitus, 219, 239
Hermeticism, 58
Hesse, Herman, 1
Hick, John, 72-73
Hillman, James, 48, 81, 92, 213, 217, 322
  archetypal psychology of, 342, 351
Historical validity of past lives. *See* Past lives—history and
Hitchcock, Alfred, 32
Hobbes, Thomas, 39
Hoffman, Dustin, 342
Holistic health movement, 164, 352
Holistic therapy, past life therapy as, 314-15
Holography, 108
Holonomics, 108
Home, Daniel Dunglas, 56
Homer's *Odyssey*, 248
Homosexuality in

"Wayne," 228, 233-35, 240-41
Hospice movement, 281
Hugo, Victor, 57
Hume, David, 42
Hungry ghosts, 300
Huxley, T.H., 42
Huxtable, Graham, 84-85
Hypnosis, 62, 352
  in past life research, 84-85
  See also Trances
Hypnotherapy, 122, 352, 338, 340
  psychoanalysis compared to, 88-89
Hypnotic regression, 352

Iamblichus, 72
I Ching, 48, 77
Imitation of Christ, The, 289
Incest, 18
Inquisition, the, 8, 61
Insecurity, 17
  maternal, 18
Isis Unveiled, 58
Iverson, Jeffrey, 85

James, William, 63, 64, 337
Janet, Pierre-Marie-Félix, 340
Janov, Arthur, 127, 247, 354
Jesus, 72-73
  in after death visions, 296
  reincarnation and, 72-73
John of the Cross, St., 61, 134, 327
Journal of the Society for Psychical Research, 7-9
Joyce, James, 202
Judaism, reincarnation in, 61, 73
Jue, Ronald Wong, 77
  "Foreword" by, xiii-xv
  on reincarnation, 74-75
Jung, Carl Gustav, 5-7, 45, 68, 77, 121, 308, 316, 318